Education Law

Vera G. McEwan
M. A. LL. M. M. Sc Barrister
Visiting Lecturer, School of Education University of Durham

CLT Professional Publishing Ltd
A CLT Group Company

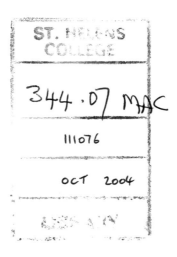

© Vera McEwan

Published by
CLT Professional Publishing
A division of Central Law Training Ltd
Stonehills House
Howardsgate
Welwyn Garden City
AL8 6PU

ISBN 1 85811 192 7

Typeset by Saxon Graphics Ltd, Derby
Printed in Great Britain by Alden Press, Oxford

Contents

Preface

Since the first edition of Education Law the pace of change in education law has continued relentlessly. The labour party, prior to the 1997 general election, adopted the mantra, 'education, education, education', as the expression of its main concerns. Critics have said that 'learning, learning, learning' might have been more appropriate.

The two slogans are a useful reminder that education and learning are not necessarily the same. Education law has traditionally concerned itself with the structure of education: the School Standards and Framework Act 1998 is an illustration of that fundamental involvement in the shaping of educational institutions. As the name of that Act implies there is also now some legalistic concern with the learning process. In the last ten years the law has become more closely involved with the curriculum and the inspections regime. Although that involvement has not resulted in much litigation in other areas, such as special educational needs and duties of care, there has been a considerable increase in the volume of case law, for example, *Phelps* v *Hillingdon London Borough Council*, see Chapters 7 and 13. It is of vital importance that both prospective and practising teachers have some understanding of education law and that time is made for this in the teacher training curriculum.

The law relating to special educational needs appears to be under permanent review by Parliament and the Courts and the complexities of that subject have meant that Chapter 13 should be regarded as merely an overview. Similarly, Chapter 14 deals with an area of education law which is becoming a specialism in its own right. In the Queen's Speech of November 1998 the government confirmed that education will continue to be its main priority. The structure of the teaching profession is to be reviewed although that process has already begun with the Teaching and Higher Education Act 1998.

Some, but not all of the legislation of the previous government, has been repealed. Care must be taken, as always in areas of rapid change, because much litigation will be based on the previous legislation for some considerable time. It is therefore necessary to know what the law was as well as what it is and is going to be. The education lawyer necessarily has to look backwards and forwards, often at the same time, to get a complete picture. As with the previous edition of this book care must be taken with the law in Scotland, Northern Ireland and Wales. As greater devolution of powers has occurred the differences in education law are likely to become more pronounced.

Vera G McEwan
August 1999

Acknowledgements

The author and publishers wish to thank the following for their kind permission to reproduce extracts from their publications:

Education Law Reports (Jordans Publishing)
Administrative Law by Peter Cane (1986) (Oxford University Press)
The Times (Times Newspapers Limited)

Table of Cases

Table of Statutes

Practice Directions

Table of Statutory Instruments

Table of Circulars

Abbreviations

CEF	College Employers Forum
CPR	Civil Procedure Rules
CTC	City Technology College
DES	Department for Education and Science
DFE	Department for Education
DfEE	Department for Education and Employment
EAZs	Education Action Zones
ELAS	Education Law Association
ELR	Education Law Reports
ERA 1988	Education Reform Act 1988
FAS	Funding Agency for Schools
FEFC	Further Education Funding Council
GTC	General Teaching Council
HEFC	Higher Education Funding Council
HMCI	Her Majesty's Chief Inspector of Schools
HMIs	Her Majesty's Inspectors
LEAs	Local Education Authorities
LMS	Local Management of Schools
OCA	Ofsted Complaints Adjudicator
Ofsted	Office for Standards in Education
PFI	Private Finance Initiative
PRU	Pupil Referral Unit
QCA	Qualifications and Curriculum Authority
RSC	Rules of the Supreme Court
SACRE	Standing Advisory Council on Religious Education
SCAA	School Curriculum and Assessment Authority
SSA	Standard Spending Assessment
SSFA 1998	School Standards and Framework Act 1998
THEA 1998	Teaching and Higher Education Act 1998
TTA	Teacher Training Agency

Chapter 1

Introduction:
The Nature of Education Law

Introduction:
The Nature of Education Law

History of education law

The foundations of modern education law are to be found in the late nineteenth century, with the introduction of a series of Acts of Parliament which created both the structure of the educational institutions designed to provide compulsory education and the administrative mechanisms to regulate the new system. The Education Act 1870, known as the 'Foster' Act, created new locally elected school boards with the sole purpose of providing elementary education. By the Education Act 1902 (the 'Balfour Act') the system of local government altered so that school boards were replaced by local education authorities (LEAs).

Education Act 1944

The 'Butler' Act, as the Education Act 1944 became known, established the state system of post-war education reorganising provision of education into three stages: primary, secondary and further education. The responsibility for educational provision was placed with the LEAs, which were obliged by Schedule 1 of the Act to establish education committees. Schedule 1 set out in detail the law relating to the membership of those committees and powers of delegation of functions. A 'fit and proper' person was to be appointed as Chief Education Officer in each LEA, this appointment being made in consultation with the Secretary of State for Education.

The Education Act 1944 has been described as a great Act which formed a system of education that has lasted 40 years. The Act has also been described as a monument of vagueness. These apparently contrasting views can be reconciled if it is accepted that the 1944 Act set out two different agendas. The first was to set up the administrative framework of the post-war education system. The second was to set out certain philosophical and policy issues which underpinned the system. This involved the setting out of the many duties which were required of those who were to be involved in what was perceived to be a partnership in educational provision.

Under the 1944 Act, local authorities had specific responsibilities (e.g. under section 8 to provide sufficient schools and full-time education suitable for the requirements of senior pupils). There were also less specific duties such as those in section 7:

> It shall be the duty of the local education authority for every area, so far as their powers extend, to contribute towards the spiritual, moral, mental and physical development of the community ...

Section 55 of the Act, relating to transport, became a frequent source of litigation:

> A local education authority shall make arrangements for the provision of transport and otherwise as they consider necessary ... for the purpose of facilitating the attendance of pupils at school ... and any transport provided in pursuance of such arrangements shall be provided free of charge.

This section proved difficult to apply with the advent of 'parental preference' when parents exercised their right to indicate a preference for a school for their children which was many miles away from home.

Parents also had duties under the 1944 Act. For example, they had to ensure that every child of compulsory school age received efficient full-time education suitable to his age, ability and aptitude under section 36.

From a legal perspective, one of the most surprising aspects of the 1944 Act was the lack of litigation. Some commentators suggest that there was an understanding that education would be run with goodwill as a partnership and that this was accepted by all parties. However, with the increase in education legislation and the rise of 'consumer' awareness, there was a spate of education litigation. Commentators such as Aldrich and Leighton, in *Education: Time for a New Act?* (University of London 1985), called for the repeal of the 1944 Act. This happened only gradually until the Education Act 1996 formally repealed the residue of the 1944 Act; however, many of philosophical principles of the 1944 Act remain enshrined in the more recent legislation and it is not uncommon to see the 1944 Act referred to in recent caselaw.

Recent legislation

The 1970s saw a period of political unrest which permeated the education system. Whilst there were Acts of Parliament which changed certain aspects of education, none have had a particularly lasting effect. The 1980s saw much more radical change, with the

Education Reform Act 1988 and the Education Act 1993 reforming and consolidating much of the previous law. The latter part of the 1990s saw education policy as a high priority in the 1997 election campaign, and there was considerable legislative activity immediately before and after the election.

The most important legislative changes of the 1980s and 1990s to date in education are set out below in chronological order. The full implications of these many and various Acts will become apparent as specific issues are addressed in subsequent chapters. The Education Act 1996 lists certain statutes as 'the Education Acts' for the purposes of that Act, but there is no definitive list.

Education Act 1980 Prior to this Act, LEAs were obliged, when considering admissions or transfers to their schools, to have regard to parental preference. By section 6 of the 1980 Act they were under a mandatory duty, save in exceptional circumstances, to comply with such preference.

Education Act 1981 This Act addressed special needs assessments and provision. The Act was substantially replaced by the Education Act 1993 and repealed by the 1996 Act.

Education (Amendment) Act 1986 This is a short Act relating to expenditure.

Education (No 2) Act 1986 Parents were given equal representation with the LEA on governing bodies. Parental rights were further extended by the Education Reform Act 1988.

Education Reform Act 1988 The main aim of this Act was said to be the bringing of parents 'centre stage' in that they are given greater choice, influence over governing bodies and control of new grant-maintained schools. The powers of LEAs were decreased dramatically and schools were to be more accountable both financially and in terms of attainment. A numbers of circulars (see below) were issued under this Act to allow for implementation of the details relating to opting out and other matters.

Children Act 1989 Brought into force in October 1991, the Children Act established a new and comprehensive legal framework for the care and upbringing of children. A number of the Act's provisions are therefore of direct relevance to education, although it has been amended subsequently to deal with certain anomalous provisions. See, for example, *Re G (Parental Responsibility: Education)* [1995] FCR 53.

Education (Student Loans) Act 1990   Students in Higher Education were given access to loans to assist them with maintenance during their courses.

Further and Higher Education Act 1992   Colleges of further education, tertiary colleges and sixth form colleges were no longer to be maintained by LEAs and became part of the new further education sector.

Education (Schools) Act 1992   This Act introduced provisions relating to the inspection of schools and the dissemination of information concerning schools.

Education Act 1993   The main aim of this Act was to make it easier for schools to opt for grant-maintained status while making it more difficult for local authorities to stop them. The Funding Agency for Schools (FAS) was created. Education Associations were given powers in respect of schools which are considered to be 'failing' by the Office for Standards in Education (Ofsted). The Act also introduced 'Pupil Referral Units' for disturbed pupils who had dropped out of or had been excluded from schools.

Education Act 1994   This Act made various provisions in relation to teacher training, including the establishment of the Teacher Training Agency. The Act also made some provisions in respect of student unions.

Education Act 1996   This Act repealed the Education Acts 1944 and 1993. It consolidated the law relating to primary, secondary and further education, but is not entirely comprehensive; other 1996 legislation also contributed to the overall picture. The Act contained 583 sections and 40 schedules.

Schools Inspections Act 1996   This Act consolidated those parts of the Education (Schools) Act 1992 and the Education Act 1993 dealing with school inspections.

Education (Student Loans) Act 1996   This Act amended the Education (Student Loans) Act 1990 to provide for the payment of subsidies to those private sector bodies making loans to students.

Nursery Education and Grant-Maintained Schools Act 1996   This Act provided for the introduction of nursery education vouchers and gave grant-maintained schools the power to borrow commercially.

Education Act 1997   One of the last statutes of the Conservative government, this Act received Royal Assent on the dissolution of Parliament. Some of the provisions of the Act survived the change in government. The Act contained a number of miscellaneous provisions concerning school discipline, home–school partnership documents, baseline assessment schemes, the inspection of LEAs, careers education and the establishment of the Qualification and Curriculum Authority (known in Wales as the Qualifications, Curriculum and Assessment Authority).

Education (Schools) Act 1997   One of the first statutes of the newly elected Labour government, the Act sets out the basis for ending the Assisted Places Scheme.

Education (Student Loans) Act 1998   This Act made provision for the transfer of student loans to the private sector, prescribed terms of student loan agreements and dealt with the administration of public sector loans.

School Standards and Framework Act 1998   The Act embodies the principles of the White Paper, 'Excellence in Schools'. A major piece of legislation, the Act sets out a new structure for schools, places new duties on LEAs and governors and introduces, *inter alia*, Education Action Zones. There are provisions relating to admissions and nursery schools. Parts of the Education Acts 1996 and 1997 were repealed.

Teaching and Higher Education Act 1998   The Act introduces a requirement of a pre-appointment qualification for headteachers and induction for newly qualified teachers. A General Teaching Council is to be establised. One of the most controversial provisions in education law, the payment of tuition fees by students, was introduced by this Act. The Act repeals all previous legislation on student loans. The provisions of the Act are being brought into force by delegated legislation, see the Teaching and Higher Education Act 1998 (Commencement No 1) Order 1998 (SI No 1729).

Delegated legislation, circulars and codes of practice

As is often the case with primary legislation, power is given for the making of delegated legislation. In the case of education law, this power is mainly vested in the Secretary of State for Education who has the power to make regulations, rules and orders under various Acts; these powers are widely used.

Many policy changes in education are brought into effect through delegated legislation.

Circulars   These are used to implement important policy changes and this is perhaps more so in education law than in any other field of law. One important policy change which was introduced through a circular rather than through primary or delegated legislation was the introduction of comprehensive education. Circular 10/65 required LEAs to draw up plans for comprehensive education. Circulars have 'advisory' status only. In R v *Hertfordshire County Council, ex parte Cheung* [1986] *The Times*, 4 April, a decision was taken by the council wholly on advice given by a DES circular. It was held that although the circular could be taken into account, and indeed in most circumstances LEAs must take such advice into account, it was wrong to treat such advice as decisive. Circulars now include as part of the text an indication as to their legal effect.

Codes of practice   These also give useful practical guidance. Some codes are produced by interest groups and/or professional associations, for example the Code on Appeals produced by the Association of Metropolitan Authorities (AMA). The Department for Education and Employment (DfEE) also produces codes, as does Ofsted, which has produced a series of 'Frameworks' for the inspection of schools. The School Standards and Framework Act 1998 (SSFA) provides for two important Codes to be drawn up under the Act. One relates to admissions (ss 84 and 85), the other deals with relationships between LEAs and maintained schools (s 127).

Other legislative influences

In addition to statutory authority which relates directly to education, the provision of education is affected by other statutes and delegated legislation. For example, the Sex Discrimination Act

1975 and the Race Relations Act 1976 have relevance to education issues, as seen in *R v Northamptonshire County Council, ex parte K* [1993] *The Times*, 22 July and *R v Cleveland County Council, ex parte Commission for Racial Equality* [1993] 91 LGR 139. A number of other statutes may have direct or indirect application to schools such as the Health and Safety at Work Act 1974, the Occupiers Liability Acts 1957 and 1984, the Reverter of Sites Act 1987, the Environmental Protection Act 1990, the Asylum and Immigration Act 1996 and many others.

Common law influences

As litigation on education has increased, particularly over the last 20 years, the courts have become heavily involved in the interpretation of education legislation. Courts at all levels are involved with education issues, although cases with a criminal dimension are unusual. The civil courts have seen most of the increasing workload and courts from the magistrates' courts to the European Court of Human Rights have become involved, see, for example, *Osman v UK* [1998] *The Times*, 5 November.

Education law as a subject

Jonathan Robinson, writing in the *Solicitor's Journal*, urged solicitors (and other members of the legal profession) to treat education law as a serious subject in its own right:

> If solicitors ignore this pressing need, other professions will doubtless make an impact ... it is vital that the profession appreciates the pace and complexity of change in state schools in England and Wales (133 SJ 930).

Judicial guidance

There is some judicial authority for the view that education cases should be considered in context. In *Ex parte M (Judicial review: Education)* [1994] *The Times*, 22 March, Popplewell J in the Queen's Bench Division stated that a challenge to a decision of a schools admissions appeal committee should be supported by reference to cases on education law and not by reference to cases outside that field.

Law reports

There is now a dedicated series of Education Law Reports, (ELR) and others are to be developed. ELR extracts can be found in the *Journal of Family Law*. Many education law cases are to be found in reports dealing with local government cases, and those involving judicial review are frequently reported in the *Crown Office Digest*.

Education law texts

A detailed bibliography sets out the major texts which have been written on this subject area. Apart from standard and looseleaf works, there are newsletters which assist in keeping lawyers, teachers, governors and other interested parties abreast of changes in education law and policy.

Education Law Association (ELAS)

In 1991 an association was formed to promote the understanding of education law. ELAS seeks to enhance the status of education law through specialist and regional groups. For ELAS's address see 'Useful addresses' at p. 263 below.

Policy-making in education law

The impact of policy in education law should not be underestimated. Policy matters are formulated and information is disseminated by a variety of organisations. The DfEE is necessarily a major source, but the professional associations also produce useful information, as do bodies such as the Advisory Centre for Education.

Legal aid

The availability of legal aid in education law is patchy. Legal aid for judicial review and special educational needs advice seems set to continue, although negligence claims may well be affected by the Woolf proposals to adopt conditional fee agreements. Some legal assistance is available free of charge through schemes such as the Bar Pro Bono Unit.

Chapter 2

The Structure of Education

The Structure of Education

Department for Education and Employment (DfEE)

The Department for Education (DFE) became merged in 1995 with part of the Department of Employment responsible for training to become the Department for Education and Employment (DfEE). Prior to that the Department was known as the Department for Education and Science (DES).

The name change in 1995 was meant to reflect the link between education and training. Only those sections of the former Department of Employment which dealt with training have been allocated to the DfEE, other sections being allocated to other government departments. The DfEE maintains links with other relevant departments such as the Department of Health. As a result of greater devolution to some regions, government officers in Cardiff, Edinburgh and Belfast will have more impact on education. The Secretary of State for Wales, for example, has had considerable responsibility for regional education differences in Wales in the past. The Secretary of State for Education and Employment retains control over the provision of education by, for example, reserve powers in the School Standards and Framework Act (SSFA) 1998 to intervene when maintained schools are causing concern and of the private sector through registration requirements.

Educational providers

Together with the Education Act 1944, the Education Reform Act (ERA) 1988 and the Education Acts 1993 and 1996 had a profound effect upon the structure of education. These Acts, *inter alia*, created a new structure of those providers of education (for those of compulsory school age in particular) so that it has become more important than ever to appreciate the different types of educational institutions which exist.

One of the most important changes in recent legislation was that LEAs were no longer to be the main providers of education. The Secretary of State for Education, under section 1 of the 1944 Act, had a duty to promote education and to secure the effective execution by local authorities of the national policy for providing an education service. The 1993 Act reconsidered responsibility for educational provision and section 1 of the 1944 Act was repealed to reflect the fact that LEAs no longer had sole responsibility for provision. Section 1 of the 1993 Act stated that 'the Secretary of State shall promote the education of the people of England and Wales'.

The responsibility was a general one extending over schools and further education. It was claimed that such a change of emphasis was offset by giving more power directly to schools themselves. Some commentators claim that the recent amendments to the structure of schools contained in SSFA 1998 represent a move back to centralisation of the provision of education and removal of some of the flexibility schools have enjoyed.

Section 5 of the SSFA 1998, amending section 13 of the Education Act 1996, sets out the new duty of LEAs to:

> ... ensure that their functions relating to the provision of education [for persons of compulsory school age and for persons above or below that age who are registered at a school maintained by the authority] are (so far as they are capable of being so exercised) exercised by the authority with a view to promoting high standards.

Under sections 6 and 7 of the 1998 Act, LEAs will have to prepare education development plans, that is a statement of proposals for developing their provision of education in their area. Such a statement will have to be approved by the Secretary of State for Education. Section 8 of SSFA 1998 amends the Education Act 1996 to allow the Secretary of State for Education to intervene should he be satisfied that '... a local education authority are failing in any respect to perform any function to which this section applies to an adequate standard (or at all) ...'. The DfEE have subsequently advertised for 'contractors' who wish to express an interest in providing education and/or management consultancy and advice services. Several LEAs have been found to be 'failing' and contractors have taken over their education role.

LEAs will not have an entirely free hand in drawing up proposals; section 2 of the SSFA 1998 and the School Standards and Framework Act 1998 (Infant Class Sizes) (Modification) Regulations 1998 (SI No 1968) requires LEAs to set out arrangements to deliver the government's commitment to limit class sizes in infant schools. Under sections 24–27 (and Sched 5) of the 1998 Act the Secretary of State will be required to appoint 'adjudicators', thereby creating another tier of administration. LEAs will be required to establish school organisation committees which will formulate school organisation plans. One aim of these committees will be to consider provision of school places, rationalisation of such places being provided for under section 34 and Schedule 7 of SSFA 1998. The DfEE have produced some guidance on the working of these committees which adds some detail to the provisions of SSFA 1998. The DfEE stated in the guidance that: 'It is not our intention to be over-prescriptive about the content of the School Organisation Plan', which suggests that the DfEE clearly intends to have some input, although at that stage it was limited to highlighting relevant matters. The focus of these committees is intended to be the local determination of issues, and membership of the committees will include representatives of the LEA drawn from elected members, serving school governors, representatives from Church of England and Roman Catholic dioceses and members nominated by the Further Education Funding Council (FEFC) who will have voting rights limited to matters affecting provision for pupils aged over 16.

The committee is intended to give formal effect to the local partnership in the provision of school places.

Ajudicators will be called upon where:

- the school organisation committee could not agree the terms of a school organisation plan;
- the school organisation committee could not agree a decision on a school organisation proposal; or
- there is a dispute between local admission authorities over admission arrangements.

Adjudicators will be able to hold local inquiries on such matters. They will be independent and will come under the supervision of the Council on Tribunals. The precise nature of the relationship which will develop in the light of these requirements remains to be seen. The code of practice on LEA-School relations sets out the basic principles and aims in relations with schools giving examples of good and poor practice. The code of practice on the relationship between LEAs and schools should provide a useful insight. Some LEAs are relatively new, being unitary authorities, and detailed transitional arrangements are detailed in the Local Government Changes for England (Education) (Miscellaneous Provisions) Regulations 1996 (SI No 710). The inspection of LEAs by Ofsted and involving the collaboration of the Audit Commission can require action planning by LEAs to address problems (Education Act 1997, ss 38–41). The DfEE announced that 16 LEAs were to be inspected in 1998, 24 in 1999 and 30 in 2000.

The idea of promoting local partnerships in education provision is further demonstrated by section 9 of SSFA 1998, which requires LEA education committees to include representatives of parent governors. Similarly, the introduction of education action zones (EAZs) provided by sections 10–13 of SSFA 1998 anticipates the involvement of private companies in the provision of state education by virtue of their membership of Education Action Forums. See the Education Action Forum (Proceedings) Regulations 1998 (SI No 1964).

Educational provision

Maintained schools

Under section 8 of the Education Act 1944, each LEA had to provide a sufficient number of schools providing a variety of education for children of compulsory school age (i.e. 5–16 years). The bulk of educational provision has therefore been that established by LEAs. The duty (as amended) may involve the closure of schools as the concept of rationalisation suggests. Closure of schools on a temporary basis was considered in *Meade* v *Haringey London Borough Council* [1979] 2 All ER 1016 where schools were closed during a period of industrial action. Eveleigh LJ stated:

> It is a tenable view that the authority were genuinely trying to do their best under section 8 by closing schools for a time not to exacerbate an industrial situation which might result in greater detriment to the children's education.

The SSFA 1998 repealed Part II of the Education Act 1996 which concerned the establishment and conduct of maintained schools.

The phrase "maintained schools" is commonly used and traditionally included "county" schools provided wholly by the LEA and "voluntary" schools (see below) and maintained special schools. Care should be taken with this phrase, as it may (depending on the context) include not only those schools but also special schools not so maintained and grant-maintained schools as, for example, in the Education (Partnership Grant) Regulations 1998 (SI No. 1222). The new categories of maintained schools for the purpose of the SSFA are set out in section 20 of the Act. Provision of primary and secondary schools has also traditionally included "middle schools" which partly overlap primary and secondary provision and which were authorised by the Education Act 1964, although section 20(6) of SSFA 1998 which defines "school", refers only to primary, secondary or special schools (including special nursery schools). Nursery schools and pupil referral units are excluded from the definition.

Community schools

The SSFA 1998 introduced the community school (effective from the "appointed day"), a category made up of former county schools according to Schedule 2 of that Act, which sets out the allocated categories of schools. The governing body may accept such an allocation or opt for an allocation to a different category. The premises of a community school will continue to be owned by the LEA.

In performing their statutory duties under previous legislation, LEAs could take into account a number of factors. In *R v Birmingham City Council, ex parte Equal Opportunities Commission (No. 2)* [1993] 91 LGR 14, it was held that the LEA could look at all educational provision in the area when determining what was appropriate; that included looking at the likely impact of a grant-maintained school in the locality. Watkins LJ stated that:

> While the council's section 8 functions were carried out not in relation to the grant-maintained school but in relation to the children in its area they could not be carried out in blinkers.

Similar issues were under consideration in *R v Northamptonshire County Council, ex parte K* [1993] *The Times,* 22 July where closure of a single-sex school was the subject of a dispute. In future education development plans, the work of the school organisation committees will have a considerable impact on the number and location of community schools, and closure of schools remains one way in which the LEA may satisfy its duty to promote high standards in education if school inspections deem closure appropriate.

The establishment, alteration and discontinuance of maintained schools is dealt with under sections 28–35 of SSFA 1998. Sections 36–44 set out the provisions relating to the governance of maintained schools. Previously, each maintained school had Articles and Instruments of Government. The Instruments of Government set out the constitution of the governing body. The Articles set out in detail matters relating to the conduct of the school, the curriculum, public examinations, special needs, term dates, discipline, appeals, premises, reports and meetings, admissions and health and safety matters. It was possible for schools to adopt block Instruments and Articles under Circular 7/87, *Education (No 2) Act 1986, Further Guidance.* Under SSFA 1998, Articles are effectively abolished.

Section 38, whilst stating that the conduct of a school is a matter for the governing body, provides for regulations to be made setting out terms of reference for the governing bodies of maintained schools. Under section 41, the LEA shall determine the dates of school terms whilst the governing body shall determine the times of school sessions. Instruments will be required to be in standard form; Schedule 12 of SSFA 1998 provides what Instruments should contain.

One important issue in many LEAs has been whether secondary (or indeed other) education should be provided on the basis of selection or by means of comprehensive education. The traditional view was that this was a matter of policy to be determined in conjunction with the Secretary of State as decided in *Secretary of State for Education v Metropolitan Borough of Tameside* [1976] 3 WLR 641.

The Education Act 1996 set out detailed arrangements for ballots to be held to establish grammar schools. Under section 104 of SSFA 1998, a school may only be designated a grammar school if it was a maintained school with selective admission arrangements at the beginning of the 1997–1998 school year. This is seen to signal the end of the short-lived return of the grammar school, but is likely to stimulate some litigation. A recent case involving the proposed establishment of a new grammar school considered the role of the county council in the context of the new unitary authorities. In *R v Buckinghamshire County Council, ex parte Milton Keynes Borough Council* [1997] *The Times,* 13 November, the local authority issued proposals to establish a grammar school knowing that it would be replaced as the LEA by Milton Keynes Borough Council before the school was due to open. The borough council "would therefore be saddled with the establishment of a grammar school to which it was strongly opposed". On appeal to the Court of Appeal, it was held that the county council had the power to set in train the new school, but the county council were urged to re-think their proposal in the light of the borough's objections.

The new arrangements for ballots in respect of grammar schools under SSFA 1998 are set out in the Education (Grammar School Ballots) Regulations 1998 (SI No 2876).

The question of selection generally is addressed in section 99 of SSFA 1998. There is a general restriction on selection by ability or aptitude except in certain circumstances provided by sections 100–102 of the Act. These sections cover pre-existing arrangements, pupil banding and aptitude for particular subjects.

Voluntary schools

There were traditionally three types of voluntary school: controlled, aided and special agreement schools. The main difference was in the provision of expenditure. Such schools are not "provided" as such by LEAs, but they assist in the running of these schools. They were therefore traditionally referred to as "maintained schools". Voluntary aided schools often served a particular religious persuasion. In 1993 it was reported that there were 2,000 Church of England, 2,100 Roman Catholic, 21 Jewish and 4 Methodist voluntary aided schools. The creation of such schools has been the subject of some litigation, as has their closure. In *R v Secretary of State for Education, ex parte Islam* [1992] COD 448, the DES was found to have acted with "manifest unfairness" in dealing with proposals to establish an Islamic primary school.

In *R v Governors' of the Bishop Challenor Roman Catholic Comprehensive Girls School, ex parte Choudhury* [1992] 3 WLR 99, the status of voluntary schools was considered in some detail by Lord Browne-Wilkinson who was quoted extensively in *Board of Governors of St Matthias Church of England School* v *Crizzle* [1993] IRLR 472.

State funding through grant-maintained status was made available for a Muslim school for the first time in 1998; under SSFA 1998 the school is likely to become voluntary aided. Special agreement schools status has been abolished under SSFA 1998, and any such remaining schools will become voluntary aided. Schedule 2 of the Act sets out which schools will be allocated voluntary status, and there are provisions similar to those for community schools set out in sections 28–35.

There are some special provisions relating to schools with a religious character throughout SSFA 1998 such as the requirement to set out the "ethos" of the school in the Instruments, as required by Schedule 12 and section 60 which refer to the religious opinions of staff at schools with a religious character. Representatives of dioceses will be appointed to school organisation committees and admissions to voluntary schools with a religious character will be decided by the adjudicator.

In broad terms, aided schools will own their own premises, but it was felt that "consistency of ownership" would create too much turbulence and that the guiding principle should be that schools should continue to hold what they owned prior to the 1998 legislation. The Education Transfer Council will deal with any necessary land transfers. This non-departmental government body was established under ERA 1988 as the Education Assets Board to deal, *inter alia*, with schools leaving LEA control. The name and role of this body was changed under SSFA 1998.

Independent schools

"Independent school" is defined in section 463 of the Education Act 1996 as:

> any school at which full-time education is provided for five or more pupils of compulsory school age (whether or not such education is also provided at it for pupils under or over that age) , and which is not—
> (a) a school maintained by the local education authority,
> (b) a special school not so maintained, or
> (c) a grant-maintained school.

In *R v Headmaster of Fernhill Manor School, ex parte Brown* [1992] *The Times,* 5 June, the legal status of private schools was considered for the purposes of a judicial review application. It was contended that a private school was not a public body and that the relationship between pupils and independent schools is solely a private agreement between the school and the parents. It was recognised that private schools operate within a statutory system of control, but Brooke J agreed with the contention that relationships were based on the private law of contract. As a result such schools were not open to scrutiny by the courts. The governing bodies of such schools should take care to ensure that rules relating to disciplinary matters were fair: "The relevant principles of fair play had been repeatedly stated by the courts."

The Education Act 1996 provides for the registration and regulation of independent schools in Part VII and Schedule 34. See also the Education (Particulars of Independent Schools) Regulations 1997 (SI No 2918).

Some independent schools attract charitable status and the general law of charitable trusts applies. In *Commissioners of Income Tax* v *Pemsel* [1891] AC 531 "charity" was defined by Lord MacNaghten. Charitable trusts must be for:

- relief of poverty
- the advancement of education
- the advancement of religion
- other purposes beneficial to the community.

Many education trusts will fall under the second item, but the other types of charitable trusts may be applicable. According to *Incorporated Council for Law Reporting* v *Attorney-General* [1972] Ch 73 "education" in this context is much wider than classroom teaching. It includes the imparting and disseminating of knowledge as well as the encouragement of conventional academic and commercial subjects. A trust which merely provides for sporting facilities may be charitable under this head if linked to education. See for example *Re Mariette* [1915] 2 Ch 284, where a Fives Court was provided at a public school under a trust.

The ability of parents to sue a charitable trust was considered in *Gunning* v *Buckfast Abbey Trustees* [1994] *The Times*, 9 June. In this case it was held that parents of children at a fee-paying preparatory school run as part of a charitable trust were neither subscribers to nor beneficiaries of the charity; they had a greater interest than ordinary members of the general public in securing the proper administration of the trust. As a result they were not barred from bringing proceedings under section 33(1) of the Charities Act 1993. The parents wished to challenge the proposed closure of the school.

It had been suggested that the charitable status of independent schools was under threat; however, the Charity Commission confirmed in 1998 that there were no plans to press for a change in the law, although an independent review would take place to ensure that charities satisfied legal requirements. The removal of some tax benefits has had important financial implications at a time when independent schools are facing increasing competition and funding difficulties with the abolition of the Assisted Places Scheme. It is claimed that charitable status is worth £40 million to independent education.

Provision for "partnership schools" involving independent and maintained schools which group together for educational purposes are regulated by The Education (Partnership Grant) Regulations 1998 (SI No 1222).

Foundation schools

Grant-maintained schools directly funded by the state were established by the Conservative government in an attempt to increase local choice and to take education out of LEA control. They were commonly referred to as schools which have "opted out" i.e. they were no longer under LEA control.

These schools received better state funding than other state schools, with transitional grants, more favourable capital allowances and the funds released by not requiring specialist LEA support. The ERA 1988 gave the Secretary of State the power to approve applications for grant-maintained status. In *R v Secretary of State for Education and Science, ex parte Newham London Borough Council* [1991] COD 277 it was held that neither the courts nor the LEA could interfere with this power even when the change of status was regarded as 'experimental' and where there was no evidence that the quality or range of teaching would change as a result. In July 1995, the government announced a common funding policy for grant-maintained primary schools as part of a drive to increase the number of schools opted out in that sector. Special schools could also be grant-maintained (see below). In 1995, there were 1,000 grant-maintained schools. Part III of the Education Act 1996 consolidated the law on grant-maintained schools, but this has been repealed by the SSFA 1998 which effectively brings to an end the "experiment" of grant-maintained schools and introduces a new category of school, the "foundation school". It is expected that most grant-maintained schools will become foundation schools as anticipated by Schedule 2 SSFA 1998, although grant-maintained schools which were formerly an aided or special agreement school or a school established by promoters under Part III of the Education Act 1996 have been allocated voluntary aided status. The Education (Allocation of Grant-maintained and Grant-maintained Special Schools to New Categories) Regulations 1998 (SI No 1969) set out the procedure in detail.

Foundation schools will have a "foundation" which will be a body of trustees or a body corporate (other than the governing body) which holds property for the purposes of the school. Existing schools which are not grant-maintained will not be able to become foundation schools until the Secretary of State provides by regulations that they may do so. The Education Transfer Council will deal with matters relating to the transfer of property.

City Technology Colleges

Section 105 of ERA 1988 provided for the creation of City Technology Colleges (CTCs). In *R v Governors of Haberdashers' Aske's Hatcham College, ex parte Tyrell* [1995] COD 399, Dyson J. described CTCs as:

> ... publicly funded non-fee paying urban schools for pupils drawn wholly or mainly from the areas in which the schools are situated, whose curriculum was broad but with an emphasis on science and technology.

There is also provision for CTCs where the syllabus has an arts bias.

The legal status of CTCs has been the subject of litigation; it seems that it was originally anticipated that they would attract the status of independent schools, but this proved contentious. In *ex parte Tyrell* (above) it was held that "the position of CTCs was materially different from that of private schools". The legal status of CTCs (and other educational institutions) is an important matter when considering the application of public law remedies. *Ex parte Tyrell* established that CTCs were liable to judicial review. The "public law" dimension was also recognised in *R v Governors of John Bacon School, ex parte Inner London Education Authority* [1990] 88 LGR 648, despite the fact that the CTC in that case was described as "an independent school set up by agreement between private sponsors and the [DES] under the Education Reform Act 1988". The matter seems to have been resolved by the inclusion of CTCs in that part of the Education Act 1996 which deals with independent schools.

Nursery education

Nursery education is defined in section 117 of SSFA 1998. It means "full-time or part-time education for children who have not attained compulsory school age (whether provided at schools or elsewhere)".

Under previous legislation there was no duty to provide such education, although section 18 of the Children Act 1989 set out the duty of the local authority in respect of day care for the under-fives who are not yet attending schools. The duty under this section was to provide such day care: however, "day care" was defined as any form of care or supervised activity for children during the day, and can therefore include care within the home.

The "nursery school voucher scheme" introduced by the Nursery Education and Grant Maintained Schools Act 1996 was an attempt to give parents the right to some form of nursery education. Under sections 118–124 of SSFA 1998 there is a duty on all LEAs to secure the provision of sufficient nursery education for their area (whether made by them or not) for children below compulsory school age but above such age as may be prescribed. There is a requirement to establish a body known as an "early years development partnership", the function of which will be to work with the LEA to review provision and to prepare "early years action plans" which are subject to the Secretary of State's approval. From 1999, all LEAs are expected to meet targets for places for 4-year-olds in schools, playgroups or with private providers.

Special educational provision

The duty to provide for various kinds of education requires LEAs to consider, for example, how special educational needs can be met.

The duty, now set out in the Education Act 1996, has resulted in a vast amount of litigation, discussed in detail in Chapter 13 below. Many LEAs have had a policy of closure in respect of special schools, preferring instead to integrate pupils into mainstream schools. This has been reinforced by a policy of integration reflected in the legislation. Special needs may also be provided for in independent, non-maintained and (former) grant-maintained special schools. The first grant-maintained special school opened in 1994. Schedule 2 of SSFA 1998 allocates maintained special schools, community special school status and grant-maintained special schools will become foundation special schools. Independent schools may still be suitable for the admission of "statemented children" under section 347 of the Education Act 1996, replacing section 189 of the Education Act 1993.

Special educational needs provision is constantly under review and has been the subject of a recent Green Paper, "Excellence for all children".

Education of sick children

Section 19 of the Education Act 1996 (replacing similar provision under the Education Act 1993) allows LEAs to make exceptional provision of education by way of home tuition in the case of children who are too ill, *inter alia*, to attend school. Detailed guidance was also given in Circular 12/94. The provision of home tuition was recently considered in *R* v *East Sussex County Council, ex parte Tandy* [1998] 2 WLR 884. Should a child be detained in hospital for a lengthy period, the LEA should be notified under the provisions of the National Health Service and Community Care Act 1990, section 661 and Schedule 9. Schools established in hospitals are often exempt from requirements placed on other schools; see for example Schedule 30 of SSFA 1998 which excludes such schools from target-setting requirements.

Part IX of the Education Act 1996 mentions the medical inspection and treatment of pupils in school, while Circular 14/96 (jointly issued with the Department of Health) deals with supporting pupils with medical needs in school.

Education of disruptive children

Pupil Referral Units (PRUs) for those children who do not attend school because they are disturbed or excluded were introduced by the Education Act 1993. The arrangements were based on pre-existing provision. Circular 10/94 set out the proper use by schools of the sanction of exclusion and Circular 11/94 gave guidance on the education of such children through individual and home tuition, as well as through pupil referral units. The Education Act 1997 has had a considerable impact on the education of such children. Section 9 of that Act placed a new duty on LEAs to "prepare, and from time to time review, a statement setting out the arrangements made or proposed to be made by the authority in connection with the education of children with 'behavioural difficulties'", amending section 527 of the Education Act 1996. The term "behavioural difficulties" is not defined in the Act, but seems to include not only those excluded from school but those with special educational needs. LEAs are given no additional powers, but are obliged to inform schools in one document of their policies and arrangements regarding such children.

Education of children in care

It was reported in 1997 that more than a third of children in care or with foster parents were receiving no education at all. Circular 13/94, *The Education of Children being Looked After by Local Authorities,* set out the relevant guidance for the education of such children.

Schools run by education associations

Schools which were considered to be failing following inspection by Ofsted could be taken out of local authority control by virtue of the provisions of section 220 of the Education Act 1993. Control was given to teams, normally of teachers and business people, who had three months to produce a recovery plan. Within two years the schools should either close or become grant-maintained. In July 1995, the first school to have such a team assigned to it was Hackney Downs. Under the SSFA 1998 the Secretary of State may make such arrangements as are necessary to intervene in the case of a school causing concern, or may create an EAZ in cases where it is "expedient to do so".

Tertiary education

Tertiary colleges provide both full- and part-time courses for those aged over 16. They differ in that respect from sixth form colleges, which generally offer full-time courses only.

Tertiary colleges have developed from further education colleges and have achieved "independent" status in that they are now free from local authority financial control and are centrally funded. Regulations made under the Further and Higher Education Act 1992 prescribe the form of Instruments and Articles to be adopted by tertiary colleges and deal with the incorporation of the same.

Adult education

There is no statutory or common law definition of "adult education" but it is a term commonly used to denote non-vocational educational and recreational provision. The Further and Higher Education Act 1992 amended the Education (No 2) Act 1986 to give governors of county and voluntary schools the power to provide part-time education for those aged over 16 and/or full-time education for those aged over 19. Maintained special schools could also make such provision, but only with the LEA's consent. Grant-maintained schools were allowed to make similar provision by virtue of section 128 of the Education Act 1993.

Adult education is also provided by university departments, the Workers' Educational Association and other voluntary associations and commercial providers; recent impetus has been provided by the government's promotion of the concept of "lifelong learning".

Higher education

Since the implementation of the Further and Higher Education Act 1992 the bifurcated system of universities and polytechnics has disappeared, with the latter taking on the status of universities. The new universities have corporate status. The effect of corporate status was considered in an employment law context in *Leicester University* v *A*, [1999] *The Times*, 23 March. Many Universities also have charitable status and have been similarly affected by the changes in taxation referred to above. Universities are often regulated by statutes (e.g. University of London Act 1994).

Miscellaneous provision

Some schools, such as British schools abroad and schools for HM forces, fall outside what may be considered to be mainstream education.

Challenging Decisions

Challenging Decisions

Appeal committees

The education lawyer will often be asked to advise on the prospects of mounting a successful challenge to decisions taken by LEAs and governing bodies. Parents, professional associations and pressure groups may wish to challenge decisions made about education. The introduction by the SSFA 1998 of adjudicators creates a further potential party in legal proceedings.

Because education law is based on primary and delegated legislation, it is important when challenging a decision to investigate the possibility of a statutory appeal. Failure to do so may have serious consequences. A premature request for judicial review disregarding a statutory appeal can result in loss of time, possible loss of remedies and, ultimately, actions against the lawyer for lack of care.

Statutory appeals procedures are commonly found in the legislation: see, for example, sections 496 and 497 of the Education Act 1996. Procedures often provide for an initial appeal to governors and then to an appeal committee (or panel). In *R v Essex County Council, ex parte Bullimore* [1997] ELR 327 it was held that the applicant should have availed himself of the procedure for complaint to the Secretary of State under sections 496 and 497 rather than launching an application for judicial review.

The system of appeals to committees was revised by the Education Act 1997 in certain respects and fundamentally overhauled by the SSFA 1998. Most appeals concern issues relating to admissions or exclusions, both being part of the same appellate structure. However, the nature of each appeal varies according to the type of school and the issues involved.

Community schools

Admissions will continue to be dealt with by the LEA and governors (known as the admissions authority under SSFA 1998) in accordance with published criteria. Admissions policies in general terms may be challenged by referring them to the adjudicator.

In specific cases, parents may appeal to an appeal committee if, for example, they are denied the exercise of parental preference in accordance with the provisions of the Education Act 1980 (now section 86 of SSFA 1998). In 1996/97 there were 72,700 appeals to committees with 19,800 being decided in favour of the parents, 51,300 having been heard by a committee.

Appeal committees were formerly made up of councillors, lay members (in the education sense) and LEA representatives. The SSFA 1998 provides that councillors will no longer be able to act as members and governors of schools will not be able to sit on panels involving their own schools. There has been a gradual move towards this procedure over recent years with councillors being unable to chair committees and governors voluntarily removing themselves from committees. The duty to advertise for lay members of committees in the Education (Lay Members of Appeal Committees) Regulations 1994 (SI No 1303) required LEAs to advertise in local newspapers for lay members. Further provisions relating to advertisements may be made under Schedule 24 of SSFA 1998.

Aided schools

Admissions are dealt with by the governing body. Under section 91 of SSFA 1998, such schools may impose admission criteria to preserve their religious character. Such arrangements must be agreed with the LEA and the school may appeal to the adjudicator. The necessary arrangements for an appeal by parents should be made by the governing body, but no members of the governing body should be on the appeal committee. The governing bodies of aided and former special agreement schools are also bound by the requirements to advertise for lay members (see above).

Independent appeal committees should be set up by the governors to deal with appeals against exclusions.

Foundation schools

Governing bodies may draw up their own criteria on admissions. Decisions may be challenged by appeal to a governors' appeals committee which includes a majority of independent members. Independent appeal committees deal with appeals in respect of exclusions.

Appeals procedure

Appellants will often be parents who may feel that the appeal committee has not dealt with their case properly, in which case a complaint may be made to the Secretary of State for Education or, in the case of LEA schools, to the Local Government Ombudsman.

Under sections 496 and 497 of the Education Act 1996, complaint can be made to the Secretary of State on the grounds that the LEA or governing body was unreasonable in the setting-up of the appeal arrangements. Appeal committees are considered to be "statutory tribunals", and as such they are subject to the scrutiny of the Council on Tribunals. Guidance on the constitution and procedure of these committees can be derived from a number of sources, including the Council on Tribunals and the Association of Metropolitan Authorities (AMA). A new code of practice has been produced by the government to implement the SSFA 1998 provisions with effect from September 2000. Voluntary implementation of the new procedures from September 1999 is encouraged by the DfEE. The Secretary of State is obliged to issue "such practical guidance as he thinks fit" in relation to the discharge by LEAs, the governing bodies of maintained schools, appeal panels or adjudicators under sections 76–89 of SSFA 1998.

Appeal committees must be constituted with care and should adhere strictly to the rules of procedure and natural justice. If they do not, an application for judicial review may be possible. The courts have been keen to point to the "lay" nature of these committees. For example, in *R* v *Commissioner for Local Administration, ex parte Croydon London Borough Council* [1989] 1 All ER 1033, the appeal committee procedure had been followed as set out. In that case it was said to be important to remember that these were lay committees (in the legal sense) and as such the standard which attached to them were those appropriate to lay proceedings:

> The court should not approach decisions and reasons given by committees of laymen expecting the same accuracy in the use of language which a lawyer might be expected to adopt. This was a lay committee with a lay clerk.

A similar approach was taken in *R* v *Hackney London Borough Council, ex parte T* [1991] COD 454, in which the system of admissions was challenged together with the appeal procedure. The suggested unfairness was held not to be a basis for challenge, "rather it was a blemish which must be accepted". It was held that the appeal committee had given adequate reasons for their decision. They had explained their conclusion in broad and simple terms, which indicated a correct appreciation of the task they had and a correct approach to its resolution: "It must be remembered that they were an appeal committee not a judicial body and that they did not have the advantage of a legally qualified chairman." Writing in the *Head*

Teacher's Briefing (Issue No 68, 20 February 1995), Robert Morris has suggested that the committee might feel vulnerable if the clerk were not a lawyer, especially if there were legal representations made on behalf of the parties. Morris states:

> Only commonsense and the need to avoid unnecessary expenditure ... keep the scale of operations at the level of businesslike informality which the framers of the original legislation intended.

The question of legal representation can be an issue. In complex cases legal representation may be deemed to be appropriate. The AMA code pointed out that whilst it would be appropriate for parents to have the assistance of a "friend" before a committee, it would be an exceptional circumstance for that person to be a lawyer. However, the Education Act 1997 provided that legal represention in exclusion appeals should always be considered as a matter of course.

Admissions appeals

Admissions appeals begin with an explanation, mainly for the parents' benefit, of the procedure. The first stage is based on guidance by the Director of Education which should have been sent to the appellants. This will usually include information about the criteria used by the LEA, admission limits, standard numbers and physical capacity of the school. The criteria may be considered directly. The Director's representative, normally an education officer, presents the LEA's case first and the parents may then ask questions, as may the panel. The parents then put their case, which is likely to be based on personal circumstances, and questioning may again take place. A brief period of summing up on each side follows with the parents having the last word. In admissions appeals there may be several cases all dealing with the same issues (i.e. appeals for the same year group in the same school). In such circumstances these cases should be heard individually and then determined when all the appeals have been heard. This is the procedure preferred by the Council on Tribunals and recommended by the AMA code, despite the rather time-consuming nature of such a procedure. This procedure requires the education officer to state the same cases perhaps several times. A grouped appeal may be possible where the LEA's case is put only once and then the parents make their representations; however, this can also cause difficulties where the parents wish their case to be heard in private. The education officer's task is to establish prejudice in the sense that either efficient use of resources or efficient education would be prejudiced by the admission.

The parents may prove that there would be no such prejudice or that any prejudice would be overridden by their personal circumstances.

The importance of the two-stage procedure was established in *R v Commissioner for Local Administration, ex parte Croydon London Borough Council* (above) and recently confirmed in *R v Appeal Committee of Brighouse School, ex parte G & B* [1997] ELR 39. It is considered good practice (mainly derived from Ombudsman's reports) for committees who find that there is prejudice to determine the degree of prejudice.

The content of the decision letter was considered in *R v Birmingham City Council, ex parte M* [1998] *The Times*, 13 October.

The procedure which relates to appeals conducted in respect of admissions to infant classes is quite different. The new schools admissions regime applies from September 1999 for those applying for places in reception years. Parents will have to show that the admissions criteria were applied unreasonably to succeed, see Appendix 2 which sets out some interim guidance issued by the DfEE. Details of the new rules can be found in the Education (Infant Class Sizes) (Transitional Provisions) Regulations 1998 (SI No 1947), the Education Act 1996 (Infant Class Sizes) (Modification) Regulations 1998 (SI No 1948), the School Standards and Framework Act 1998 (Infant Class Sizes) (Modification) Regulations 1998 (SI No 1968), and the Education (Infant Class Sizes) (England) Regulations 1998 (SI No 1973).

Exclusion appeals

The procedure for appeals against exclusion or reinstatement is similar to that of admissions appeals, except that the school is likely to be represented at the hearing by the headteacher and legal representation may be appropriate for parents under the provisions of the Education Act 1997. See further Chapter 6 below on exclusions generally.

Judicial review

Many texts on the subject of constitutional and administrative law refer to judicial review as if it were a relatively recent topic; texts dating from before the 1970s scarcely refer to it at all. In relation to education law this is probably a genuine reflection of the position, but with increasing amounts of education legislation, both primary and delegated, judicial review is of fundamental importance in education matters.

Judicial review is the fastest growing area of law in recent years. The High Court has seen an increase in the number of judicial review cases generally: in research funded by the Public Law Project a report found that the number of judicial review cases had increased four-fold since 1981. Out of a total number of applications in 1992–93 of 2,600, immigration and homelessness cases accounted for approximately 600 applications. The only other areas of law which generated more than 5% of applications were planning law and education.

The remedies

Judicial review is an area of law which has been described by David Pannick QC as one which: "provides remedies for administrative decisions, whether of central, local or private government, which are illegal, irrational or procedurally unfair" (*The Times*, 5 May 1992). The origins of judicial review are among the oldest in English law and the basis of the subject is to be found in "prerogative writs" of certiorari, mandamus and prohibition. These writs were originally available to the king against his officers to compel them to exercise their functions properly or to prevent them from abusing their powers.

Mandamus is the writ which is used to compel the performance of duties by a public body. The Secretary of State for Education and Science applied for mandamus in *Secretary of State for Education v Metropolitan Borough of Tameside* [1976] 3 WLR 641 requiring compliance with a DES policy decision. It was refused as it was held that LEAs were entitled to have a policy of their own and could not be expected to abandon it merely because the Secretary of State did not agree with it.

Prohibition is used to prevent the abuse of powers.

Certiorari is used most frequently and has the effect of quashing a decision made in an improper way. In *R v Rochdale Metropolitan Borough Council, ex parte Schemet* [1993] 91 LGR 425, certiorari did not issue despite a successful challenge to a local authority policy on travelling expenses because the effect of quashing the decision would retrospectively affect the previous two years' education budget. In those circumstances the court decided that a more appropriate remedy would be a declaration.

The power which derived from these writs eventually transferred to the courts, particularly the High Court, which assumed a "supervisory jurisdiction" based on the prerogative writs and other remedies which became available to it such as damages, injunctions and declarations. As a direct result the High Court has an extensive "inherent" right to supervise or review governmental decision-making.

In addition, other remedies such as declarations, injunctions and damages are also available. The use of these remedies in 'public law' has been the subject of some discussion. Declarations may more properly be a private law rather than a public law remedy as considered by Carol Harlow writing in *Modern Law Review* in 1986 (p 49).

The discretionary nature of the remedies is of particular interest. As stated above and confirmed in *R v Barnet London Borough Council, ex parte B* [1994] FLR 592, even where good grounds exist for judicial review the court will not exercise its discretion to grant a remedy where the proper course of action is deemed to be the making of representations as set out by statute. In *ex parte B*, the closure of a day nursery was challenged. The Court of Appeal held that the proper procedure was to make representations under section 26 of the Children Act 1989.

Review procedure

In recent years the inherent jurisdiction referred to above has been refined. In 1977, the Law Commission produced a report on "Remedies in Administrative Law" (Working Paper No 40). In 1978, the procedural rules of the Supreme Court were altered to free the remedies from the formalities and limitations which attached to them. RSC Order 53 specifically related to judicial review. The procedure was put on a statutory basis by the Supreme Court Act 1981. It should be noted that the procedure has been effected to some extent by the Civil Procedure Rules (CPR) 1998 (SI No 3132) which came into effect on 26th April 1999.

Initial application

The procedure now involves the submission of an application to a single High Court judge, usually in the Queen's Bench Division, but an application may be heard in the Chancery Division. As cases are brought in the name of the Crown, cases are heard by judges nominated to hear the "Crown Office List". The role of the single judge is to consider if the case is appropriate for judicial review. Only those cases given leave by the single judge will be heard in full. The initial application is part of a "filter system" by which inappropriate or frivolous cases can be rejected without the resources of the courts being unduly stretched. However, such is the increase in the number of applications for judicial review that applicants have only 20 minutes before the single judge to convince him or her of the suitability of their case. According to a Practice Direction issued in 1991 in respect of the Crown Office List (*The Times*, 21 March 1991), applications are listed on the footing that the application will take no more than 20 miznutes with an additional 10 minutes for reply by the respondent. Special arrangements have to be made in advance where the hearing is likely to be of greater length. Recent research has shown that approximately 60% of applications in areas other than immigration and homelessness cleared "the leave hurdle". Between 31 and 42% of all applications were withdrawn before the final hearing. One reason for this may be the length of time taken to hear applications through to a final conclusion delays of 18–22 months are not uncommon (see Sunkin, Bridges and Meszaros, *Judicial Review in Perspective: An Investigation of Trends in the Use and Operation of the Judicial Review Procedure in England and Wales,* Public Law Project, London, 1993).

Abuse of the system

Judges are clearly concerned to prevent abuses of the judicial review system. One abuse to be avoided is that of using judicial review as an appeal. In a strict legal sense judicial review and the system of appeals are quite distinct. The consequences of judicial review are quite different from that of an appeal. Certiorari, as previously mentioned, lies to quash an improperly made decision. The High Court, in making such an order, will not substitute its own decision or even remit the case to the decision-making authority. A litigant, an aggrieved parent perhaps, might well make a successful application for judicial review only to find that no real progress has been made. At best the process of review provides a second bite at the cherry.

The single judge should always check to see that all appeals available to the applicant have been exhausted before the application for judicial review is made (see *R v London Borough of Barnet, ex parte B* above) Several recent cases have failed to proceed on this basis. In *R v Secretary of State for Education, ex parte Banham* [1992] Fam Law 435, judicial review proceedings were taken in respect of school closure plans. Macpherson J. stated that "care should be taken to assess whether what was being sought was not an oblique appeal". Similarly, in *R v Salford City Council, ex parte L* [1992] *The Times,* 17 April, the court decided that "it was more appropriate to follow the appellate procedure provided for in the statute (the Education Act 1981) and appeal in writing to the Secretary of State rather than apply to the High Court by way of judicial review". In *R v Staffordshire County Council, ex parte Ashworth* [1997] COD 132, the ability of a court to control its own processes was stressed.

The separation of judicial review from the appeals procedure does not always operate against the litigant. In some statutes the decision of a government minister might be said to be "binding" (e.g. s 7 (5) of the Education Act 1980), indicating that such decisions are incapable of challenge. The courts have ruled that such a statement does mean that there is no appeal, but that this does not preclude judicial review.

Private law

There are other reasons which may frustrate an application for judicial review from the outset. Despite David Pannick's assertion that judicial review provides remedies for "private government" the courts have recognised that their jurisdiction is not all-embracing. Judicial review is primarily a matter of public law and has been used for centuries to supervise the decisions of those who are in positions of public power such as government ministers and local government officers and members. Organisations and institutions which regulate their own affairs are, as a general rule, immune from judicial review. This is important in relation to educational institutions. The status of any institution under discussion is paramount. Most of the cases have concerned independent schools and universities.

In *Kent* v *University College London* [1992] 156 LG Rev, an application was made to review the decision of the college's "Visitors", the disciplinary body of the college. The High Court held that they had no jurisdiction in issues of private law and as in this case a contract of employment was involved the court determined that they had no jurisidiction. In *R* v *Board of Examiners of the Council of Legal Education, ex parte Joseph* [1994] COD 318 and *R* v *Council of Legal Education, ex parte Halstead* [1994] *The Independent*, 9 August, complaints against the Council for Legal Education were held not to be appropriate matters for judicial review.

In *R* v *Headmaster of Fernhill Manor School, ex parte Brown* (1992) *The Times*, 5 June, it was decided that an application by a 16-year-old girl to challenge her expulsion from a public school was misconceived. According to Brook J, the "only remedy available was a writ action in private law by the pupil's parents". However, a "pupil at a state school was in a different position".

Thus judicial review is available to parents of children excluded from state but not private schools, although see *R* v *Cobham Hall School, ex parte S* [1997] *The Times*, 13 December in Chapter 10 below. It was decided in *R* v *Governors of Haberdashers' Aske's Hatcham College Trust, ex parte Tyrell* [1995] COD 399 that decisions made in relation to CTCs could be reviewed, as could those in relation to grant-maintained schools. However, in both cases it is interesting to note that in policy terms both of these types of institutions were to be hybrids (i.e. part state and part independent). The Education Act 1996 suggests that CTCs have independent status. For the purposes of judicial review the courts have felt able to treat decisions made by and about such institutions as matters of public rather than private law.

As a matter of course it is still important in practical terms to consider the legal status of any institution before considering if judicial review is likely to be available.

Locus standi

Another obstacle to overcome in the making of an application for judicial review is that the applicant must satisfy the court that he or she has the appropriate legal standing, or "locus standi" to bring the case.

The procedure is not open to "interfering busybodies"; applicants should be a "person aggrieved". They must have a personal interest in the issue and must have suffered some harm as the result of the decision they seek to challenge. Traditionally, "harm" was limited to loss of expectation, particularly loss of livelihood. "Loss of legitimate expectation" is the phrase used most often today. Headteachers in admissions cases often make statements to parents which subsequently raises the issue of legitimate expectation. A recent case is *R* v *Beatrix Potter School, ex parte K* [1997] ELR 468, in which it was held that a promise made by a headteacher to a parent had created a legitimate expectation for the purposes of locus standi, but as far as the hearing itself was concerned it was a matter to be taken into account by a committee, though it was not a determinative factor. Lord Wilberforce in *R* v *Inland Revenue Commissioners, ex parte Federation of Self Employed* [1981] 2 WLR 722 spoke of a "threshold requirement" in relation to RSC Order 53, rule 3 (5) which required applicants for judicial review to have a "sufficient interest". Lord Wilberforce said that this requirement did not remove the whole and vitally important question of locus standi into the realm of pure discretion. The question of locus standi must be considered before the action proceeds.

As a general rule, it is desirable that parents rather than children should be applicants. In *R* v *Hackney London Borough Council, ex parte T* [1991] COD 454, the Legal Aid Board were put on notice that a young boy had been made a party to an action possibly as a means of acquiring legal aid to which the parents may not have been entitled.

The question of what constitutes a "legitimate expectation" on the part of parents was discussed at some length in the cases. In *R v Rochdale Metropolitan Borough Council, ex parte Schemet* (above), in which the applicants challenged the LEA's policy on transport provision, one of the arguments was that the parents should have been consulted about the new policy which affected the education of their elder child. It was held that there was no obligation of the LEA to consult, but there was a legitimate expectation on the part of the parents that they would be consulted in such circumstances: "Legitimate expectation was not confined ... to situations where there had been a promise or practice of consultation."

A similar conclusion had been arrived at in *R v Brent London Borough Council, ex parte Gunning* [1986] 84 LGR 168 in respect of a proposed schools closure and in *R v Barnet London Borough Council, ex parte Pardes House School Ltd* [1989] COD 512 where it was held that the applicant who had submitted a tender for the purchase of land had a legitimate expectation when the plans to sell were dropped and later revived. The applicant should have been allowed to submit another tender, it being held that such a legitimate expectation involved simply an obligation on the part of the decision-maker to act fairly.

In *Bostock v Kay* [1989] 87 LGR 583 (see below) the locus standi of the applicant, Mr Bostock, was considered by the court. He was the chairman of the board of governors. As he would have to decide who was to speak at meetings, and in what order, he had a legitimate interest in bringing a case to resolve a dispute. Additionally, there is a time limit; cases must be brought within three months, although this period may be extended for "good reason".

Grounds for review

Should an applicant be successful in overcoming the filter process, the case can then proceed to a full hearing. This is when the basis for the application is considered in detail. Lord Diplock in *Council for Civil Service Unions v Minister for the Civil Service* [1985] 1 AC 374 said:

> Judicial review has I think developed to a state today when ... one can conveniently classify under three heads the grounds on which administrative action is subject to control by judicial review. The first ground I would call illegality, the second irrationality and the third procedural impropriety. That is not to say that further development on a case by case basis may not in the course of time add further grounds.

Lord Diplock went on to discuss in some depth the various attributes of these grounds. Traditionally, the High Court has sought out instances of "ultra vires" or breaches of natural justice as a starting point.

The ultra vires doctrine relates to the abuse of power. Powers such as those conferred on local authorities and government ministers are necessarily limited. The exercise of these powers must be intra vires, that is within the powers conferred by statute. Ultra vires means that a person or body has gone beyond these powers. There are two types of ultra vires, procedural and substantive.

Procedural ultra vires

This is a relatively straightforward concept and is, in essence, the third of the grounds referred to by Lord Diplock (above). If an Act or a piece of delegated legislation sets out a procedure to be followed, then that procedure must be followed.

Several recent cases have concerned the conduct and constitution of committees in relation to school admissions. For example, in *R v Camden London Borough Council, ex parte S* [1991] 89 LGR 513 a committee was appointed to hear a number of appeals against refusals to admit children to a school. The appeals began on one day and the next day one of the committee members could not attend. He was replaced and the appeals continued. It was held that S's appeal had been decided by a committee differently constituted from that which had heard part of the appeal. The decision of that committee was therefore unlawful and was quashed.

Not all procedural irregularities may be challenged: some may be "cured" by a properly constituted appeal hearing as in *R v Governors of St Gregory's Roman Catholic Aided High School, ex parte Roberts* [1995] *The Times*, 27 January.

In *R v Wandsworth London Borough Council, ex parte Andrew Milne* [1992] 90 LGR 515, a dispute arose concerning the proposed closure of a primary school. Section 12 (3) of the Education Act 1980 provided the procedure for objections. For objections to be valid under that section, at least ten people had to sign, each being local government electors for the area. In this case two objections had been submitted. Both had been signed by persons who were not local government electors for the area in question and several signatories had signed both objections. The Court of Appeal held that the objections were not valid.

Decision-making bodies are often required to "consult" interested parties before reaching a decision. Whilst it is important that such consultation should be carried out, there is no requirement to take into account the opinions of those consulted in making a decision: see for example *R v Secretary of State for Education and the Governing Body of the Queen Elizabeth Grammar School, ex parte Cumbria County Council* [1994] COD 30.

Substantive ultra vires

Substantive ultra vires also relates to the legality of a decision. Lord Diplock referred to irrationality and also to unreasonableness. Both are aspects of illegality. If a person or body makes a decision which they are not entitled to make, then that decision would be void. The courts have gone further and taken upon themselves the task of investigating how lawful decisions are by applying the principles of reasonableness and rationality to the decision-making process (see e.g. *Associated Provincial Picture Houses v Wednesbury Corporation* [1948] 1 KB 223 and the more recent cases of *R v Lancashire County Council, ex parte Foster* [1995] COD 45 and *R v Wiltshire County Council, ex parte Razazan* [1997] ELR 370).

One very important basic point is that for a decision to be reviewed the decision must have been made. In *R v Gwynedd County Council, ex parte W* [1994] 158 LG Rev 201, a challenge was made in respect of a decision of whether a child was to be placed in a class where the teaching was predominantly English or in a Welsh-speaking class. It was held that at the time of challenge no decision had been taken on the matter and as such there was no decision capable of being reviewed.

If a decision is made, it is open to the courts to consider whether that decision has been made taking into account only 'relevant considerations'. In *R v Inner London Education Authority, ex parte Westminster City Council* [1986] 1 All ER 19, a local authority subcommittee authorised a media campaign costing £651,000. Westminster City Council sought a declaration that the action of the subcommittee was ultra vires. The High Court found that the subcommittee had taken into account an irrelevant consideration in reaching its decision (i.e. publicising the alleged unsuitability of government policy), and that decision was therefore unlawful.

There are many examples where the courts appear to shape policy as well as deciding issues on a case-by-case basis. There are two areas of special interest to education lawyers. The first relates to educational provision with particular reference to special educational needs; the second relates to school admissions policies. Note that current reported cases are still dealing with cases issues under the Education Acts 1981 and 1993 with respect to special educational needs, although these Acts have been replaced by the Education Act 1996.

In *R v Secretary of State for Education and Science, ex parte E* [1992] FLR 377 the Court of Appeal confirmed a decision of the High Court made in respect of a boy, E, aged 13. E had learning difficulties that could be grouped under the headings of dyslexia and discalcula. The local authority statement in respect of E's special educational needs included both his literacy and numeracy difficulties. However the local authority felt that it was only obliged under the Education Act 1981 to provide special educational needs in relation to E's literacy difficulties. E's parents argued that both special needs should be addressed and challenged the decision. Nolan J in the High Court agreed with the parents and held that in the case of children with more than one special educational need it is the LEA's duty to make special educational provision for a child in respect of each special need identified.

The Education Act 1993 introduced the Special Educational Needs Tribunal (SENT) to deal with appeals on such issues: see further Chapter 13.

The second body of caselaw involves school admissions policies and parental preference. In *R v Cleveland County Council, ex parte Commission for Racial Equality* [1993] 91 LGR 139, the Commission claimed that the council had committed an act of discrimination by transferring a child at her parent's request from one maintained school to another. Macpherson J dismissed the Commission's application stating that the Race Relations Act 1976 did not qualify the LEA's duty under section 6 of the Education Act 1980.

Another case in this context is *R v Governors of the Bishop Challenor Roman Catholic School, ex parte Choudhury* [1992] 3 WLR 99. A problem arose when a school was over-subscribed. It was held that in such circumstances there was no need to comply with the duty relating to parental preference. There was no error of law. Similarly, there was no procedural ultra vires. The courts have recently taken the opportunity to consider the importance of parental preference. In *R v Rotherham Metropolitan Borough Council, ex parte Clark* [1998] 96 LGR 214 it was held that although it was not unlawful for an LEA to have an admissions policy based on, *inter alia*, 'catchment areas', parental preferences should be ascertained by the LEA before addressing the question of catchment areas. Circular 6/96 (*Admissions to Maintained Schools* – now withdrawn) required schools to give priority to local children.

Natural justice

A concept which is related to, though separate from, ultra vires is natural justice. An important aspect of natural justice is that justice must not only be done but must be seen to be done (*R v Sussex Justices, ex parte McCarthy* [1924] 1 KB 256). Natural justice involves two principles:

Nemo judex in causa sua – the rule against bias

In *Hannam* v *Bradford Corporation* [1970] 1 WLR 937 the plaintiff taught at a voluntary aided school. He absented himself and then refused to return. The governors dismissed him, although the LEA had power under section 24 of the Education Act 1944 to prohibit his dismissal. The Corporation's staff subcommittee met to consider the issue. The chairman and two other committee members were also members of the school governing body. The decision of that governing body was affirmed. The plaintiff sued for damages on the basis of the likelihood of bias and was successful. Per Sachs LJ: "The governors did not, upon donning their sub-committee hats, cease to be an integral part of the body whose action was being impugned." The remedy of damages in this case was awarded on the basis of breach of contract. The case was heard before judicial review cases were commonplace and before RSC Order 53 encouraged such cases to be brought in the High Court. The case is still of interest as the "bias" element is quite clear and because of the recent revived interest in private law remedies.

In *Bostock* v *Kay* (above) there were proposals to replace a school with a CTC. Members of staff were likely to earn more if they were subsequently employed by a CTC. It was held that certain teacher governors had a direct pecuniary interest in the outcome of a governor's meeting on the subject and that they were not able to vote. The case considered in some detail the construction of the phrase "pecuniary interest" including whether such an interest had to be a present interest or whether it could be something which may happen in the future as in this case. Jowitt J held:

> These words are given a wide ambit in order to avoid, firstly the possibility of advantage to the person voting, secondly, (and this is important), to avoid the appearance that anyone might be voting on an issue on which he has an axe to grind.

There would be no "future" pecuniary interest if the possibility of there being such an interest was so remote as to be "simply speculative, purely hypothetical and very unlikely to materialise". That was held not to be the case here, where the prospect of the increased salaries was very real.

Audi alteram partem – the right to a fair hearing

In *R* v *Brent London Borough Council, ex parte Assegai* [1987] 151 LG Rev 891 it was held that the principle that justice not only had to be done but had to be seen to be done had to be applied with caution, as if it had been applied too strictly it might have led to some committees being frustrated in their tasks. In this case, members of a subcommittee witnessed an ugly scene involving the applicant, who was taking part in a discussion. The next day the subcommittee met and removed the applicant from his appointment as a community governor. It was held that as a matter of fairness he should have been told in advance of the subcommittee's concerns and that he should have been allowed to make representations. The resolutions which had been made by the subcommittee were quashed.

Another example of this rule is to be found in *R v Secretary of State for Education, ex parte Islam* [1992] COD 448, in which the governors of a school in Brent had not been given the opportunity to comment on new information which was material to the Secretary of State's decision to approve or reject proposals by the governors that the school should become voluntary aided. Both certiorari and mandamus were issued to quash the Secretary of State's decision and to direct that the proposals be reconsidered.

A similar case is that of *R v Secretary of State for Education, ex parte S* [1995] 2 FCR 225, where it was held that if the Secretary of State relied on further expert advice before making a decision (in this case in relation to special educational needs provision), this advice should be disclosed to the parties so that they could make submissions. This duty was limited to situations where a new point arose and where there had been no opportunity to consider it previously.

In *R v Newham London Borough Council, ex parte X* [1994] *The Times*, 15 November, a child had been expelled from school without being given the opportunity to make representations to the headmaster. It was held that the decision could be reviewed as it had been *prima facie* unfair.

The future of judicial review

The system of judicial review is under almost constant scrutiny. In 1994, the Law Commission produced a report detailing proposals to streamline the procedure further (*Administrative Law: Judicial Review and Statutory Appeals* (No. 226)). According to Richard Gordon QC writing in *Public Law* (Spring 1995), the report "flirts with the idea of radical reform". Part of the proposed streamlined procedure is that oral preliminary hearings should be exceptional.

The use of judicial review is the subject of some considerable debate, although the principles seem entrenched and are regarded as important. According to Cane (1986):

> The autonomy of judicial review has an important implication which should be made explicit, namely that, in controlling administrative activity, the courts are asserting and exercising, in their own right and in their own name, a power to limit and define the powers of other governmental agencies.

There seems little doubt that this autonomy will be increasingly used by parents, governors and local authorities to challenge various decision-making processes. The grounds on which they do so may be apparently legal and technical, but in reality many challenges are often politically motivated, and in looking at education cases it is often important to appreciate that there may well be a political dimension. In *R v Secretary of State for Education, ex parte Avon County Council (No 2)* [1990] 88 LGR 716, an application for judicial review based on the differences of opinion between an LEA and the Secretary of State on education policy was misconceived:

> The minister ... was acting under powers given by Parliament in the Education Reform Act 1988. If he was acting lawfully within those powers, there was no purpose in seeking to demonstrate that the proposals put forward by Avon County Council were ... superior ... Parliament did not entrust the making of that judgment to the court but to the Minister who was answerable in respect of his decision to Parliament.

The courts have recognised that they do have considerable flexibility in the making of decisions in public law cases; other wider issues may be relevant and may take precedence over the letter of the law. In *R v Governors of John Bacon School, ex parte ILEA* [1990] 88 LGR 648 it was held that:

> The court in exercising its discretion in public law cases had to strike a balance between the need to protect the long term public interest in protecting the integrity of decisions such as those of school governors and the danger of treating regulations and their observance as sacrosanct where there might be a countervailing public interest.

Breach of statutory duty

The interrelationship between public and private law rights was considered in detail in the composite appeals of *X v Bedfordshire County Council* [1995] 3 WLR 152 *et al*. It was held by the House of Lords that a breach of statutory by a local authority did not, by itself, give rise to any private law cause of action: "it was not just and reasonable to superimpose a common duty of care on the local authority in relation to the performance of its statutory duties". Actions have to be framed with care, and in education law it should not be assumed that the usual negligence and/or breach of statutory duty approach can be adopted.

Legal redress outside the courts

Many bodies other than the courts may become involved in the resolution of disputes in education law. These include:

- education tribunals (such as SENT)
- employment tribunals
- Commissioner for Local Administration (Ombudsman)
- The Commission for Racial Equality
- The Equal Opportunities Commission
- The Health and Safety Executive and Commission

A useful article on this subject is to be found in the *British Journal of Educational Studies* by V Hanon, October 1983.

The European courts

The European courts are becoming increasingly involved in education law. One issue which has concerned these courts is corporal punishment. In *Campbell and Cosans* v *United Kingdom* [1982] 4 ECHR 293 the European Court of Human Rights ruled that inflicting corporal punishment where the parents were philosophically opposed to it was a breach of Article 2 of the First Protocol and might even be a breach of Article 3, which refers to torture or degrading treatment or punishment. Corporal punishment by a step-father was considered in *A* v *United Kingdom* [1998] *The Times*, 1 October (see Chapter 6). In *Osman* v *United Kingdom* [1998] *The Times,* 5 November, although regarded as exceptional, it was held that any rule (known as an exclusionary rule) which prevents access to a civil remedy on policy grounds, as in *Hill* v *Chief Constable of West Yorkshire,* [1989] AC 53 will be a breach of Article 6 of the European Convention on Human Rights.

The European courts have also considered cases involving the rights of those in higher education (e.g. see *X* v *United Kingdom* [1982] 4 ECHR 252 and *Landesamt Für Aubildungsförderung Nordrhein-Westfalen* v *Gaal* [1995] All ER (EC) 653.

Governing Bodies

Governing Bodies

Relevant legislation

The Education (No 2) Act 1986 (the 1986 Act) and the Education Act 1993 contained detailed provisions concerning governors supplemented by the Education (School Government) Regulations 1989 (SI No 1503) and the Education (School Government) (Amendment) Regulations 1996 (SI No 2050). Generally, the powers of governing bodies increased to meet the demands placed upon them by virtue of, for example, delegated budgets. The Education Act 1994 enabled governing bodies to become involved in teacher training. The SSFA 1998, in sections 36–44 and Schedules 9–13, makes further provision in respect of governors to reflect the alterations to the structure of education made by that Act.

Role of governors

Section 38 of SSFA 1998 makes clear the role of governing bodies. With respect to maintained schools, the conduct of such a school will be under the direction of the governing body; further, in section 38(2), the school shall be conducted with a view to promoting high standards of educational achievement at the school.

Categories of governors

Governing bodies are made up of a number of different types of governors. The number of governors varies according the type of school and the number of registered pupils. Under the SSFA 1998 every school must have its own individual governing body. The Secretary of State is able to allow for exceptions. Governing bodies in community, foundation and voluntary aided schools all have different attributes.

The categories of governors are defined in Schedule 9 to SSFA 1998. Parent governors may be elected or appointed. Under Schedule 9 such governors should be elected by parents of registered pupils at the school and the governor should also be a parent of a pupil registered at the school at the time of election. It seems likely that the last requirement will have to be satisfied by an appointed parent governor, although the SSFA 1998 states that such an appointment should be made in accordance with regulations. Parent governors are to be represented on LEAs under the SSFA 1998.

Teacher governors are elected by teachers from their own number. Such governors must be teaching at the school at the time of election, although the Schedule refers to those employed under a contract of employment or a contract for services, "or otherwise engaged to provide his services as a teacher". Head teachers can choose not to be governors. Should the head teacher choose to be a governor, he will be treated as an *ex officio* governor. In a voluntary aided school the head may be counted as one of the foundation governors (see below).

LEA governors are appointed by the LEA.

Foundation governors were originally only to be found in aided schools, although the terminology was also adopted by grant-maintained schools. The term will now be applied in relation to schools with a particular religious character or those with a trust deed. Such governors are appointed to secure either the religious character of the school or the purposes of the trust deed. Additionally, where the school has neither a religious character nor a trust deed a foundation governor may be appointed, otherwise than by the LEA. Foundation governors in foundation schools which do have a foundation may be referred to as "partnership governors".

Staff governors are to be appointed from the non-teaching members of the staff at the school. Such persons should be so employed at the time of election and here employment is limited to a contract of employment or a contract for services.

Co-opted members may be members of the local business community or, in maintained special schools, members of a voluntary organisation. They should be appointed by governors who have not been so appointed themselves.

Eligibility

Under Schedule 11 to SSFA 1998, regulations relating to election or appointment are likely to follow the requirements of the Education (School Government) Regulations 1989 (SI No 1503). These regulations disqualified certain categories of persons, such as those aged under 18 years, at the time of election or appointment, although there was formerly no upper age limit. A person who is bankrupt was disqualified, as were persons with certain criminal convictions. Teacher governors were to cease to be teacher governors if they left the school during a term of office, although parent governors were not required to leave if their child left the school during their term of office. A governor could also be disqualified from office at a particular school if he or she failed to attend any meetings of that governing body for six months. Governors were prevented from being members of more than two governing bodies, but an exception applied in respect of governors appointed under section 214 of the Education Act 1993 which concerns governors of schools "requiring special measures".

The appointment of governors has resulted in some litigation: for example, in *Champion* v *Chief Constable of Gwent Constabulary* [1990] 1 WLR 1 it was held that the appointment of a serving police officer to a governing body was unlikely to give the public the impression that he would not be able to discharge his police duties impartially. The political balance of school governors may also be a consideration; see *R* v *Warwickshire County Council, ex parte Dill-Russell* at p 52 below.

Terms of office

Governors, except those who are *ex officio*, will hold office for terms specified in regulations made under the SSFA 1998. Under the 1986 Act, such governors held office for not more than four years.

Dismissal

Section 8 of the 1986 Act provided:

> Any foundation governor of a voluntary school, or governor of a county, voluntary or maintained special school appointed otherwise than by being co-opted, may be removed from office by the person or persons who appointed him.

In *R* v *Trustee of the Roman Catholic Diocese of Westminster, ex parte Mars* [1988] 86 LGR 507, it was held that it was lawful for the trustees of a voluntary aided school to dismiss governors who opposed changes to the character of the school as proposed by the trustees. However, in *R* v *Governors of Haberdashers' Askes' Hatcham Schools, ex parte ILEA; sub nom Brunyate* v *ILEA* [1989] 2 All ER 417, the Court of Appeal and subsequently the House of Lords held that an LEA cannot remove governors mid-term solely because of their failure to promote the LEA's policies. Bridge LJ held that "non-compliance with the wishes of the authority ... is a usurpation of the governors' independent function". As a result the Court of Appeal reversed the decision in the *Mars* case when it came before that court as *R v Westminster Roman Catholic Diocese Trustee, ex parte Andrews* [1990] COD 25.

Although these cases relate to the removal of governors mid-term, they do not establish limitations on the reappointment or replacement of governors. In *R v Warwickshire County Council, ex parte Dill-Russell* [1991] COD 375, the Court of Appeal held that following local authority elections, council-appointed school governors could, under the provisions of section 8 (5) of the 1986 Act, face reappointment or replacement so as to ensure that the number of governors nominated by each political party stayed in proportion with the representation of those parties on the council.

Where an appointing authority dismisses a governor, it must follow the rules of natural justice (see p 42 above). In *R v Brent London Borough Council, ex parte Assegai* [1987] 151 LG Rev 891, it was held that a local authority could not dismiss a governor before the end of his term of office without first informing him of the intention to dismiss and giving him the opportunity to reply in writing to the complaints made against him.

Structure of governing bodies

The number of governors depends on the type of school and the number of pupils. The following tables set out the position indicated in Schedule 9 to SSFA 1998 with regard to community and foundation secondary schools, although there are further tables relating to primary schools, voluntary controlled schools and further provisions relating to special schools.

	Community schools	
Category of governor	Secondary school – normal basis	Secondary school – option if less than 600 pupils
Parent	6	5
LEA	5	4
Teacher	2	2
Staff	1	1
Co-opted	5	4

| Category of governor | Foundation schools | |
	Secondary school – normal basis	Secondary school – option if less than 600 pupils
Parent	7	6
LEA	2	2
Teacher	2	2
Staff	1	1
Foundation	5	4
Co-opted	3	2

Note: Head teachers may choose to be governors as mentioned above.

The procedure for the appointment and election of governors will be set out by regulations, although it was previously the case that elections must be by secret ballot.

Groups of schools

Although the 1986 Act required schools to have individual governing bodies under section 10, the Secretary of State could approve the grouping together of schools for the purposes of school government. Similar provision was made under the Education Act 1993 for grant-maintained schools. Such a provision may be made under the SSFA 1998 regulations.

Articles and Instruments of Government

Under section 1 of the 1986 Act, Articles set out the way in which a school was to be conducted and they contained such provisions as the allocation of functions between the governors, head teacher and the LEA. The Instruments set out the composition of the governing body and under section 1 contained information about the size of the governing body, composition and the procedures for elections. Block (i.e. standard form) articles and instruments were available to schools as set out in Circular 7/87. A review of articles and instruments was undertaken by the DfEE in 1997 (see Prof N Harris with M Mokal, *The Legislative Basis for School Governance*).

Under the SSFA 1998, Articles of Government are effectively abolished (in the Bill they were specifically abolished). The Technical

Consultation Paper on the Education White Paper, *Excellence in Schools* (1997) stated that the powers, duties and functions of governing bodies across the range of school activities would be applied directly through legislation rather than having to operate through Articles. It has been suggested by Sean Williams in 'Levelling Down' (Centre for Policy Studies, 1998) that "an important and valued means for schools to define their individual character is being sacrificed to ease the burden of officials in the DfEE".

Under section 37 of SSFA 1998 every maintained school must have an Instrument of Government which determines the constitution of the governing body and other matters. See the Education (Government of New Schools on Transition to New Framework) Regulations 1998 (SI No 3097) and the Education (Transition to New Framework) (New Schools, Groups and Miscellaneous) Regulations 1999 (SI No 362). However, Schedule 12 to the Act regulates the contents, making, review and variation of such Instruments. In effect, schools are left with very little input into the making of this document of governance and critics suggest that this is further evidence of centralisation. Under Schedule 12 it is the LEA's duty to secure the making of the first Instrument of Government made in accordance with the Schedule.

Schools conducted by education associations

The Education (Schools Conducted by Education Associations) (Initial Articles of Government) Regulations 1993 (SI No. 3101) prescribed the initial Articles of Government for schools run by education associations under section 220 of the Education Act 1993. Governors of such schools were exempted from the requirement that they should only belong to two governing bodies (see above).

Meetings

Schedule 11 to SSFA 1998 makes provision for the making of regulations relating to meetings and proceedings. Under the 1989 and 1996 Regulations, governors had to meet at least once per term and, except in emergencies, seven days' notice had to be given of a meeting. A meeting might also be required by any of the governors. Usually, a chairman and vice-chairman had to be elected at the first meeting of each school year. A teacher or other employee of the school or a pupil could not be appointed to these posts.

A quorum consisted of at least three governors or one third of the total membership. Decisions were taken by a majority of those present and, where there was a tie, the chairman had a casting vote.

Public access to governor's meetings was not barred. The governing body were entitled to say who could attend. Written minutes must be taken and agendas and minutes must be published for inspection at a school. Confidential material could be excluded, such material being defined by the governors. Certain members may be required to withdraw, not take part in discussions or vote. These matters are set out in the Schedule to the regulations.

Under the SSFA 1998 committees may be established which include members other than those on the governing body. Schedule 11 sets out the issues which the regulations are to have particular regard to, but states that subject to the regulations governing bodies may regulate their own procedure.

In *Bostock* v *Kay* [1989] 87 LGR 583 it was held that teacher governors could not participate in discussion of a proposal to close a school and replace it with a CTC or vote on any issue concerning it because they had a pecuniary interest in the outcome. However, in *R* v *Governors of Small Heath School, ex parte Birmingham City Council* [1990] COD, 23 August, the Court of Appeal distinguished the *Bostock* case. It was held that the teacher governors had no pecuniary interest in discussions on a proposal to seek grant-maintained status. A change to grant-maintained status was said to be far less fundamental a change than to a CTC. In such a case the school would cease to exist and a new institution would take its place. Staff might not be re-engaged and they might have to work longer hours for less pay.

Clerk to the governors

The SSFA 1998 specifically mentions the role of the clerk to the governors. Under Schedule 11, regulations may be made for the appointment, dismissal and attendance of the clerk at meetings.

Delegation

A governing body could resolve to delegate to a committee, to any member of the governing body or to the head teacher any of its functions under the 1989 Regulations, although there were certain excep tions. Similar provisions are anticipated by the SSFA 1998.

Governors' powers and duties

Governors' powers have been extended considerably since the 1986 Act. The ERA 1988 had the most effect, introducing the national curriculum, local management of schools, grant-maintained status, open enrolment and charging policies. Under Schedule 10 to SSFA 1998, the powers of the governing body are stated to be to "do anything which appears to them to be necessary or expedient for the purposes of, or in connection with, the conduct of the school". However, such apparently wide-ranging powers must be seen in the context of the rest of the SSFA 1998 and the anticipated regulations, which make it quite clear that in reality governing bodies will have to exercise their powers within a tightly regulated framework.

Change of status

In *R* v *Tameside Metropolitan Borough Council, ex parte Governors of Audenshaw High School* [1990] *The Times,* 27 June, the LEA wished to bring into operation a scheme which would ensure that the land and buildings of a school remained in local authority control even if the governors were successful in bringing about a plan to opt out. It was held that the LEA were under a duty to consult the governors before bringing the scheme into operation and to consider the educational implications of such a scheme. The Queen's Bench Divisional Court set out how the question of educational implications could be tackled. It was suggested that one approach which could be adopted by the courts was to ask a "hypothetical politically neutral board of governors" what would be in the pupils' best interests.

Under section 28 of SSFA 1998, proposals for new foundation or voluntary schools may be made by persons referred to as promoters, which may include the governing body. Governing bodies are specifically referred to in respect of alterations to existing foundation and voluntary schools. Section 29 refers to proposals for the discontinuance of community, foundation, voluntary or maintained nursery schools.

Both sections refer in detail to the provisions for publication of information and consultation requirements. Section 31 makes similar provision in relation to special schools. Schedule 8 sets out the basic procedure to be followed by a governing body seeking to alter the status of a school. Regulations will make further detailed provision. Governing bodies may also become involved in the balloting arrangements in respect of grammar schools, as set out in sections 104–109.

Previously, in relation to transfer to grant-maintained status, there were complex provisions for ballots of parents which resulted in some litigation. In *R v Governors of Astley High School, ex parte Northumberland County Council* [1994] COD 27, a ballot was held on whether to seek grant-maintained status under the provisions of the ERA 1988. In all, 383 voted against and 385 in favour. The council challenged the decision on the basis that the parents had been given insufficient information. It was stressed in this case that "guidance notes" which were issued were strictly "for guidance only". In *R v Governors of John Bacon School, ex parte ILEA* [1990] 88 LGR 648, the role of the governors in relation to a proposal to become a CTC were considered (see further Chapter 3).

Information

Section 42 of SSFA 1998 requires a governing body to produce an annual "governors' report". Regulations will make further requirements in respect of publication. Governing bodies will be enabled to consider which language(s) the reports should be in. The governing body can require from the head teacher information relating to the discharge of his functions for the purposes of the report which itself should relate to the discharge of the functions of the governing body. Any information requested by the LEA must be provided either on a regular basis or from time to time. An annual parents' meeting must be held.

Section 43 sets out who may attend. The meeting shall provide "an opportunity for discussion" of various topics listed in the section including, *inter alia*, the governors' report, standards of educational achievement and how the spiritual, moral, cultural, mental and physical development of pupils is to be promoted at the school. In very exceptional circumstances (i.e. in hospital schools and schools with at least 50% boarding pupils) the governing body need not hold such a meeting. Regulations will further set out the procedure to be followed at such meetings.

Admissions

Under section 88 of SSFA 1998, admissions are to be dealt with by the "admissions authority". This may be the LEA or the governing body of a community or voluntary controlled school. The LEA may delegate its functions to the governing body with its agreement. The admissions authority will be the governing body in foundation or voluntary aided schools. The admissions authority must determine admission arrangements at the beginning of the school year which are to apply for that year. The Act sets out detailed requirements in respect of consultation. Other admission authorities should be consulted where appropriate, see the Education (Relevant Areas for Consultation on Admission Arrangements) Regulations 1999 (SI No 124).

If the admissions authority is the LEA, it must consult the governing body on proposed admission arrangements. Under section 90 of SSFA 1998, objections to the proposals can be made to the adjudicator or to the Secretary of State. Section 92 provides for the publication of admission arrangements by the governing body. Special arrangements can be made to preserve the religious character of schools under section 91. The admissions authority may fix relevant admission numbers as set out in section 93, but must now have regard to the duty to comply with limits on class sizes for infants. Under section 97, the governing body may be consulted prior to the LEA directing the admission of a pupil and should be informed in writing if any decision to do so. (See also Chapter 5 on school admissions.)

Exclusions

The functions of the governing body in relation to excluded pupils are set out in section 66 of SSFA 1998. The governors in considering an application to reinstate the pupil should take into account the reasons for the exclusion and representations made to them by the LEA, parents or by the pupil if over 18 years old. The head is under a duty to inform the governing body of the duration of a fixed period of exclusion or a decision to permanently exclude.

Curriculum

A governing body can modify the LEA's curriculum policy to match their statement of aims so far as this is compatible with the "basic curriculum" (see p 125). There must be a policy on sex education; if there is none provided, reasons must be given. The basic curriculum as set out in the ERA 1988 (as amended by Part V of the Education Act 1996) must be implemented and complaints from parents regarding the curriculum must be dealt with (see below). Representations may also be made by members of the public and the police in respect of the curriculum. Parents may appeal to the governing body about a decision to modify or suspend the national curriculum in relation to their child; the governors can overrule the decision of a head teacher in this respect. The head must consult the governing body on arrangements for collective worship and under section 69 of SSFA 1998 the governing body, *inter alia*, have a duty to secure the provision of religious education within the provisions of section 352(1) of the Education Act 1996.

In aided schools the governing body decides on the secular curriculum, having considered LEA policy. The curriculum must be compatible with the basic curriculum which must be implemented and any complaints must be considered (see below). The governing body is responsible for the provision of religious education.

Target setting

Under section 63 SSFA and the Education (School Attendance Targets) (England) Regulations 1999 (SI No 397) the governing body must secure a reduction in the level of unauthorised absences.

School meals

Section 116 of SSFA 1998 (amending the Education Act 1996) provides for the transfer of certain functions in relation to the provision of school meals and milk from LEAs to governing bodies by order of the Secretary of State. Section 114 states that regulations may prescribe nutritional standards for school meals.

Length of school sessions

Section 115 of ERA 1988 (as amended by the Education Act 1996) gave governing bodies the responsibility of fixing the times of the school day. The LEA was to determine term and holiday dates. Section 41 of SSFA 1998 preserves this position in relation to community, voluntary controlled or community special schools. In a foundation, voluntary aided or foundation special school the responsibility for both dates lies with the governing body. The procedure involved in the making and publication of changes to dates and times will be detailed in regulations.

Special educational needs provision

Part IV of the Education Act 1996 sets out the duties on schools regarding the identification, assessment, statementing, integration and information of children with special educational needs. The governors must ensure that the LEA is aware of any pupils with special educational needs for whom it ought to consider making a statement. All teachers should be made aware of the importance of identifying and helping pupils with such needs. A "responsible person" must be named to ensure that all who teach a statemented child are aware of their needs.

Finance

Section 49 of SSFA 1998 provides that every maintained school shall have a delegated budget. The effect of financial delegation is set out in section 50, and in particular provides that the governing body may spend any amounts as they think fit for any purposes of the school (as defined).

The governing body may delegate their powers to the head teacher. Section 50(7) specifically states that governors shall not incur any personal liability in respect of these functions as long as they have acted in good faith.

Staffing

Under section 54 of SSFA 1998 the number of teaching and non-teaching staff will be determined by the LEA and dismissals will similarly be a matter for the LEA in schools without a delegated budget. Schedules 16 and 17 to SSFA 1998 set out detailed provisions in respect of the appointment, disciplining and dismissal of staff by a governing body in consultation with others.

Discipline

The governors should provide the head with a written statement about general rules of discipline having consulted the head and parents. According to section 61(6) of SSFA 1998, the standard of behaviour which is to be regarded as acceptable at the school shall be determined by the head teacher, so far as it is not determined by the governing body. A failure to comply could lead to the LEA using its reserve powers to prevent a breakdown of discipline; section 62 details the circumstances in which this may occur and the information which would have to be given to the governing body. Under section 110 of SSFA 1998, the governing body shall adopt a home–school agreement for the school and shall take reasonable steps to ensure that the parental declaration associated with such agreements is signed by every qualifying parent.

School premises

The governing body shall control the occupation and use of the school premises, both during and outside school hours, subject to any directions of the LEA in respect of community schools as provided for by Schedule 13 to SSFA 1998. Similar provisions are made in respect of foundation and other schools.

The governing body shall have regard to the desirability of making the premises available, outside school hours, for community use.

In *Islwyn Borough Council* v *Newport Borough Council* [1994] 158 LG Rev 501 it was held that section 42 of the 1986 Act, which provided that school premises are under the control of the governing body except for "school sessions", did not operate to frustrate a prior agreement under which the plaintiffs and defendants jointly ran a leisure centre on school premises for public use outside school hours. Security matters should be discussed with the LEA. One further matter which has been of interest is the responsibility of the governing body in respect of litter; see for example 'Governors, litter and the law' by Celia Wells, *Education and the Law,* 1993, (5)(3) p 135. See generally responsibility in relation to safety matters in Chapter 7.

Complaints procedures

The governing body must establish procedures for the handling of complaints relating to the school and must publicise those procedures under section 39(1) and (2) of SSFA 1998, unless specific statutory provision is otherwise made.

Training and expenses

Allowances payable to governors should be made in accordance with Schedule 11 to SSFA 1998 and regulations made thereunder. Under the same provision, LEAs are to ensure that such training and support as is necessary for the discharge of their functions is available to governors free of charge.

Corporate status

The Education Act 1993 gave governing bodies corporate status. Section 36 of and Schedule 10 to SSFA 1998 confirm that status. Personal liability exists for acts by members in bad faith (see provisions relating to finance above). Care should be taken in the exercise of all the functions of the governing body, in 1994 the governors of a grant-maintained school were fined £2,100 after a crash in which 12 pupils were hurt while travelling in a school minibus. The governors had failed to insure the vehicle, which was on loan from a local scout group.

Parents

Parents

Definition of 'parent'

Admissions registers (rather than attendance registers) record the name and address of the child's parents and other information. The Education Act 1944 was amended by the Children Act 1989 so that a parent might be any person with parental responsibility under that Act. The Education Act 1996, section 576, defines a parent as either a parent or someone who has parental responsibility or someone who has care of the child. A distinction must be made between a person who has parental responsibilty for a child or day-to-day care and a person who has "delegated" care of a child, such as a teacher. This could also include a person who, for example, has permission to pick up the child after school. It is important for schools and teachers to know who the registered parents are as the day-to-day running of the school may involve the need to obtain consents, for example in relation to school visits. It is also useful to know if there are any potential problems relating to contact (see below).

In admissions cases the relevant address for the purposes of measuring distance from a school is that of the parent and not, for example, that of a childminder. Any claims that a person other than a parent has day-to-day care of a child should be verified in such cases. The term "step-parent" is often used informally and does not necessarily indicate any permanent or established relationship.

Disputes between parents

Matters relating to education may form the basis for applications under the Children Act 1989. Often there will be an application for a section 8 order to resolve matters between parents themselves and other persons with parental responsibility.

In *Re G (Parental Responsibility: Education)* [1995] FCR 53, the father of a boy with learning difficulties decided to send his son to a special school. The mother learned of his decision the day before and applied to prevent it. She applied for a prohibited steps order which was refused and she appealed. The appeal was dismissed, although it was held that she should have been consulted. There was no evidence, however, that the first instance judge's decision had been clearly wrong: "There was a strong argument for the view that the judge made the right, or at least the least wrong order." Schools should be aware, as far as is possible, of any restriction of contact to a child, such as where an order of the court has imposed such a restriction.

See N Harris (1992); 'The Children Act 1989: Parental responsibility and decisions concerning a child's education', *Education and the Law* 4(1), 1–6.

Parental duties

Ensuring education

Under section 444 of the Education Act 1996 (replacing section 36 of the Education Act 1944, as amended):

> It shall be the duty of the parent of every child of compulsory school age to cause him to receive efficient full-time education suitable to his age, ability and aptitude and to any special educational needs he may have either by regular attendance at school or otherwise.

The Education (Start of Compulsory School Age) Order 1998 (SI No 1607) sets out when a child has reached compulsory school age by reference to the child's age at the end of August, December and March of each school year. A child ceases to be of compulsory school age on the official school leaving date, but only if he or she has attained the age of 16 years, or will do so before the beginning of the next school year. The Education (School Leaving Date) Order 1997 (SI No 1970) applies. It is possible for children under 5 years of age to be registered in school, but the duty to secure attendance does not apply until the child is 5 years old. A child is presumed to be of compulsory school age unless the parent proves to the contrary under section 445 of the Education Act 1996.

One of the most contentious aspects of section 444 is that parents are not under a duty to send children to school, since education can be provided "otherwise" than at school. Section 7 of the 1996 Act requires that the education received is suitable to the child's age, ability and aptitude and to any special educational needs the child may have. It is possible for the parent to take the child out of school; this is sometimes referred to as "deschooling".

If a child is taken out of school, LEAs have a duty to ensure that the education received is "efficient full-time education". The LEA can make inquiries into the education being received by a deschooled child. Home teaching arrangements can be inspected even if the parents object (*Tweedie* v *Pritchard* [1963] Crim LR 270).

The courts may decide that a child is being educated efficiently even if that child could be educated more efficiently at school. In *Bevan* v *Shears* [1911] 2 KB 936, Lord Alverstone CJ stated that:

> In the absence of anything in the by-laws providing that a child of given age shall receive instruction in given subjects, in my view it cannot be said that as to a particular child there is a standard of education by which that child must be taught.

The difficulty today is there are, by virtue of the national curriculum, precisely those standards of attainment by age expected of a child at school. Furthermore, many schools outside the state system, such as independent schools, have adopted the provisions of the national curriculum, and it may be much more difficult today to establish that any form of alternative education satisfies the requirements of section 444.

Education partly at school and partly otherwise is not appropriate according to *Osborne* v *Martin* [1927] 91 JP 197. In certain circumstances the LEA may well condone the teaching of the child at home, often with tutorial support from home tutors provided by the LEA. The most obvious situations would be where the child is ill and unable to attend school for long periods or where the child has been excluded.

The European courts have occasionally become involved in disputes relating to the nature of education. In *Family H* v *United Kingdom* [1984] ECHR Decisions and Reports, Vol 37, July 1984, the LEA threatened to take a child into care when the parents removed the child from school. The child had dyslexia and the parents found the regime of corporal punishment at the school the child attended repugnant. In that case it was held that there had been breach of the European Convention on Human Rights and the role of the state was clarified:

> No person shall be denied the right to education. In the exercise of any functions which it assumes in relation to education and to teaching, the state shall respect the right of parents to ensure that such education and teaching is in conformity with their own religious and philosophical convictions.

Thus there is merely a right, under Article 2 of Protocol 1 to have wishes respected. This accords with section 76 of the Education Act 1944, which established the principle of parental choice in relation to education matters generally:

> In the exercise and performance of all powers and duties conferred and imposed on them by this Act the Secretary of State and local education authorities shall have regard to the general principle that, so far as is compatible with the provision of efficient instruction and training and the avoidance of unreasonable expenditure, pupils are to be educated in accordance with the wishes of their parents.

This was preserved in section 9 of the Education Act 1996. Under section 437 of the Education Act 1996 LEAs can serve a school attendance order if they are not satisfied with the arrangements for a child's schooling.

Under section 447, before serving a school attendance order the LEA must give the parent notice requiring him or her to satisfy the LEA within 15 days that the child is receiving "efficient full-time education …". If the parent fails to satisfy the LEA, notice must be given of the intention to serve the order (s 438), then an order must be served naming a school which the child must attend. Written notice of the intention to serve the notice must be given together with the name of the school(s) to be specified in the order. The parent then has an opportunity to select an alternative school if named in the notice or to secure a place at an LEA or other school which may then be named in the notice, subject for example to availability of places. The governing body and head teacher must be informed once a school has been so named. The school must accept the child. The school named should not be one from which the child has been excluded and the naming of a school does not prevent that school from subsequently excluding that child. It is possible to seek amendment of an order. The order will remain in force until the child ceases to be of compulsory school age or it is revoked, or is superseded by an education supervision order (see p 70). Non-compliance is a criminal offence punishable by a fine, imprisonment or a parenting order under the provisions of section 8(1)(d) of the Crime and Disorder Act 1998. Parenting orders have been introduced so that parents may be ordered to attend for such counselling or guidance sessions as may be specified.

Securing attendance

Where a child is registered at a school, the parent must ensure the regular attendance of the child at that school under section 444 of the Education Act 1996. "Regular attendance" is not defined but is taken to mean that the child must be present for the school sessions as identified by the school governing body and, as such, strict adherence to the requirements regarding registration of attendance is important.

Persistent lateness could constitute non-attendance. Lateness may be authorised or unauthorised depending on the reason and the time; guidelines suggest that 30 minutes after registration should be the cut-off point. The Education (Pupils' Attendance Records) Regulations 1991 (SI No 1582), the Pupils' Registration Regulations 1956 (SI No 357) and section 80 of the Education Act 1944 all required the school to keep registers and to inform the LEA of children whose attendance is poor. The relevant regulations are now the Education (Pupil Registration) Regulations 1995 (SI No 2089), as amended by the Education (Pupil Registration) (Amendment) Regulations 1997 (SI No 2624). Registration must take place at the beginning of the morning session and at any time during the afternoon session. The 1991 Regulations introduced the concept of "authorised" and "unauthorised" absences. Every authorised absence must contain a code in the register to show on what grounds authorisation was given.

The categorisation of absence into authorised or unauthorised lies with the school and not the parents. Funding is to be made available to computerise the registration system. Under section 63 of SSFA 1998, regulations may be made to ensure that annual targets are set to reduce the level of unauthorised absences in maintained schools.

Breach of section 444 is an offence of strict liability, so that the ignorance of the parent is no excuse (*Crump* v *Gilmore* [1969] 68 LGR 56 *Hinchly* v *Rankin* [1961] 1 WLR 421). There may however be reasonable causes for absence. These are set out in the Regulations and include:

- sickness (of the child, not the parents or a relative) or other unavoidable cause, such as an emergency involving home or family (in 1997 a magistrates' court decided that a parent should not be liable for her daughter's failure to attend school because her daughter had become pregnant at 13 and stayed off school to look after her child);
- leave of absence granted by a person authorised by the governing body: examples of an authorised absence would be work experience, interview, public performances, off-site activities, exclusion and study leave, some of which are regarded as "approved educational activity" under the 1997 Regulations and therefore do not require leave of absence, such as work experience in the last year of compulsory schooling; no more than 10 days' leave in a school year should be granted unless there are exceptional circumstances;
- days of religious observance;

- holiday periods (by agreement and subject to the leave provisions above);
- the school is not within walking distance and no suitable arrangements have been made for transport;
- the parent's trade or business requires the parent to travel from place to place subject to the child attending school for a minimum period;
- the child is of no fixed abode (under the 1997 Regulations the children of traveller families can be registered at a base school and another school).

In *R v Dyfed County Council, ex parte S* [1995] FCR 113 it was held that it was not possible for parents to use the alleged unsuitability of a school as a defence to an allegation that they failed to secure the attendance of their children at a school under section 39 of the Education Act 1944. In this case, a Welsh LEA refused to provide a mainly English speaking school when there was a school closer to the children's home which was predominantly Welsh speaking. It was held that the LEA did not act unlawfully.

Transport is often an important issue in relation to choice of school (see p 111 below).

Many LEAs have "non-attendance procedures". These are often in four stages:

- Office interview
- Governors' meeting
- Non-attendance panel
- Magistrates'/Family Proceedings Court.

Under section 444 of the Education Act 1996, a failure to secure a child's "regular" attendance at school may result in a criminal prosecution. Before initiating criminal proceedings the LEA should consider the possibility of applying for an education supervision order.

Section 36 of the Children Act 1989 allows the court on the application of the LEA to make an order placing a child under the supervision of that authority where the court is satisfied that the child is of compulsory school age and is not being properly educated. The social services committee or department must be consulted before the making of the application and the general principles of the Children Act must be taken into account (i.e. it must be for the welfare of the child which is the paramount consideration and the court must make no order unless it is necessary and in the child's interests).

Once an order is made, the supervisor is under a duty to "advise, assist, befriend and give directions to the child, the parents and any person with parental responsibility ... in order to ensure that the child is properly educated". Failure to comply with the supervisor's directions is a criminal offence punishable by a fine.

An education supervision order is intended to transfer the primary obligation to educate the child from the parent to the local authority. Therefore, once an education supervision order is in effect an attendance order will cease to have effect, as will any other relevant provision in the Education Acts.

An education supervision order will have an effect for an initial period of one year, but it can be extended. The order ceases to have effect when the child ceases to be of compulsory school age or if a care order is made.

The purpose of the education supervision order is said to be that local authorities should be encouraged to take a more conciliatory view when a child is not being properly educated and that this order might be used instead of prosecuting the parents or taking the child into care. A care order is still available and the court must make such an order if the child's welfare so demands.

In *Re O (A Minor) (Care Proceedings)* [1992] 1 WLR 912, a 15-year-old regularly failed to attend school over a two-year period. The local authority failed to secure her attendance and made an application for a care order under the Children Act 1989. The magistrates made the order but granted a stay pending an appeal. It was subsequently held that they had no power to order such a stay. On appeal it was held that the local authority were justified in making their application, but an education supervision order under section 36 of the Children Act 1989 was said to be the most appropriate method of securing a child's attendance at school. If a care order were to be made then the likelihood of "harm" would have to be considered:

> In determining whether the harm suffered was significant comparison was to be made with a child of equivalent intellectual and social development who was going to school ... Where a child was missing her education by not attending school justices were entitled to conclude that her intellectual and social development were suffering significantly.

In *Re B (A Minor) (Supervision Order: parental undertaking)* [1996] 1 WLR 716 it was held that the county court had no jurisdiction to accept undertakings from the parent of a child who was the subject of a supervision order under section 31 of the Children Act 1989. The order had contained an undertaking to take the child to school on time and to notify the school of any illness, *inter alia*.

A conviction under section 444 of the Education Act 1996 can lead to a parenting order being made, as mentioned above.

Home–school agreements

Traditionally, parents had to comply with any rules that are reasonable for the running of the school, although the rules had to be lawful (see *Spiers* v *Warrington Corporation* [1954] 1 QB 61; *Jarman* v *Mid-Glamorgan Education Authority* [1985] 82 LS Gaz 1249). Several disputes have concerned corporal punishment: see further Chapter 6.

In *R* v *Headmaster and Governors of Westminster Junior School, ex parte Stewart* [1995] COD 111, the conduct of a parent at a school was thought to be an important factor. It was held that:

> As to whether the fact of the mother's conduct was an irrelevant consideration in the decision to exclude the applicant the furthest the court would go was to say that it was idle to suppose that a mother's attitude towards a head teacher and/or governors of a school as expressed by her defiant conduct must of necessity be an erroneous matter to consider when determining that an exclusion, formerly indefinite in duration, should become permanent. Education was not simply a two way process between child and school but a three way partnership between child, school and parent ... it was also a matter of simple worldly experience and common sense.

The Education Act 1997 introduced the "home–school agreement". Under section 13 of that Act (amending the 1996 Act), schools could refuse to admit the child of a parent who refused to sign a home–school partnership document. Sections 110–111 SFFA, the School Standards and Framework Act 1998 (Home–School Agreements) (Modification) Order 1998 (SI No 2834). The School Standards and Framework Act 1998 (Home–School Agreements) (Appointed Day) Order 1998 (SI No 2877) specifies 1st September 1999 as the date upon which the new rules will come into force. This date will apply to many of the SSFA changes.

The governing body shall take reasonable steps to secure the signature of every qualifying parent of the parental declaration, a document recording that the parents accept their parental responsibilities as set out in the document. Importantly, the 1998 Act states in section 111(4) that signing of the parental declaration will not be a condition in the admissions process, and in section 111(5) that "no person shall be excluded from such a school or suffer any other adverse consequences on account of any failure to comply with the invitation to sign the parental declaration".

Parental rights

Participation

Parents have had a right to representation on the governing body since the Education (No 2) Act 1986 and may vote in a secret ballot for the election of members of governing bodies. They could previously initiate the procedure for a change in the status of the school, although under Schedule 2 to SSFA 1998 it is the governing body which take preliminary decisions on status; however, the intention seems to be that parents will be involved in the consultation and balloting procedure which may follow. Parental involvement in requesting and voting in ballots in respect of grammar schools is specifically mentioned in section 106 of SSFA 1998. Parent governors will be represented on LEA education committees as provided for by section 9 of SSFA 1998, and representatives of parents should be consulted under the Local Education Authority (Behaviour Support Plans) Regulations 1998 (SI No 644).

Educational provision

Where an LEA makes educational provision it must be of a type which discharges its duty under section 5 of SSFA 1998. The duty may be discharged by the closure of schools on either a temporary or a permanent basis (*Meade* v *Haringey* [1979] 2 All ER 1016). The school organisation committees established by section 24 of and Schedule 4 to SSFA 1998 do not specifically refer to parental membership, although regulations will be made to clarify who will be eligible for membership.

Parents have a right to expect that provision to be free, subject now to certain charging provisions (see further Chapter 10).

The duty on the LEA and others to provide a certain standard of education is much less clear, and until recently it was a generally accepted view that there was little or no prospect of there being a tort of "educational malpractice" in the United Kingdom. The possibility has been considered (e.g. see A Wolfgarten (1990), "Educational malpractice: A potential problem for LEAs or teachers", *Education and the Law* 2(4), 157–161). The prospect seemed more real following the collective appeals of *E (a Minor)* v *Dorset County Council, Christmas* v *Hampshire County Council* and *Keating* v *Bromley London Borough Council,* discussed in Chapter 7. See also J Holloway (1995), "The Liability of the local education authority to pupils who receive a defective education", *Education and the Law* 7(3), 125–131.

The requirement on LEAs in section 5 of SSFA 1998 to "promote high standards" applies generally rather than to individual pupils, but parents will no doubt use that requirement to challenge proposals in school organisation plans to close schools and may be able to use it more specifically in relation to individual educational provision.

Information

In *R* v *Governors' of Small Heath School, ex parte Birmingham City Council* [1990] COD 23, the parents challenged the nature of the information they had received in connnection with a ballot issued to parents under section 61 of ERA 1988. In particular, the parents complained that the information had been distributed in English only amongst parents in a multicultural area reflected in the school. It was held that whilst publication of notices in other languages would have been desirable, there was no breach under section 61. See also *R* v *Birmingham City Council and the Secretary of State for Education, ex parte Kaur* [1991] COD 21 (below). Section 42 of SSFA 1998 specifically refers to the making of regulations which will allow governing bodies to determine the language or languages in which governor's reports may be produced, and it seems likely that other documents may have to take into account the language requirements of the local community.

Under the "Parents' Charter" and the Education (Schools) Act 1992, the information to be given to parents began to be formalised. From the summer of 1992 parents were to receive five key documents:

- a school report about their child at least once a year
- regular reports from independent inspectors
- performance tables for all local schools
- a prospectus or brochure about individual schools
- an annual report from school governors.

Regulations frequently determine the precise nature of information to be given to parents from time to time. See for example the Education (Individual Pupils' Achievements) (Information) (Amendment) Regulations 1998 (SI No 877). The draft Freedom of Information Bill, published in 1999, will allow parents greater access to information e.g. about why a school has refused admission to a child. It is proposed that a charge will be made for information obtained.

Withdrawal from curriculum

Under section 9(3), of ERA 1988 parents were given a right to withdraw children from religious worship and instruction. Sections 69–71 of SSFA 1998 now deal with the provision of religious education and withdrawal from that provision.

In *R v Secretary of State for Education, ex parte R and D* [1994] ELR 495, the mothers of two children asked that they should be partially excused from religious education. They later complained that the schools' integrated curriculum with religious and secular subjects being taught together meant that children could not be withdrawn from religious education without also depriving them of some secular education. The court refused to give any direction under sections 68 or 99 of the Education Act 1944 as the children had left the school and were too old to return, although the general comments of the Secretary of State in relation to the nature of collective worship were endorsed. Section 405 of the Education Act 1996 allows for withdrawal from sex education except where it forms part of the national curriculum. Sex education is defined in the Act. Sections 365 and 366 of the Education Act 1996 deal with temporary suspension of the national curriculum in respect of a pupil by the head teacher.

Parental preference

The general principle of parental preference was set out in section 76 of the Education Act 1944, as mentioned above. However, Lord Butler has stated that section 76 was part of the 1944 "religious settlement" and that it was not the government's intention to introduce universal "choice" by section 76 "the objective of that settlement and of section 76 was to give Roman Catholic and Anglican parents a choice of school" (*Hansard*, House of Lords, Vol 353, Col 580, 10.7.74).

Under section 6 of the Education Act 1980, parents were given a right to express a preference for a school. LEAs and governors were required to honour this preference unless: it would prejudice the provision of efficient education or the efficient use of resources; it would be incompatible with any arrangements for admission made between the LEA and the governors in respect of a voluntary aided school; or unless in a selective school the child had not met the requirements as to ability and aptitude. Under section 7, local appeal committees had to be established to deal with disputes and the decisions of these committees was said to be "binding" although this is not the case in practice. Parents could opt for a school in another area and the home LEA could not refuse to pay recoupment.

LEAs and governors were required to publish their recruitment criteria, including the numbers to be admitted, and to assist parental preference schools were to publish information about their curriculum, organisation, discipline, examination results or any other matters as required by the Secretary of State through regulation (s 8). Information about the comparative performance of schools in an area became available with provison of league tables under the Education (Schools) Act 1992. Since the introduction of the Special Educational Needs Tribunal, admissions relating to children with special educational needs are now dealt with under the provisions as set out in Chapter 13 below.

In *R v Cleveland County Council, ex parte Commission for Racial Equality* [1993] 91 LGR 139, a parent requested that her child be transferred to a preferred school because the school her daughter had attended had a large number of Asian pupils. The preferred school was predominantly white. The council was reluctant to comply with the request, which it considered had been made on racial grounds, but on taking legal advice found that it was bound to do so. The Court of Appeal held that the mandatory duty to comply with parental preference imposed by section 6 of the Education Act 1980 was not qualified by the Race Relations Act 1976. In the Queen's Bench Division, Macpherson J held that the parents' motives were irrelevant when expressing a preference: "Otherwise the burden imposed upon the authority would be intolerable, because ... they would have to exercise value judgments as to the motivation behind a parent's request ..." *See* G Mead (1992), 'The Cleveland Dispute', *Education and the Law*, 4(1), 25–26.

The ERA 1988 sought to expand the opportunities for parental choice through open enrolment, grant-maintained status and CTCs. Section 30 of ERA 1988 amended section 6 of the 1980 Act. The introduction of the national curriculum limited parental preference in that there is little diversity in the curriculum on offer, but the introduction of league tables has given parents information on which they can make an informed decision and the number of appeals has risen dramatically. One concern has been that vociferous parents can "play the system" and thereby secure their preference at the expense of less articulate parents (see also Tipple p 81 below). The government anticipates that the system as refined by the SSFA 1998 will be more transparent and fairer to parents.

The duty to comply with parental preference may be mandatory, but it is not absolute. The main problem with parental choice, or more properly parental preference, is that popular schools soon become over-subscribed and parents find it difficult to find a place in their first choice school. Recent reports have highlighted the lengths to which some parents are prepared to go in an effort to secure the school place of their choice:

> ... parents are going to extraordinary lengths to secure places for their children at the best schools. Some are using the addresses of relatives to demonstrate that they live within the natural catchment areas; others are inventing house purchases. (*The Times*, 19 September 1995).

The reference to "catchment areas" is of interest. In *R v Greenwich London Borough Council, ex parte Governors of the John Ball Primary School* [1989] 88 LGR 589 it was held that LEAs and schools had to give pupils from outside the borough an equal chance to attend. According to the same *Times* editorial:

> The result is a mess. Schools cannot deny a place to a pupil who does not live within the right borough. They can, however, admit applicants on the ground that they live near to the school ...

The *Greenwich* decision was followed in *R v Bromley London Borough Council, ex parte C* [1992] 1 FLR 174, where it was held that:

> The effect of section 6(5) of the Education Act 1980 was that a local education authority could not in any circumstances favour children living within its area as against children living outside its area when considering applications for places at maintained schools.

However, it was also stated that:

> Their Lordships saw much practical difficulty and it did not surprise them to learn that representations had been made to the Secretary of State which sought to bring about a change in the law.

The "irrelevance" of boundaries was also considered in *R v Kingston upon Thames Royal Borough Council, ex parte Kingwell* [1992] 1 FLR 182.

The position in relation to voluntary aided schools was set out in *R v Governors of Bishop Challenor Roman Catholic Comprehensive Girls School, ex parte C* [1992] 3 WLR 99. Section 6(2) of the 1980 Act imposed the duty to comply with parental preference on governors of voluntary aided schools. It was held that the school could exempt itself from these provisions by using section 6(3), which permitted non-compliance if it would prejudice the provision of efficient education or the efficient use of resources. It was held that a voluntary aided school could operate an admissions policy intended to preserve the character of the school and thereby exempt itself under section 6(3). It was considered by the Court of Appeal that over-subscription could prejudice efficient education.

Similarly in *R v Royal Borough of Kingston upon Thames, ex parte Emsden* [1993] 1 FLR 179, Schiemann J held that:

> ... section 6(3)(c) of the Education Act 1980 envisaged a situation in which "the arrangements for admission to the school [were] based ... partly on selection by reference to ability or aptitude".

The school in question here was a voluntary controlled secondary school wholly maintained by the LEA. It was also considered that geographical location might well be a factor:

> There was nothing intrinsically or inevitably unlawful in a local education authority maintaining a selective school basing the admissions policy of its pupils upon their ability and their geographical distance from the school.

Similar admission arrangements were considered in relation to a grant-maintained school in *R v Governors of Pate's Grant-Maintained School and Appeal Committee, ex parte T* [1994] COD 297. The admissions procedure provided for pupils to be admitted on the basis of an admissions test and provision was also made for priority to be given to pupils living within a certain designated area. The applicant pupil had passed the admissions test, but lived outside the priority area. It was held by Judge J that the appeal panel which had refused the appeal had been right to have regard to all the admission arrangements, including the location of the parental residence.

It seems that the idea of the catchment area was effectively being revived, and there is further evidence of this in *R v Bradford Metropolitan Borough Council, ex parte Sikonder Ali* [1995] 159 LG Rev 81. Here, the LEA had a policy of catchment areas in relation to over-subscribed schools and the applicant's address was outside the catchment area of a particular school. The policy was "multi-stage" in that it involved allocating places to children with siblings at a school and then on catchment areas:

> If the number of parental preferences was sufficiently low the catchment areas were widened to give effect to more preferences but if they were increased the catchment areas could shrink.

Jowitt J held:

> In the case of over-subscription no policy could provide all applicants with an equal chance of success, unless places were awarded by lottery. There had to be some system of selection. In defining such a system it would be possible to delineate catchment areas on the basis of traditional ties between certain schools and certain areas.

The legality of a policy of admissions based on catchment areas was further considered in *R v Rotherham Metropolitan Borough Council, ex parte Clark* [1998] 96 LGR 214. Under section 411 of the Education Act 1996, the LEA was obliged to give parents the right to express a preference in a positive sense. Here, parents living within the catchment area had been written to indicating which school their child had been allocated to and they were told if they were happy they need take no further action. It was held that the LEA had not performed its duty under section 411.

The SSFA 1998 sets out in sections 84–98 new admissions procedures, including parental preferences in section 86. Under that section, the LEA must make provision for the expression of preferences and must enable the parent so doing to give reasons for his or her preference. The LEA and governing body shall comply with such a preference; however, exceptions still apply where compliance would prejudice the provision of efficient education or the efficient use of resources, if there are special arrangements concerning the religious character of the school under section 91, and if the school is selective and the preference does not comply with selection arrangements. There are further constraints on the operation of parental preference provided by the committment to reduce class sizes (s 1 of SSFA 1998) and section 87 states that there is no duty on a school to admit a pupil permanently excluded from two or more schools. Under section 96, the LEA may direct admission to a school. Detailed guidance in a new Code of Practice is awaited and it remains to be seen to what extent local variations will be considered.

In *R v Lancashire County Council, ex parte Foster* [1995] COD 45 the LEA refused to comply with the parental preference. It was held that it was not unlawful for an LEA to consider Roman Catholic children who had attended Roman Catholic primary schools for places at county secondary schools only after other applicants had been placed where such a policy was required in a particular area. This was despite government policy set out in DFE Circular 6/93, *Admissions to Maintained Schools,* which said that where non-denominational schools were over-subscribed, criteria which assigned priority to applicants of one faith as compared to another were unacceptable. The LEA's policy was not so unreasonable as to be interfered with, especially in the light of the particular arrangements in the diocese. The LEA was not bound to comply with the parental preference as this would prejudice the provision of efficient education and efficient use of resources: "If preference were to be given to Roman Catholic children to attend non-denominational schools, problems would arise."

The main problem would seem to have been the lack of opportunity for non-Roman Catholic children to attend Roman Catholic schools, there being very few places available for such pupils. In this case the parent had been seeking to have her son placed in a maintained county school situated opposite his home. This had been refused and he had been offered a place in a school several miles away.

Choice of school also has implications in respect of transport (see above and Chapter 6). Referring to one instance where a mother had said she was going to change her child's religion so that she could get a free bus pass to attend a Roman Catholic school some miles from her home where her parents thought she would receive a better education, a council official said: "... we are not obliged by law to provide free travel to children whose parents choose to send them to schools outside their normal catchment area" (*The Times*, 9 September 1995).

Clearly, the admission of children to schools in an era of so-called parental choice is difficult and impossible without some method of selection. The idea of the catchment area which seemed to be rendered out-dated by the *Greenwich* case would appear to be thriving and along with other criteria. Some commentators suggest that catchment areas are still the major deciding factor in allocating pupils to schools and that there is little real choice or even preference. According to David Tytler, writing in *The Times* on 29 August 1995:

> Parental choice, once the core of the Government's education reforms, has given way to parental preference. The reality is that while there may be preference, there is often very little real choice. The only way to be sure of getting your child into the state comprehensive that you want to is to move next door. Whatever the criteria for admission, it is inevitable that closeness to the school will be the first.

In general terms this is probably correct, but the *Foster* case (above) demonstrates that in certain cases not even proximity to the school will assist.

Complaints

The various Education Acts have given parents numerous opportunities to have complaints considered. For example, under sections 94 and 95 of SSFA 1998 parents have a right of appeal to a local appeals committee against a decision by the LEA or the governors as to the school their child is to be sent to. This is of particular importance when the parent has expressed a preference which has been refused. The procedural aspects of such appeals are considered in Chapter 3 above. Under the ERA 1988, complaint could be made where it is considered that a school is failing to implement the provisions of the national curriculum and in respect of religious education under section 23 (as amended by the Education Act 1996). Under section 68 of the Education Act 1944 (also amended by Education Act 1996), parents could appeal to the Secretary of State for Education where it was considered that either a governing body or LEA were acting or proposing to act unreasonably. Such procedures may be of importance in considering whether an application for judicial review is appropriate, as mentioned in Chapter 3, although Tim Kaye in *Education and the Law* (1998), 10(1), 19, "Admissions to school: Efficiency versus parental choice notes that section 496 of the Education Act 1996 "plays no meaningful part in the admissions process".

The SSFA 1998 makes it compulsory for schools to have a published complaints procedure, and generally it is intended that parents should become much more informed than they have been previously about what can be done when they wish to complain. Applications can also be made by parents for judicial review and to the local ombudsman. Private law actions in the courts are now being actively used by parents following cases on breaches of duty of care (see Chapter 7). Tipple (1990) makes an interesting point in relation to complaints generally:

> Experience suggests that a few parents will seek to exploit these procedures to the utmost, and consume a highly disproportionate amount or resources. However, a number of less articulate and less well informed parents will not be able to take advantage of the new machinery, even though they may well have a good case, simply because of the sophistication of the procedure and the complex nature of the issues.

See *R v Essex County Council, ex parte Bullimore* [1997] ELR 327 where complaint to the Secretary of State was encouraged, and *R v Governing Body of the Rectory School, ex parte WK (A Minor)* [1997] ELR 484 where judicial review was thought preferable to the appeals procedure in certain circumstances.

Consultation

In certain circumstances parents may have a right to be consulted, the most obvious process being through parents meetings. In *R v Birmingham City Council and Secretary of State for Education, ex parte Kaur* (above) it was held that an LEA was not under a duty to provide interpreters to translate at a parents meeting and that a failure to do so was not an act of racial discrimination: "A presentation only in English ... could not cause a flaw in the consultative procedure."

The decision in *R* v *Governors of Small Heath School, ex parte Birmingham City Council* was relied upon (see p 74 above).

In many cases there will be a "legitimate expectation" of consultation. In *R* v *Rochdale Metropolitan Borough Council, ex parte Schemet* [1993] 91 LGR 425, declarations were granted in respect of an application by parents who were not informed of an LEA change to their policy on travelling expenses. No other remedy was granted because that would have had an adverse effect on the previous two years' education budget, so the court in this application for judicial review exercised its discretion not to award certiorari in circumstances where it might otherwise have been appropriate. The parents were informed that although there was no obligation to consult, there was a legitimate expectation that they would be consulted.

See also *Re G* [1995] FCR 53 as to the expectation of consultation between parents or those with parental responsibility, and *R* v *Beatrix Potter School, ex parte K* [1997] ELR 468.

Pupils

Pupils

Definition of "pupil"

For the purposes of the Education Acts a distinction must be made between the definitions of a "pupil" and a "child" in those Acts and the definition of a "child" under the Children Act 1989. Pupils are divided into "junior" and "senior", there being no statutory requirement to separate juniors into "infants" and "juniors" as is often the practice. A junior pupil is a pupil aged under 12 years (Education Act 1996, section 3). A senior pupil is one who is aged 12–18. A pupil aged over 18 is still considered to be receiving secondary education if he or she is continuing a course he or she began before attaining that age. A child for the purposes of the Education Acts is a person who is not over compulsory school age; however, under the Further and Higher Education Act 1992 a "pupil" was defined as any person for whom education is being provided at a school other than a person:

- aged 19 or over for whom further education is being provided; or
- for whom part-time education suitable to the requirements of a person over compulsory school is being provided.

It is possible for a child of 4 years to be registered at an infant school. A child for the purposes of the Children Act 1989 is anyone under 18 (s 105). In section 131 of SSFA 1998 (see below) the word "child" is used rather than "pupil".

Pupil choice

In *Re P (a Minor)* [1992] 1 FLR 316, it was held that in family proceedings it was the duty of the court when making decisions about the future of a child to listen to and respect the wishes of older children. Although this case pre-dates the implementation of the Children Act 1989, that Act had reinforced rather than reduced the rights of children in this respect. In *Re P*, a "mature and sensible" boy aged 14 wished to attend a local day school rather than attend a boarding school. The boy was able to give sound reasons for his decision and this carried such weight as to tip the balance in his favour.

Pupil numbers

The ERA 1988 introduced the concept of open enrolment as a way of increasing parental choice. Section 26 of ERA 1988 stated that the authority with control of admissions to county and voluntary schools could not fix a number of pupils below the "standard number" as defined in the Education Act 1980. However, the discretion which LEAs had had previously to increase this number was swept away, although some powers to increase the number of pupils and procedures were set out to indicate how this might be achieved (e.g. by changing the character of the school, by it becoming selective). The net effect of this, according to some critics, is that while parental preference was extended for some parents, for others it was limited. The SSFA 1998 contains in section 1 a commitment to limit class sizes in infant schools to less than 30 pupils, and parental preference will be affected by such a policy. The increased capital expenditure for the provision of more teachers and classrooms should mean that parental preferences are more likely to be met, although appeal committees will not be able to direct that a school takes 'qualifying measures' – see Appendix 2. Section 93 of SSFA 1998 deals with admission numbers and Schedule 23 to the Act deals with standard numbers, both of which are relevant in admission appeals.

Change of name

A Practice Direction issued in February 1995 set out guidelines about how the surname of a child aged under 18 might be changed. The Practice Direction (Child: Change of surname) states that where a person with 'parental responsibility for a child applies to have that child's surname changed, the application has to be supported by the written consent of every other person with parental responsibility. Any such change as a matter of course should be referred to the school for the register to be altered. Further consideration was given to this important matter by the House of Lords in *Dawson* v *Wearmouth* [1999] *The Times,* March 26.

Transport

Provision of free transport

Under section 509 of the Education Act 1996 (formerly section 55 of the Education Act 1944), the LEA are required to consider whether transport arrangements are necessary in order to facilitate the attendance of a child at school and to provide those facilities free of charge. Sections 509 and 444 of the 1996 Act are linked (as were previous provisions) so that if the shortest route between the parental home and school is more than three miles, then the LEA have to make free transport provision for a child over 8 years of age (two miles for a child under 8 years of age). If no such provision is made a parent cannot be convicted under section 444 for failing to secure the attendance of a child at school (see Chapter 5).

In *Rogers* v *Essex County Council* [1985] 1 WLR 700, the parents of a 13-year-old girl were charged with failing to secure her attendance at a local school under section 39 of the Education Act 1944. The LEA had designated the shortest route from the child's home to school as 2.94 miles.

The designated route was an isolated one along a partly unmade track which would have been difficult to cross in winter and which would have involved some danger for a young girl. An education welfare officer called to give evidence, stating that he would not allow his daughter to walk the route unaccompanied. The parents were originally convicted, but their appeal was allowed. It was held that a route which was unsafe was not an "available route" under section 39 and that the school was not therefore within walking distance. Parker LJ reviewed the situation and stated that:

> "Walking distance" varies with the age of the child. It clearly contemplates routes which the child can use on foot. To regard Parliament as having intended that there should be regarded as an available route something, such as a public footpath, which was dangerous even for adults, and which was so dangerous for children that no responsible parent would allow a child of the relevant age to use it is, in my view, to impute to Parliament an unacceptable disregard for the safety of children.

However, the House of Lords allowed the council's appeal. Lord Ackner, giving the leading judgment, said that a route did not fail to be available because of dangers which might arise if the child used it unaccompanied. The Education (No 2) Act 1986 amended section 55 by the insertion of subsection (3), which stated:

> In considering whether or not they were required ... to make arrangements in relation to a particular pupil the authority shall have regard, amongst other things, to the age of the pupil and the nature of the route, or alternative routes, which he could reasonably be expected to take.

In *R v Devon County Council, ex parte George* [1989] AC 573 Lord Donaldson, MR found that:

> The amendment of 1986 has no application to children who lived outside the walking distance from school. Under s55(1) the local authority continued to be under an obligation to provide them with transport free of charge. But in relation to children living within the walking distance the authority now had to apply its mind to the question of whether it was necessary to make arrangements to facilitate their attendance at school ...

If it was found necessary to make such arrangements, the parents were entitled to have them made free of charge.

In this particular case where the child lived just under three miles from the school which could be reached along a rural road, it was held that it was completely unreasonable for the child to walk unaccompanied. His mother could not go with him because of younger children, and the father would have to walk nearly 60 miles a week.

The fact that an elder child was already receiving free transport on health grounds could create disunity in the home. The appeal against a decision to refuse judicial review of the council's decision was allowed, although in the circumstances there was no need to formally quash the decision, as "no doubt the council would take account of the views expressed by the court". The Court of Appeal was keen to stress that each application of this type was to be considered on its own merits and that "stress and strain" on the child, even if induced by the stress of the parent, was to be avoided.

The courts seem to have become reluctant to adjudicate in matters such as this. In *R v Essex County Council, ex parte Bullimore* [1997] ELR 327 the High Court told the applicant to take her case to the Secretary of State instead. McCullough J stated: "This court has no means of judging safety. There's no question of the court going to the road and having a look. The Secretary of State can do exactly that through her officials" (See further Chapter 3.)

There are still problems where the child's parents choose to send the child to a school beyond the walking distance limit. In *R v Essex County Council, ex parte C* [1994] 1 FCR 773, it was held that an LEA was not obliged to provide a child with free transport to the school of his or her parents' choice irrespective of the distance involved or the existence of an equally suitable school nearer to his or her home. As mentioned in Chapter 5, the notion of parental choice is regarded as something of a myth. Russell LJ in this case stated:

> While Parliament had accepted that parental choice of schooling was important, the legislation did not give parents a right to decide the school at which a child would be educated.

The "nearest suitable school" was further considered in *R v Kent County Council, ex parte C* [1998] ELR 108 where a pupil was selected to attend a school further than a school nearer to her home. It was held that as long as the LEA considered the nearer school "suitable", their decision not to provide free transport was lawful. The fact that the selective school was "more suitable" for the pupil was not a relevant consideration.

Under section 76 of the Education Act 1944 parental choice was subject to the avoidance of unreasonable public expenditure and as such the Court of Appeal could find nothing in section 55 of the 1944 Act, nor in section 39, which it was argued gave an obligation by implication to provide transport, which meant that the local authority had to provide free transport to this child.

Even if no arrangements are made under section 509 of the Education Act 1996, the LEA may pay the whole or part of the pupil's travelling expenses.

Section 55 was further amended by the ERA 1988. Subsection (4) was inserted by section 100(3) of the 1988 Act and considered in *R v Rochdale Metropolitan Borough Council, ex parte Schemet* [1993] 91 LGR 425. Subsection (4) made Parliament's intention clear that an education authority was not to discriminate in favour of schools it maintained itself as against schools that were grant-maintained or maintained by other education authorities. Transport arrangements under section 55(1) had to include "provision for pupils at grant-maintained schools which is no less favourable than the provision made in pursuance of the arrangements for pupils at schools maintained by the local education authority".

Withdrawal of free transport provisions

In Rochdale, a new policy was introduced in 1990 as a result of constraints on the council's expenditure. It stated that the council would not pay travelling expenses if a child was to attend a school not maintained by the authority, even if it was the nearest suitable school. This policy was found to be unlawful; however, this did not mean that the withdrawal of travel passes as a general policy was unlawful. Again, the potential conflict with parental choice was an issue, per Roch J:

The parents' wishes were an important consideration but they were not the sole consideration and the education authority might conclude that they could make suitable arrangements for the child to be registered at a school closer to his home despite a conflict with the parents' stated preference, provided that the authority took account of that preference in reaching its conclusion.

In this case the parents had a legitimate expectation of consultation and they should have been given rational reasons for the withdrawal of the passes and should have been given the opportunity to comment. Ultimately the outcome may well be the same, which again demonstrates the limited value of challenges by way of judicial review as mentioned in Chapter 3.

Private provision of transport

The private provision of transport has also caused some difficulties. In *DPP v Sikonder* [1992] *The Times*, 19 May, a father preferred to take his own children to school in his car together with other children. Payments for this were never demanded but were made irregularly. He was stopped by the police who found 11 girls in his car. He was subsequently prosecuted for various offences relating to the use of a "public service vehicle" under the Public Passenger Vehicles Act 1981 and the Road Traffic Act 1988. It was held that such a person was operating a public service vehicle because the activities described "went beyond the bounds of mere social kindness".

Disciplinary rules

The conduct of the school, as seen in Chapter 4, is under the control of the governing body, subject to the delegation of specific functions to any other person. Under section 110 of SSFA 1998, the governing body shall adopt a home–school agreement which specifies, *inter alia*, the school's expectations of its pupils, namely as regards the conduct of such pupils while they are registered there. In certain circumstances the pupil may be asked to sign the parental declaration (s 110(5)). Under sections 61 and 62 of SSFA 1998 the head teacher is responsible for the internal organisation, management and control of the school, particularly:

- promoting, among pupils, self-discipline and proper regard for authority;
- encouraging good behaviour and respect for others on the pupils' part;

- securing that the pupils' standard of behaviour is acceptable; and
- otherwise regulating the pupils' conduct.

In achieving the above the head teacher should act in accordance with any written statement of the governing body on such matters and any guidance which that body offers. It is the head teacher's duty to make such rules generally known throughout the school. The governing body and the head teacher should inform the local authority if there are any matters which may affect finance or the authority's duties as employer. The right of the head teacher alone to exclude a pupil is set out in section 64 of SSFA 1998.

Section 28 of the 1986 (No 2) Act provided that the LEA had reserve powers to intervene in the event of a breakdown of discipline in maintained schools; this is preserved in sections 14,15 and 62 of SSFA 1998. LEAs also have a duty under the Education Act 1997 to draw up behaviour support plans to set out the arrangements for the education of disruptive children: see further the Local Education Authority (Behaviour Support Plans) Regulations 1998 (SI No 644).

Independent schools can make their own disciplinary rules as a matter of contract (*R* v *Headmaster of Fernhill Manor School, ex parte Brown* (below). However, see the law on corporal punishment (below).

Homework

In 1995 the DfEE confirmed that the "amount of homework and its frequency is a matter for individual schools and teachers to decide" (*The Times,* 28 October 1995). However, the present government has made homework the subject of DfEE guidance. In September 1998 it was stated that schools should consider introducing homework from the age of 4 and that children of 8 years should do 40 minutes a night; GCSE students should complete up to two hours a night.

Uniform

Decisions relating to uniform are a matter for the governing body, but any policy would need to take into account the provisions of any other enactment, such as the Race Relations Act 1976. Cases involving school uniform have tended to concentrate on discrimination issues. A leading case is *Mandla* v *Dowell Lee* [1983] 1 All ER 1062, where the House of Lords held that a head teacher of a private school had indirectly discriminated against a boy by refusing to admit him unless he went without his turban and had his hair cut. The boy was a Sikh and it was held that such a demand was not "justifiable". In certain situations, such discrimination might be justifiable, for example where the wearing of items might constitute a risk to health and safety (e.g. the wearing of jewellery in physical education).

The Equal Opportunities Commission has suggested that banning girls from wearing trousers in school may be discrimination under section 22 of the Sex Discrimination Act 1975.

Punishment

In general terms, the right of teachers to administer punishment is well established, subject to certain basic principles such as the law relating to trespass, assault and false imprisonment.

Corporal punishment

The long legal debate on corporal punishment has continued, mainly in the European courts. According to C Barton in "Time to spare the child", *The Times,* 13 April 1993:

> As long ago as 1669 a "Children's Petition" was presented to Parliament, complaining of the school practice of whereby "our secret parts, which are by nature shameful, and not to be uncovered, must be anvil exposed to the immodest eyes and filthy blows of the smiter".

The right of teachers to administer corporal punishment was, however, well established and based on the principle of *loco parentis.* In *R* v *Hopley* [1860] 2 F&F 202 it was held that lawful parental chastisement must be "moderate and reasonable" and in *Mansell* v *Griffin* [1908] 1 KB 160 the punishment given to a child in school was said to be moderate, not dictated by the wrong motives and "it was such as is usual in the school and such as the parent of a child might expect that it would receive if it did wrong".

In 1967, the Plowden Report had recommended the abolition of corporal punishment in primary schools and the Society of Teachers Opposed to Physical Punishment (STOPP) was established in 1968. Little changed as a result. In *Jarman* v *Mid-Glamorgan Education Authority* [1985] 82 LS Gaz 1249, children were taken into care when their mother was prosecuted for their non-attendance at school. The children had been suspended when one of them had been caned and the mother refused to retract a written statement declaring her opposition to corporal punishment.

In *Campbell and Cosans* v *United Kingdom* [1982] 4 ECHR 293, the European Court of Human Rights ruled that inflicting corporal punishment where parents were philosophically opposed to it was a breach of Article 2 of the First Protocol of the European Convention on Human Rights, and might even be a breach of Article 3 which relates to torture or degrading treatment or punishment. (See also *Family H* v *United Kingdom* [1984] ECHR Decisions and Reports, Vol 37, July 1984, 105). In *A* v *United Kingdom* (1998) *The Times*, 1 October, it was held that the law of reasonable chastisement was not adequate to protect children and that the beating of a child by his step-father constituted a breach of Article 3 of the Convention.

In 1992, a private school pupil who sued in the European Court of Human Rights over a caning he received from his headmaster settled out of court. He was awarded £8,000 and the government paid £12,000 costs (see *The Times*, 14 November 1992, 'Pupil wins £8,000 for caning').

Matters relating to corporal punishment were considered further in *Costello-Roberts* v *United Kingdom* [1994] 1 FCR 65 by the European Court of Human Rights. The pupil in this case attended a private boarding school. The facts of the case occurred in 1985 when domestic law did not feature in the European Court judgment as it was accepted that domestic law did not address the issues of privacy and degradation. As in *Campbell and Cosans* (above), the issue was whether the European Convention on Human Rights was breached. The court held (by five votes to four) that the punishment received did not constitute degrading punishment under Article 3 "as it did not reach the minimum threshold of severity". The boy in this case had received a "slippering" (i.e. hit three times on the buttocks, through his shorts, with a rubber-soled gym shoe). His parents complained to the police and the NSPCC, but they told the parents that no action could be taken given that there were no visible marks. The child was subsequently removed from the school by his parents. In the case of *A* (above), the step-parent had been acquitted by a criminal court of assault (the defence of reasonable chastisement being successful), but the beating took the form of caning and there were several physical scars left by the canings, which took place over a period of years. This seems to have reached the minimum threshold of severity anticipated by *Costello-Roberts*, but it remains to be seen what impact this case will have, if any, in respect of so-called "trivial assaults".

The Committee of Ministers of the Council of Europe encouraged member states to review their legislation on the power to punish children in order to prohibit corporal punishment; section 131 of SSFA 1998 abolishes corporal punishment at "any school".

Section 47 of the Education (No 2) Act 1986 effectively abolished corporal punishment in schools maintained by LEAs, non-maintained special schools and independent schools maintained or assisted by a government department. Pupils on the assisted places scheme could not receive corporal punishment.

Section 131(4) of SSFA 1998 defines corporal punishment as the "doing of anything for the purpose of punishing the child ... which, apart from any justification, would constitute battery". Under section 131(4), corporal punishment shall not be taken to be anything done to avert immediate personal injury to the person or property of any person, including the child.

Guidance on the restraint of unruly pupils is relevant in this context. The Education Act 1997 provided for the restraint of such pupils and further guidance has been issued by the DfEE. Any force used should always be the minimum needed to achieve the desired result and the degree of force must always be in proportion to the circumstances. LEAs and schools should develop their own policies to be understood by both parents and pupils on actions which may be taken to control pupils. See further section 550A of the Education Act 1996 and Chapter 7 below.

Corporal punishment may not be administered in CTCs (see the Education (Abolition of Corporal Punishment) Regulations 1987 (SI No 1183), as amended). See also generally A Khan (1995), "Corporal punishment in schools", *Education and the Law* 7(1), 1–11.

Detention

In *R v Rahman* [1985] *The Times,* 5 June, it was held that a parent could not detain a child if it is for such a period or in such circumstances as to take it out of the realm of reasonable parental discipline. Such detention can amount to unlawful imprisonment. In *The Times Educational Supplement*, 29 September 1995, the Secretary of State for Education announced that the law relating to detention was to be reviewed:

> At present it is thought that schools have no power [to detain] if parents refuse their permission ... We do want to look again at that advice. It's perhaps less clear in legal terms than the impression we have given.

Education Act 1997 inserted section 550B into Section 5 of the Education Act 1996 clarifying the position and making after-school detention lawful in certain categories of schools subject to the requirements of the section. Whilst the Act does not require parental permission, one of the requirements is at least 24 hours' notice in writing.

Removal to a school

Under section 16 of the Crime and Disorder Act 1998, a local authority can designate premises to which children and young persons can be removed. A constable can remove a person of compulsory school age if he or she has reasonable cause to believe that he or she is absent from school without lawful authority (established by reference to s 444 of the Education Act 1996) from a public place to designated premises or to the school from which he or she is absent.

The impetus for such a provision is the link between truancy and youth crime; however, it does appear to make truancy an offence committed by the child, whereas the offence of failure to secure attendance can only be committed by a parent. It is not clear what powers or duties a school would then have to detain such a child on the premises.

Confiscation

Confiscation is not unlawful and in some circumstances may be necessary for the health or safety of a particular pupil or other pupils, for example where weapons or drugs are found. In April 1995, a draft circular suggested that where illegal drugs are found teachers should confiscate the substances and hand them over to the police. Section 4 of the Offensive Weapons Act 1996, amending section 139 of the Criminal Justice Act 1988, gave the police powers of entry, search and seizure on school premises (as defined by the Further and Higher Education Act 1992) in respect of weapons, but not drugs.

Exclusion

Exclusion is the usual name now for both expulsion and suspension. Expulsion used to represent "the end of the line" for both pupil and school. The most common offences leading to exclusion include disobedience, verbal abuse or insolence. Other instances include attacks on teachers and other staff and bullying or physical aggression towards other pupils. The framework for exclusions is now set out in sections 64–68 of SSFA 1998. Under section 64, the head teacher of a maintained school may exclude a pupil for a fixed period or permanently.

The head must inform parents immediately about what kind of exclusion has been made and the reasons for it. Failure to do so may be a breach of natural justice (see below). Parents (and pupils) have a right to make representations to governors and there is a further right of appeal to local appeal committees.

In 1998, research found that more than 12,500 pupils were excluded from school in 1997, the most dramatic rise being in primary schools. The subject of exclusions was due to be reviewed by the government's Social Exclusion Unit because of the long-term implications of such figures. There has been some concern pupils were being excluded to prevent their impact on academic league tables. Inspections of LEAs will identify those with a record of high exclusions. The first official inspection (following a voluntary scheme) found that Manchester schools had 142 permanently excluded pupils and the authority could not tell the inspectors what alternative provision was being made for 140 of those pupils.

Governments have persistently threatened financial implications for over-use of exclusions. In 1993 it was announced that the government planned proposals to tighten up the exclusions system and to abolish indefinite exclusions provided for by section 261(1)(a) of the Education Act 1993. The only exclusion options which are now available are fixed or permanent exclusions. Fixed periods should not be used to exclude a pupil for more than 45 days of the school year (s 64(2) of SSFA 1998).

In 1994, following on from research and recommendations made in the 1992 Elton Report, "Discipline in Schools", a series of six related circulars was produced by the DFE (and in some cases jointly with other government departments). Circular 8/94 dealt specifically with *Pupil Behaviour and Discipline*. It aimed to limit the need for pupils to be excluded and offered guidance to head teachers and governors. The idea of "whole school policies" in matters such as bullying is promoted. Circular 9/94, *The Education of Children with Emotional and Behavioural Difficulties* offered advice on the early identification of special needs in mainstream schools which might be beneficial in dealing with "disruptive children". Circular 10/94, *Exclusions from School*, elaborated on changes in the law introduced by the Education Act 1993 and offered guidance to schools on the proper use of the sanction of exclusion. It suggested model procedures for head teachers, governors and LEAs and it explained the rights of pupils and parents, especially on appeal.

Circular 11/94 *The Education by LEAs of Children Otherwise than at School*, included, *inter alia*, the provision of Pupil Referral Units (see below). LEAs may provide home tuition for pupils who are "out of school" and the Circular gave some information on that aspect. The question of home tuition in respect of disruptive children has been a matter of some concern lately, with both quality and duration coming under attack. The two other circulars in the series, *Pupils with Problems*, do not refer to discipline as such and are mentioned below in other contexts. Additional funding was announced in 1998 by the DfEE to encourage schools to retain disruptive pupils in mainstream schools.

There has been some concern about the grounds on which a pupil may be excluded. The question of "parental misdemeanours" such as the giving of a false address to gain admission to a chosen school is referred to in Chapter 5. A DfEE spokeswoman in *The Times Educational Supplement*, 22 September 1995 said:

> The removal of a child actually at school, for other than disciplinary problems is a serious action to take. At the same time we would not condone any application made on inaccurate information as such an application could result in another more eligible child being denied a place.

See also *R v Headmaster and Governors of Westminster Junior School, ex parte Stewart* [1995] COD 111 with respect to the effect of a parent's conduct on the nature of an exclusion.

Some teacher associations have expressed concern that there is no general policy on exclusion where a pupil has broken the law. Nigel de Gruchy of the NASUWT, quoted in *The Guardian*, 25 April 1995, said:

> People should automatically be suspended if they have violated the law ... Not necessarily permanently excluded for the first offence, but if we are going to run discipline properly then anyone committing a criminal offence on school premises must receive some kind of suspension.

The Schools Minister, Estelle Morris, caused some controversy in 1998 when she suggested that the "zero tolerance" approach to drugs in school was not always appropriate, and that drug-taking or possession might also be regarded as a welfare issue and should not lead to automatic exclusion.

The appropriate procedure for exclusion was considered in *R v Newham London Borough Council, ex parte X* [1994] *The Times*, 15 November. It was held that where a child had been expelled from school without the opportunity to make representations, the head-master's decision could be reviewed by way of judicial review as it had been "prima facie unfair".

The duty of appeal committees in exclusion cases is that they ask the right questions so that they do not reach an irrational decision, as established in *R v Solihull Borough Council, ex parte W* [1997] ELR 489.

In *R v Governing Body of Rectory School, ex parte WK (A Minor)* [1997] ELR 484, it was held that there had been procedural irregularity in not allowing the pupil's mother to make representations and importantly that this was not a case where the established appeal procedure should be exhausted before resort was to be had to judicial review. The appeal procedure was not appropriate for dealing with issues of procedural irregularity, whereas the court was.

If the appeals procedure is used then it may be that any "defect" is "cured". In *R v Governors of St Gregory's Roman Catholic Aided High School, ex parte Roberts* (1995) *The Times*, 27 January, a boy was indefinitely excluded having sworn at a teacher. On appeal, the governors decided that the exclusion was a reasonable response and the head then ordered the exclusion be permanent. There then followed an appeal to an appeals committee. On an application for judicial review, it was held that the original appeal before the governors had been flawed in that the governors had misunderstood that the boy himself could be heard, albeit that his mother represented his interests. However, this was deemed to be a minor defect which could be cured by a proper hearing before the appeals committee. As that appeal had been properly conducted, the decision was valid. It has been suggested that this ability to cure defects would only be appropriate where there was no serious defect, such as manifest bias, and is only effective where a subsequent hearing takes the form of a complete rehearing.

An excluded pupil may apply for reinstatement and such applications are also subject to appeal procedures. In *R v London Borough of Camden and the Governors of the Hampstead School, ex parte H* [1996] ELR 360, it was held that the effect of the excluded pupil's return on the "victim" of such a pupil should be investigated and considered.

In *R v Headmaster of Fernhill Manor School, ex parte Brown* [1992] *The Times*, 5 June the rules relating to children in independent schools was considered. Despite the ruling in *Costello-Roberts* (see p 93 above), the *Brown* case determined that there was a distinction to be drawn between pupils in state and those in dependent schools. The school's brochure provided the terms of the contract between the school and parents. One of the terms was that:

> The head reserves the right of requiring the removal of any pupils whose influence is found to be detrimental to her companions or whose conduct and application to work is unsatisfactory.

The applicant for judicial review had been expelled from the school for alleged bullying and alleged intimidatory behaviour. She was not informed of the reasons for the decision to expel, nor was she given the right to make representations before the headmaster and the board of governors. It was held that public law could offer her no remedy; the only remedy available was to her parents, who could issue a writ in private law. The matter was considered to be one wholly of private rather than public law as described in Chapter 3. Brook J. did recognise the impact that expulsion (presumably from either a public or state school) could have:

> Expulsion from school was and always had been a stigma; it might hamper the education of a child perhaps at a crucial stage and could lead to later difficulties in employment.

The judge hoped that independent schools would draw up their disciplinary rules according to the principles of natural justice and the courts had given some guidance as to what those rules were.

Section 87 of SSFA 1998 applies to the admission of children when they have been permanently excluded from two or more schools. The duty to admit in section 86(2) of the Act does not apply to such children.

The funding implications of permanent exclusion are dealt with in the Education (Amount to Follow Permanently Excluded Pupils) Regulations 1999 (SI No 495), made under section 494 of the Education Act 1996.

Pupil referral units

Section 298 of the Education Act 1993 defined a pupil referral unit (PRU) as a maintained school other than a county or special school organised to provided education for children who by reason of exclusion or otherwise may not receive suitable education unless exceptional arrangements are made for them. A total of 309 PRUs were set up under the 1993 Act for pupils "out of school" mainly because of exclusion. Not all of these were new institutions, some of them being former "special units".

In June 1995, Ofsted reported that only two of the ten PRUs inspected were "working well". Four were "unsatisfactory" and four were "pretty poor". The Education Act 1996 (s 19 and Sched 1) and the Education Act 1997 (s 47) made further provision for PRUs; section 48 of the 1997 Act created management committees for PRUs to address their problems.

The Pupils' Registration (Amendment) Regulations 1994 (SI No 2128) amended the Pupils' Registration Regulations 1956 (SI No 357) to permit a pupil to be registered at a PRU and a mainstream school simultaneously.

Bullying

Bullying of other pupils may well form the basis of an exclusion (see above).

In 1994, a disabled student claimed that she suffered post-traumatic stress disorder as a result of bullying at school. In *Walker v Derbyshire County Council* [1994] *The Times*, 7 June, it was alleged that the local authority had breached its duty of care by failing to prevent the bullying. The case, which was regarded as a test case in the county court, found that there was no negligence. A spokesman for the education committee involved said in *The Times*, 16 July 1994:

> If this case has achieved anything it may have put the issue of bullying higher on people's agendas. Where bullying arises schools must act immediately and, in this case, the authority was found to have addressed appropriately the issues that were raised.

Sick and disabled pupils

Circular 12/94 of the series on "Pupils with Problems" deals with the question of sick children in the light of the duty on LEAs under section 298 of the Education Act 1993 (as amended) to ensure suitable education for all children of compulsory school age. The circular gives details about provision whether at home or in hospital, guidance on curricular matters, staff training, the recording of progress, and liaison between medical, educational and adminstrative staff.

Circular 3/97 gave guidance on the implications of the Disability Discrimination Act 1995 for schools and LEAs. The requirement in relation to pupils is that governing bodies, in their annual report to parents must explain their policies in relation to disabled pupils.

Pupils in care

Circular 13/94 of the "Pupils with Problems" series deals with children who are being "looked after by local authorities". This phrase is now being widely used instead of "in care". The circular seeks to promote close links between educational and social services to remedy educational disadvantages of children whether in foster homes, children's homes or some other form of residential care.

The government has announced a review of services for children in care and education is likely to feature in that review.

Results

The provision of information relating to schools generally and individual pupils is now regulated by the Parent's Charter (updated in 1994) and the Education (Schools) Act 1992. See, for example, Circular 15/94, *The Parent's Charter: Publication of Information about Primary Schools in 1994.* The Education (School Records) Regulations 1989 (SI No 1261) as amended allow for parents and pupils (but only where aged over 16) to see the pupil's curricular record. Written notice of inaccuracies may be submitted. Detailed information is given in the Education (Individual Pupils' Achievements) (Information) (Amendment) Regulations 1998 (SI No 877) about the content of the annual report to be given to parents or pupils over 18.

In *R* v *Governors and Appeal Committee of Pate's Grant-Maintained Grammar school, ex parte T* [1994] COD 297, a pupil passed an admission test to a selective school. She was told that she had passed the aptitude test but was refused admission on other grounds (see Chapter 5). The parents claimed that there had been a breach of natural justice in that her marks had not been disclosed. It was held by Judge J that there were "good reasons" for not disclosing the applicant's actual marks.

Individual students may apply to external examination boards to have their examinations re-marked and schools may appeal on the behalf of groups of pupils. A pilot scheme was announced in 1999 to allow pupils to see their marked GCSE and A Level papers.

Awards

Under various enactments it is possible for pupils to apply for some financial assistance in connection with their studies. In *R* v *Lambeth London Borough Council, ex parte Ghous* [1993] COD 302, a muslim boy from a poor family applied for a discretionary financial award to enable him to attend a single sex boys school in Wandsworth to study for his A levels. He was refused by Lambeth council, which would only continue his previous financial support if he went to a co-educational school in Lambeth. It was held by Potts J that it was unreasonable to ignore parental preference in this case and that the council's policy was unreasonable in the sense of *Associated Provincial Picture Houses* v *Wednesbury Corporation* [1948] 1 KB 223 (see further Chapter 3).

Employment

The Children and Young Persons Act 1933 and sections 558 and 559 of the Education Act 1996 as amended by the Children (Protection at Work) Regulations 1998 (SI No 276) set out the law relating to the employment of children. Local authorities may make by-laws in respect of such employment and teachers may have a role to play in assisting the authorities if e.g. some illegal employment comes to their attention or if leave of absence is sought.

Immigration

Under the Statement of Changes to the Immigration Rules (HC 395) as amended, made under the Immigration Act 1971 (as amended), a person can be refused leave to enter the United Kingdom as a visitor for the purpose of attending a maintained school (para 40). Under paragraph 57, permission to enter as a student may be granted (subject to information on funding) if the person is undertaking a full-time course of study at an independent fee-paying school. Such a person may be under the age of 16.

Chapter 7

Duties of Care, Safety and Supervision

Duties of Care, Safety and Supervision

Duties and educational provision

Traditionally, duties of care in relation to education have been limited to those duties established under the principles of *Donoghue* v *Stevenson* [1932] AC 562 as applied to the safety and welfare of children and others at school. These applications of the law are discussed below. The House of Lords has considered whether there might be liability concerning the standard of care in making educational provision. At a time when standards in education are very much in the spotlight, these are important developments.

In Chapter 3, the public law dimension of education law is discussed. When any statutory appeals have been exhausted, parents and others are encouraged to use the public law remedies through the process of judicial review to challenge decisions. Private law remedies, such as actions for damages commenced by writ, are encouraged in cases of contract, for example by employees in certain circumstances and by parents of children at private schools as in *R* v *Headmaster of Fernhill Manor School, ex parte Brown* [1992] *The Times*, 5 June. In some cases the judges have taken the opportunity to consider whether damages based on a breach of duty are appropriate. LEAs, and others, have their responsibilities expressed as "duties" frequently in the various Acts. Whether this expressly or by implication involves any "duty of care" in the performance of those duties is a moot point.

In *Meade* v *Haringey* [1979], a group of parents made a complaint to the Secretary of State under section 99 of the Education Act 1944 that the education authority had failed to discharge the duty imposed upon them by section 8 of the Act to make schools available for full-time education. Schools had been closed locally because of industrial action. The Secretary of State refused to direct the LEA to perform their duty because it was considered that there had been no breach of that duty. Lord Denning MR in the Court of Appeal contended that it was right that such applications could come before the courts after the section 99 procedure had been complied with, but that if the duty had been shown to have been broken here the LEA's actions would have been considered ultra vires and any remedies would have not been founded on negligence claims.

The question was further considered in *Holtom v Barnet London Borough Council* [1993] *The Times*, 30 September. The plaintiff had been taken into the care of the local authority at age 3 years and was assessed as being "mentally handicapped and severely subnormal". She was in fact of normal intelligence and in later life obtained educational qualifications. She sued the local authority, alleging it was in breach of its duties as "parent" (i.e. *in loco parentis* (see below)) and/or negligent. Her claim was based on *Meade v Haringey* but it was held that there were statutory avenues which could have been pursued by her parents so no action in private law could lie for failure to provide adequate educational facilities, per Oddie J:

> There had been remedies under statute open to parents; for review by a local education authority with an avenue of appeal to the secretary of state, or judicial review.

However, the action was allowed in respect of the breach of the LEA's obligations *in loco parentis*.

In *R v Gloucestershire County Council, ex parte P* [1993] COD 303. Popplewell J found that there may have been an unreasonable delay in the assessment of a child with special educational needs under the Education Act 1981, but found that there was no negligence on the part of a council officer. There had been a genuine mistake and so although the issue of damages for negligence was considered there had been no "reprehensible" delay and therefore there was no negligence. In any event it was held that it would be impossible to come to a decision about whether there had been negligence, giving rise to a claim in damages on affidavit evidence.

In *Walker v Derbyshire County Council* [1994] *The Times*, 7 June, an action by a girl who claimed she had been bullied failed when it was decided that the school in question had done all that was reasonable in the circumstances at the time. It seemed therefore that there was some limited potential for actions in negligence other than in traditional personal injury cases as mentioned below, but much would depend on establishing breach of a duty of care resulting in damage, as is usual, and, importantly, there being no other available remedy. Where statute or the courts through the process of judicial review provide parents and others with avenues of appeal then private law actions are, at best, discouraged.

In 1995, the collective appeals of five cases repeated at [1995] 3 WLR 152 came before the House of Lords. In *X v Bedfordshire County*

Council and *M v Newham London Borough Council*, lack of care on the part of the local authority was alleged. In the *Bedfordshire* case a failure to identify "those in need of care proceedings" and to initiate those proceedings was alleged. In the *Newham* case it was argued that a mistaken allegation of sexual abuse by a local authority psychiatrist and social worker, which resulted in the child's removal, caused psychiatric injury. In *E v Dorset County Council,* the allegation was that parents had been wrongly advised, that the local authority failed to diagnose that a child suffered from a learning disorder and that when this was recognised the authority failed to make provision for the child. In *Christmas v Hampshire County Council* the plaintiff had learning difficulties consistent with dyslexia and behavioural problems. He claimed that the local authority owed him a duty of care to use reasonable skill and care in the assessment of his educational needs. He also claimed that his headmaster had failed to refer him for appropriate assessment. In *Keating v Bromley London Borough Council* the plaintiff claimed, *inter alia*, that the authority had failed him by placing him in a special school when he could have been educated in ordinary schools, did not pay heed to his mother's requests and failed to provide him with any reasonable education.

The *Bedfordshire, Newham* and *Dorset* cases involved consideration of the professional duties of social workers and psychiatrists. In these cases much depended on the reliance to be placed on the professionals. For example, in the *Dorset* case it was held that:

> The educational psychologists held themselves out as having special skills. They were, like any other professional, bound to possess such skills and to exercise them carefully ... The defendant authority, therefore, could be shown to be directly or vicariously liable for them.

Similarly, in the *Bromley* case, an action based on professional negligence was said to be a possibility depending on the precise nature of the facts. In the Queen's Bench Division case of *X v Bedfordshire* it had been held that:

> Hitherto, no tort of negligence by a local authority towards children was recognised, and compelling reasons of social policy had to exist before such a tort could be recognised.

In the *Hampshire* case the duty of care issue in relation to educational provision was addressed directly. In this case the claim was said to be "a pure common law claim based on a duty of care owed by a headmaster and educational adviser to a pupil". Lord Browne-Wilkinson went on:

> A school which accepted a pupil assumed responsibility not only for his physical well being but also his educational needs. The head teacher, being

responsible for the school, himself came under a duty of care to exercise the reasonable skills of a headmaster in relation to such educational needs.

It was stated that to fail to accept such a proposition "would fly in the face, not only of society's expectations of what a school would provide, but also the fine traditions of the teaching profession itself".
    The Law Lords held that:

- A breach of statutory duty by a local authority did not, by itself, give rise to any private law cause of action. Such a right might arise where a statute imposed a duty for the protection of a limited class of the public and for a breach of that duty a private right was conferred.
- Where careless exercise of a statutory duty is alleged, the plaintiff has to show circumstances which would have given rise to a duty of care at common law.
- Where a local authority had a discretion, the exercise of that discretion was a matter for the authority. If a decision fell outside the ambit of the discretion it could give rise to common law liability, but "where the factors relevant to the exercise of the discretion included matters of policy, the court could not adjudicate on them".

Rather than deciding the outcomes of the cases themselves, the matter for consideration here was whether it would be possible for the courts to hear such actions. The case of *Christmas* returned to the High Court for determination and it was held that the duty of care had not been broken in that case (see *Christmas* v *Hampshire* [1998] ELR 1). It was held that nothing "obvious" had been missed and that the more reviews that were undertaken of a child's progress the less likely it was that something would be missed.

Some commentators thought that parents would be encouraged to begin actions because of the 1995 appeals against local authorities, even if they might ultimately fail. Some, such as David Pannick QC, writing in *The Times,* felt that the House of Lords "missed an opportunity to expand the remedies provided by English law", and that the "decision of the House of Lords confirms that the common law is reluctant to provide compensation for unlawful administrative acts". (Public authorities and damages claims, *The Times,* 18 July 1995.)

Clearly, there is some danger of the floodgates being opened and policy considerations may well influence future decisions. In *Phelps* v *Hillingdon London Borough Council* [1998] 96 LGR 1, the plaintiff recovered substantial damages having shown that the educational psychologist to whom she was referred by her school failed to diagnose dyslexia. In terms of the test laid down in *Bolam* v *Frien Hospital Management Trust Committee* [1957] 1 WLR 582, the psychologist had failed to exercise the degree of care to be expected of an ordinary competent member of her profession. It was held that the plaintiff would have been "clearly dyslexic" at the age of 12. The school was not liable because remedial teaching of a standard which was acceptable given the standards of the time had been provided. The case subsequently went to the Court of Appeal and the LEA's appeal was allowed. In *Phelps* [1999] 1 WLR 500, it was held that the psychologist did not owe a duty of care unless she assumed some personal responsibility for the child. That involved more than the giving of advice, although precisely what might create such a duty remains unclear. It was also held that the type of "injury" suffered was economic loss which could not be recovered unless there had been an assumption of responsibility to protect from that type of loss. The passage of time since the events was also cited as a reason for allowing the appeal, as documents and witnesses could not be traced. The dicta of Evans LJ in *E (A Minor)* v *Dorset County Council* (above), which had raised the possibility of liability, was considered to be *obiter*. There is reference throughout the Court of Appeal judgment to policy reasons for the decision and a number of prospective plaintiffs have launched similar claims in the courts – following the High Court decision in *Phelps*, the floodgates were indeed to some extent opened by that decision. In the light of the 1998 decision in *Christmas* and the Court of Appeal decision in *Phelps*, it seems that the issues must be decided by the House of Lords.

The Parent's Charter has raised not only parental awareness, but expectations. The Charter states: at p15 "You have a **right** to a **good** education for your child." The government has pledged its support to the improvement of standards in education, as demonstrated by the duty imposed upon LEAs in section 5 of SSFA 1998, inserting section 13A into the Education Act 1996.

The widening of access to educational opportunities has also meant that local authorities have taken on more responsibilities. In *R* v *Islington London Borough Council, ex parte Rixon* [1997] ELR 66, in exercising its duty to arrange recreational and "gateway" educational facilities for a disabled person the authority was obliged to take into account guidance issued from the relevant government department. Such policy could only be deviated from with good reason.

It does seem that the more LEAs do in terms of providing educational opportunities and the higher the standards they must achieve, the more the risk of litigation will increase proportionately unless the courts make a policy decision to stem the flow of cases.

Limitation periods

The cause of action identified in the composite appeals referred to above was not recognised until 1995. Some actions based on negligence relate to incidents which took place many years ago, and whilst this may have implications for the availability of evidence and witnesses an important legal consideration is whether the limitation period operates as a statutory bar under section 11 of the Limitation Act 1981. In a Scots law case in 1998, a former pupil was awarded damages for sexual assaults which had taken place 40 years before. The courts may consider applications for an extension of the limitation period under the provisions of section 33 of the 1981 Act, but consideration should be given to the limitation issues at an early stage in any case. The Law Commission have suggested that there should be a 30-year limit to personal injury claims, including any waivers.

Loco parentis

The protection of children who may be exposed to physical harm has long been established. The case of *Holtom* v *Barnet London Borough Council* [1993] (above) suggested that actions for breach of this "quasi-parental" duty are possible by private action, and in the light of the House of Lords' decisions above this must be a correct approach. The duty is a common law duty for which there are no statutory appellate procedures in force. The two cases which have established the nature of the duty are *Fitzgerald* v *Northcote* [1865] 4 F & F 656 and *Williams* v *Eady* [1893] 10 TLR 41. In the *Fitzgerald* case Cockburn C.J held: "A parent, when he takes his child to a schoolmaster delegates to him all his own authority so far as is necessary for the welfare of the child". This would then have allowed for the disciplining of children by way of corporal punishment, but only to the extent that a parent would reasonably expect a child to be chastised. See further Chapter 6 and *A* v *United Kingdom* [1998] *The Times*, 1 October, in particular.

In *Williams* v *Eady*, Cave J stated: "The duty of a schoolmaster is to take such care of his boys as a careful father would take of his boys." The standard of care which is required is thus that of a "prudent parent"; however, see *Beaumont* v *Surrey County Council* [1968] 66 LGR 580.

In the case of a professional person such as a teacher, an inexperienced teacher is expected to exercise the same degree of skill and care as an experienced teacher. Specific issues in relation to the welfare of children and others are discussed below.

Specific provision is made in respect of protecting children from abuse: see Circular 10/95, *Protecting Children from Abuse: The role of the education service* and Circular 11/95, *Misconduct by Teachers and Workers with Children and Young Persons*.

Transport

Although safety in relation to children has been prominent of late, specific concerns have been raised about transport matters. See for example *DPP* v *Sikonder* [1992] *The Times*, 19 May on matters relating to the safety of the "school run". In *R* v *Gwent County Council, ex parte Harris* [1994] 2 FLR 1021, a mother sought judicial review of a decision of the local authority not to provide seat-belts for children using transport provided for the purpose of taking them to school. It was held that the council had not erred in law but Macpherson of Cluny J held:

> There was a positive duty upon the local authority to provide safe transport. If the local authority habitually insisted that the children should ride in second-hand vehicles and so on they would plainly be in breach of their duty.

However, in this case no such breach of duty could be based on the failure to provide seat-belts or the decisions of local authorities to allow three children to occupy two seats on buses. The judge did comment that:

> I suppose that the litigation, together with Mrs Harris' sustained campaign, will perhaps assist in the pressure which will be brought to bear upon the Government and the public generally in respect of improving the fitting of seat-belts in vehicles of all kinds which carry the public.

Since then two School Transport Safety Bills have been introduced into Parliament and withdrawn. The position is now regulated by the Road Vehicles (Construction and Use) (Amendment) (No 2) Regulations 1996 (SI No 163), which require seat-belts for each child between the ages of 3 and 16 years travelling in a coach or minibus (but not a bus) in a forward facing seat; lap belts would suffice. Three children were no longer to be allowed to travel in a double seat. The rules apply when a group of children are on an organised trip and the journey is being made for the purpose of that trip. The Department of Transport publishes guidance on vehicles used for school transport. The Royal Society for the Prevention of Accidents (ROSPA) have also produced guidance on the safety of minibuses.

The question of supervision of children using transport has also been the subject of caselaw. See for example *Ellis* v *Sayers Confectioners Ltd* [1963] 61 LGR 299 and *Myton* v *Woods* [1980] *The Times*, 11 July. In the latter case a taxi was provided by the authority for two boys with learning difficulties. They were dropped off on the wrong side of the road and one child was severely injured crossing the road. It was held that there was no liability on the part of the escort; the standard of care which was taken was that of a reasonable parent.

A failure to adhere to standards may result in criminal as well as civil proceedings. In 1994, the governors of a grant-maintained school were fined £2,100 after a crash in which a minibus overturned, injuring 12 pupils. The prosecution said: "... the governors were responsible ... for the condition and insurance of the vehicle and for the actions of their employees" (*The Times,* 20 May, "Governors fined over bus crash").

In 1998 the police and the vehicle inspectorate ordered 200 school buses to be taken off the road during a nationwide road-safety campaign.

School visits

Activity centres

The Activity Centres (Young Persons' Safety) Act 1995 was passed to provide, *inter alia*, for the licensing of activity centres. The Health and Safety Commission nominated to the Secretary of State a licensing authority under section 1(1) of the Act to deal with applications from early 1996. Inspections of premises began in mid-1996 and detailed Regulations were made under the Act, the Adventure Activities Licensing Regulations 1996 (SI No 772). The Regulations define "adventure activities" as:

- caving
- climbing
- trekking
- watersports.

All of these activities are further defined in regulation 2. Regulation 3 prescribes the persons who are required to have licences and there is an appeals system. Regulation 16 specifies what offences are created by the Act. Such offences include not only being unlicensed, but also making false statements for the purpose of holding or acquiring a licence.

Schools will not be required to apply for a licence under the Act where they are providing for their own pupils, as it was considered that education authorities, school governors, proprietors and teachers already have sufficient legal obligations of care.

Visits abroad

Some concerns have been expressed about the liability of those who either accompany and/or arrange for pupils to travel abroad for educational purposes. The mother of a girl murdered on a school visit to France commenced an action for negligence against the LEA in 1997. The detailed basis of any action is likely to be poor planning in advance of any such visits and lack of supervision whilst away. Although both could feature in any off-site visit undertaken by a school, trips abroad seem to be causing particular concern. It is important that adequate insurance cover is taken out by the school but it is much more important that all reasonable steps are taken to avoid problems. The teacher associations have produced some helpful guidance, as have LEAs. The Home Office has funded research into the abuse if children on international exchange trips abroad. At present there is no regulation or vetting of host families. It is anticipated that any regulation would be applied across Europe.

Safety on school premises

Statutory provisions

Safety of premises

Statutes imposing both civil and criminal liability apply to schools as they do to other organisations (see e.g. the Occupiers Liability Acts of 1957 and 1984 and the Health and Safety at Work Act 1974). In *Rae* v *Tayside* [1994] SLT 476 the application of the Factories Act 1961 to schools was considered in the Scots courts.

The Education Service Advisory Committee of the Health and Safety Commission have produced guidance on "The responsibilities of school governors for health and safety" (1993). According to that guidance, "The key document which will help governors of county and controlled schools deal with health and safety is the LEA's Health and Safety Policy. The LEA will expect governing bodies to comply with this." Aided schools will have to co-operate with the LEA and the diocesan authorities. Head teachers and other staff have a duty to co-operate with their LEAs and governing bodies to enable the health and safety requirements to be complied with. Governing bodies of foundation schools (former grant-maintained schools), CTCs and independent schools are responsible for health and safety aspects.

A public school was fined £21,000 in a case involving breaches of the Health and Safety at Work Act 1974 by failing to provide adequate staffing levels at a school swimming pool. The school's governing body admitted the breaches in the Crown Court (see *The Times*, 25 July 1995).

By way of contrast in *Ratcliff* v *McConnell*, [1998] *The Times*, 3 December, a student who trespassed and was injured in a college swimming pool was held to have been a volunteer and as such no liability attached to the college under the Occupiers Liability Act 1984.

The Education (School Premises) Regulations 1999 (SI No 2) and Circular 10/96 set out minimum standards for school premises covering such issues as adequate storage facilities, washroom facilities etc. In 1997 a case was successfully brought by pupils in Liverpool against the city council claiming a breach of the Environmental Protection Act 1990.

Personal safety

Prevention of assaults by pupils on other pupils and between pupils and teachers is usually a matter of common law. However, when a pupil is being disruptive, that pupil may be restrained under the provisions of the Education Act 1997 and arguably, in some cases, ought to be so restrained to avoid injury to him- or herself and others.

Section 5 of the Education Act 1997 inserts section 550A into the Education Act 1996, and section 550A(1)(b) refers to circumstances where the pupil is causing "personal injury to … any person (including the pupil himself)". In such circumstances, *inter alia,* a member of the school staff (as defined in section 550A(4)) may use such force as is reasonable for the purpose of preventing the pupil from continuing with this behaviour. One obvious problem is that where there is a fight between pupils, for example, intervention by a staff member may result in allegations that unreasonable force was used, but a failure to intervene could also result in claims that pupils were inadequately supervised. Although there is a discretion, and not a duty, under section 550A the common law might well dictate the situations in which a member of staff might be expected or even required to intervene.

Common law duties of care

The common law duties of care are essentially based on the principles of *loco parentis* mentioned above. The emphasis in the caselaw has been very much on what is reasonable in the circumstances. In *Clark* v *Monmouthshire County Council* [1954] 52 LGR 246 Lord Denning held that "the duty of a school does not extend to constant supervision of all the boys all of the time, that is not practical. Only reasonable supervision is required."

The need to put the actions of children and others into the school context was mentioned in *Lyes* v *Middlesex County Council* [1962] 61 LGR 443 where Davies J stated that the "prudent parent" principle had to take into account the circumstances of school life, including how pupils conduct themselves together with the state and conditions of the school premises.

In *Reffell* v *Surrey County Council* [1964] 1 WLR 358, the relationship between actions in negligence and the School Premises Regulations in operation then was discussed, a breach of the latter giving rise to a possible action for breach of statutory duty. The pupil in this case was hurrying down a corridor when a glass door swung towards her and she put her hand out to stop it. Her hand went through a pane of glass and she was injured. Damages were awarded, but Tony Weir, writing in *A Casebook on Tort* commented that the "decision in *Reffell* is something of a charter to the eager parents of silly children".

In *Beaumont* v *Surrey County Council* [1968] 66 LGR, Lane J preferred the ordinary language of the law of negligence to be used instead of the test laid down in *Williams* v *Eady* above. In *Beaumont* "horseplay" during a school break resulted in an injury to a pupil's eye. It was held that the prudent parent principle should not be applied to a headmaster in a school which had 900 pupils, but that rather the test in negligence should be used. Here the duty was to take all reasonable steps to prevent injury between pupils, bearing in mind the "propensities" of boys and girls. The supervision was found to be wanting and the authority were liable.

In *Wilson* v *Governors of Sacred Heart Roman Catholic Primary School, Carlton* [1997] *The Times*, 28 November it was held that where a pupil had been injured by another when leaving the school premises at the end of the school day there was no duty on the school to provide supervision. The comparison with the situation at lunchtime was not regarded as a proper comparison, per Mantell J:

> The need for supervision over the lunchtime period was obvious and accorded with standard practice in schools. The very short period in which the pupils ran or walked from the door to the exit gates was quite different even allowing for the fact that the departing pupils were likely to be high spirited.

In conclusion it was held that the confrontation might just as well have taken place outside the school gates. An example of such a situation occurred in *Nwabudike* v *Southwark London Borough Council* [1997] ELR 35 where a child ran from the school at lunchtime and was hit by a car. The court was satisfied that all reasonable steps had been taken to ensure that proper safeguards were in place and implemented. The child in this case should not have been leaving the school at lunchtime, but the court found that it was necessary "to strike a balance between maintaining security and turning the school into a fortress".

In both of the above-mentioned cases it does seem that the incidents referred to were isolated incidents, and it may be that in practice the situation in both cases would have been different if the history had been different. If there was evidence of "bullying" at the end of the school day and if pupils regularly left the school without permission at lunchtime, then it may well be that the decision in such cases would be different. Furthermore, whilst it may be undesirable to turn schools into fortresses, recent tragic events have meant that schools must develop security policies to prevent undesirable visitors gaining access to the premises, this is indeed a complex balancing exercise as egress cannot be similarly restricted because of other safety issues, such as fire regulations. The DfEE set up a working party on school security and guidance has been produced by the DfEE, LEAs and teacher associations.

Medical supervision

Part IX of the Education Act 1996 dealt with, *inter alia*, the medical inspection and treatment of pupils together with provisions relating to the cleanliness of pupils. Particular problems have concerned pupils with medical needs. Circular 14/96, issued jointly with the Department of Health, sets out guidance on how schools can support pupils with medical needs. An increasing number of children now have continuing medical needs.

In *Hippolyte* v *Bexley London Borough Council* (1994), Unreported a 16-year-old pupil suffered a severe asthma attack at school. A teacher failed to call an ambulance but did suggest that the girl went home. The girl suffered brain damage as a result of the attack. Steyn LJ stated that the education authority owed a duty of care to get medical help for a pupil, even if they were over the age of 16 years, if that pupil developed health problems at school. However, negligence was subject to the test of forseeability and in this case there could have been no forseeability of the extent of the injury. There had been no negligence in the authority not providing detailed information to the school about the pupil's hospital record. The facts of this case occurred in 1986 and it was stressed that the dangers of asthma were now better understood and that as a result teachers might be expected to take a different course of action in similar circumstances.

The increasing need for medical supervision of pupils has resulted in increasing reluctance on the part of many schools and LEAs to undertake medical supervision at all. The status of the circular as "guidance" only is frequently cited by schools and LEAs. Further, the guidance need only be adopted by those willing to supervise pupils with medical needs and many schools have chosen not to do so, with the support of their LEAs. It is considered that the ultimate responsibility rests with the parent, but there is still a grey area involving *loco parentis* and forseeability which would no doubt be considered if a teacher were to refuse to assist a pupil in medical need, if that need was known and was continuing.

School meals

Section 114 of SSFA 1998 provides that regulations may be made to prescribe nutritional standards for school lunches. Certain other duties in respect of lunches and the provision of milk are set out in section 116, inserting section 512A into the Education Act 1996.

Sports instruction and supervision

Many of the established legal authorities relate to the risks of sports instruction. In *Affutu Nartoy* v *Clarke* [1984] *The Times*, 9 February, a 15-year-old schoolboy was playing rugby at school when he was injured by a high tackle from a teacher. It was claimed that the teacher had momentarily forgotten that he was playing with schoolboys who were younger and smaller in physique than himself, but it was held that there was liability in this case. In a similar case, *Van Oppen* v *Clerk to the Bedford Charity Trustees* [1989] 3 All ER 389, it was held that the duty on the school to take only "reasonable care" was stressed. In that case it was found that as a general rule rugby coaching at the school was performed with reasonable skill and care and thus there was no liability in this case. A further issue was raised, that of insurance. It was said that the school was under no duty to insure pupils against personal injury and there was no duty to advise parents similarly.

However, in *Smolden* v *Whitworth* [1997] ELR 249 it was held that a referee could be liable if his standards had fallen below those which could reasonably be expected in dealing with dangerous aspects of the game, such as scrummages. The participants' age (in this case under-19s) was a relevant consideration.

Exposure to risks connected with sport may be many and various and need not just concern participants, but also spectators. Concerns were raised in July 1995 when a girl's parents settled a case with Staffordshire County Council out of court. The girl suffered severe sunburn on her legs after having been left outside for five hours during practice for a sports day without any protection. The parents were paid £500, although the council did not admit liability. The government stated in response that guidance had been prepared for schools by the Health Education Authority on the subject. Although this was a case in a sporting context, the main concerns have been about the risk of a teacher being accused of physical abuse and guidance from teacher associations suggest that whilst pupils may be advised about protection from the elements, physical contact should be avoided.

Defences in negligence

As the language of negligence is preferred, the defences available in negligence may be readily used. In *Barnes* v *Bromley London Borough Council* [1983] *The Times*, 16 November, a boy was found to have contributed to his injury by using an inappropriate tool when working on a sculpture. The defences would apply whether in relation to pupils or others: see below, for example, on the duties which might be owed to teachers.

Vicarious liability

In cases such as *Christmas* v *Hampshire* and *Phelps* v *London Borough of Hillingdon* (above), the liability which was in issue was the vicarious liability of the LEA for the acts of its employees, either the school, the psychology service or both. In *T v North Yorkshire County Council* [1998] *The Times*, 10 September, it was held that there was no vicarious liability for the acts of a teacher who sexually abused a boy while on a school visit abroad. It was held that this was an unauthorised act outside the course of employment.

Supervision outside school hours

In *Mays v Essex County Council* [1975] *The Times*, 11 October a child was injured on ice whilst playing in the school playground before the beginning of the school day. The injuries sustained were serious. The school gates were opened early for the convenience of parents and in the interests of the safety of pupils. There was no supervision. The court held that in this case there was no liability, as the child was 14 years old and supervision was not necessary. It was also held that parents could not impose liability on schools for activities out of school hours. Such responsibility could exist where the school voluntarily undertook such supervision, for example on school visits and other extra-curricular activities.

The government is funding a national childcare strategy to expand, *inter alia*, after-school clubs, some of which may be held on school premises. It is anticipated that each club will have to have an administrator to ensure that health, safety and educational standards are met.

In *Fowles v Bedfordshire County Council* [1995] PIQR 380, a local authority was found to be in breach of its statutory duty and negligent when young people at a youth centre were allowed to perform gymnastics without supervision. Care should be taken by governors and teachers to ensure that any "out of hours" activities on the school premises are properly supervised.

Duties of care to staff

Duties are also owed to others on school premises, not just to pupils. In *Murphy v Bradford Corporation* [1992] PIQR 68, a local authority was found to be in breach of its duties under the Occupiers Liability Act 1957 when a teacher fell on a "notorious" path made slippery by icy weather conditions. The Court of Appeal allowed an appeal against a decision that the council had taken sufficient care in the circumstances. The school caretaker had cleared and salted the path at regular intervals. A higher standard of care was not required, the standard of care was to do all that was reasonable. Here there was 'ample evidence' that the plaintiff's injuries from her fall were a result of the council's failure to take reasonable care. The judge was entitled to take into account that the path was sloping and therefore a place where it was likely an accident would occur and it was considered that cinders or grit should have been put down.

As well as physical injury to teachers and other members of staff, cases of psychological injury because of stress or workplace bullying seem likely to increase (see further Chapter 9).

Miscellaneous duties

In 1997, a cleaner who agreed to look after a duck kept by a school as a pet was prosecuted when she failed to feed it. The RSPCA brought the prosecution and the school was criticised for allowing the bird to suffer unnecessarily Although such prosecutions are rare, any pets or animals on school premises, whether kept by the school or brought in by children, should be appropriately looked after.

The duty to look after property is derived from bailment, and damage to property is specifically mentioned as one reason for the restraint of an unruly pupil, as mentioned above.

Chapter 8

The Curriculum

The Curriculum

The national curriculum

The Education Act 1944 provided that LEAs should "contribute towards the physical, mental and spiritual development of the community through educational provision" (s 7). However, control of the secular curriculum was placed in the hands of the LEA, the schools and the teachers. Under section 18 of the Education (No 2) Act 1986, control of the curriculum in county schools moved to the head teacher, although they had to take into account the LEA's curriculum policy and any statement on policy by the governors. A move towards a national curriculum was bitterly resisted in some quarters. Of all its characteristics it was the element of prescription which proved most difficult for many in the teaching profession to accept. The introduction of the national curriculum was seen by many as an attempt to make the curriculum "teacher-proof" and that was seen as an attack on the professional status of teachers. There is still some academic interest about the impact of such prescription (see e.g. N Harris (1989), "The Education Reform Act 1988 – National curriculum: framework or straitjacket?" *Education and the Law* 1(3), 105–112.

According to Maclure (1992): "The 1988 Act made it clear exactly where the legal control of the curriculum lay – with the Secretary of State. It removed the confusion built into the 1986 Act ..."

Section 1 of ERA 1988 placed a statutory responsibility on schools to provide a "broad and balanced" curriculum which:

- promotes the spiritual, moral, cultural, mental and physical development of pupils at the school and of society; and
- prepares pupils for the opportunities, responsibilities and experiences of adult life.

Section 3 of ERA 1988 designated three core subjects and seven foundation subjects which must be taught. The core subjects are English, mathematics and science. The foundation subjects are history, geography, technology, music, art, physical education and (at the secondary stage) a modern language. In Welsh schools, Welsh was to be a core subject in Welsh speaking schools and a foundation subject in non-

Welsh speaking schools. Provisions relating to the national curriculum are now to be found in the Education Act 1996.

Some teacher associations complained that some subjects were marginalised as a result; subjects such as Latin were "squeezed out" of the curriculum in state schools. Other activities such as extra curricular sports were adversely affected by the increased pressure on teachers generally. One view is that "once you have a set of legally-prescribed curriculum requirements, anything which is not prescribed and tested will be neglected" (S Maclure, *The Times*, 3 January 1994).

All maintained schools were under a general duty by section 10 of ERA 1988 (and subsequently the Education Act 1996) to ensure that the national curriculum was implemented. A duty was placed on the LEA and school governors in respect of county and voluntary schools and on the governors of aided and grant-maintained schools. Schools under the SSFA 1998 will have to provide the national curriculum unless there is provision for exemption.

Exemptions

Under sections 362–367 of the Education Act 1996, the Secretary of State has a general power to make regulations removing or modifying the provisions of the national curriculum. Specific exemptions may be made in relation to developmental and experimental work, pupils with special educational needs and individual pupils on a temporary basis. If the national curriculum is to be withdrawn or modified in respect of an individual pupil, notice has to be given to the governing body and to the child's parent by the head teacher giving the reasons for the decision.

Independent schools do not have to offer the national curriculum, but may do so in order to remain competitive. CTCs have their own curriculum provisions, originally set out in the ERA 1988.

It is intended that schools in EAZs will be exempt from the provisions of the national curriculum, and it has been suggested that in future schools performing well should have more freedom to deviate from the requirements of the national curriculum.

Implementation

Under section 4 of ERA 1988 it was the duty of the Secretary of State to establish the national curriculum as soon as practicable and to revise that curriculum whenever it was thought necessary or expedient to do so. That duty is now found in section 351(2) of the Education Act 1996. The national curriculum has in fact been under constant review and modified to some extent on an annual basis.

The Secretary of State was empowered to make orders in relation to:

- attainment targets – the knowledge and understanding expected of pupils at various ages and levels of maturity at different stages;
- programmes of study – the matters, skills and processes to be taught to pupils; and
- assessment arrangements – the arrangements for assessing pupils' achievements of the attainment targets at or near the end of each "key stage" (see below).

According to Maclure:

> The Act is at pains to describe the process by which the Secretary of State is to arrive at his curriculum Orders, the documents which he must lay before Parliament for a positive resolution in both Houses. Any proposals have to be put before the appropriate Curriculum Council. The Council then puts them out for consultation with local authorities, teachers' bodies, representatives of governing bodies and any other persons thought to be worth consulting. The Council then reports back to the Secretary of State, summarising the views of the those consulted and making its own recommendations ... The Secretary of State is then obliged to publish the Curriculum Council's report. He does not have to accept that advice but if he fails to do so he must state his reasons for not doing so. He then issues a draft Order after which there has to be yet another period of at least a month for further consultation and representation from interested groups.

The aim of this procedure was said to be to restrain the strong central powers placed on the Secretary of State by the Act. However, relations between the Secretary of State and the two Curriculum Councils which had been set up, the National Curriculum Council and the Schools Examination and Assessment Council, became strained and in due course they were replaced with one body, the School Curriculum and Assessment Authority, by the Education Act 1993 (see below). In 1995 "Final Orders" relating to the curriculum were issued, but they are subject to regular review.

The basic curriculum

Section 2 of the ERA 1988 defined the "basic curriculum", now contained in section 352 of the Education Act 1996. The basic curriculum includes the national curriculum together with religious and sex education. Guidance from the National Curriculum Council suggested that the basic curriculum should be augmented by additional subjects beyond the ten subjects of the national curriculum, with religious education as a subject in its own right, cross-curricular elements and extra-curricular activities.

The key stages

The key stages were defined in section 3 of the ERA 1988. There are four stages:

Key Stage 1 – Ages 5–7, Years 1 and 2. This stage begins on the attainment of compulsory school age and ends at the end of the school year in which the majority of the pupils reach age 7.

Key Stage 2 – Ages 8–11, Years 3–6. This begins with the school year in which the majority of the pupils are aged 8 and ends with the year in which the majority are aged 11.

Key Stage 3 – Ages 12–14, Years 7–9. As above, with ages 12 and 14.

Key Stage 4 – Ages 15 and 16, Years 10 and 11. As above, with ages 15 and 16.

Under section 113 of SSFA 1998 (amending the Further and Higher Education Act 1992) education for Key Stage 4 pupils may be provided by a further education corporation.

Assessment and testing

The government set out in detail the plans for assessment and testing in a debate in Parliament on the Education Reform Bill, recorded in *Hansard*. Assessment and testing was seen as the way to "enforce" the national curriculum. The main principles upon which assessment was to be based were as follows:

- Attainment targets will be set which establish what children should normally be expected to know, understand and be able to do at the ages of 7, 11, 14 and 16; these will enable the progress of each child to be measured against national standards.
- Pupils' performance in relation to attainment targets should be assessed and reported on at ages 7, 11, 14 and 16. Attainment

targets should be grouped for this purpose to make the assessment and reporting manageable.

- Different levels of attainment and overall pupil progress demonstrated by tests and assessment should be registered on a ten-point scale covering all the years of compulsory schooling.
- Assessment should be by a combination of national external tests and assessment by teachers. At age 16, GCSE will form the basis of assessment.
- The results of tests and other assessments should be used both formatively to help better teaching and to inform decisions about next steps for pupils, and summatively at ages 7, 11, 14 and 16 to inform parents about their child's progress.
- Detailed results of assessments of individual pupils should be given in full to parents. Aggregate results should be published.
- Assessments made by teachers should be compared with the results of the national tests and the judgement of other teachers.

On the basis of the above, the first Standard Assessment Tasks (SATs) were developed and in 1991 assessment began in earnest. The workload proved overwhelming for many teachers.

In *Wandsworth London Borough Council* v *National Association of School Masters and Union of Women Teachers* [1994] 92 LGR 91, industrial action taken by teachers who refused to carry out assessments and tests in accordance with the national curriculum was found to be a "trade dispute" within the meaning of section 244 of the Trade Union and Labour Relations (Consolidation) Act 1992 and as such protected by statute. The action had been taken to persuade the Secretary of State that an "excessive workload" had been caused by the assessment and testing procedures of the national curriculum. It was found in the Court of Appeal that:

> ... there had been increasing concern expressed by the union on behalf of its members with regard to working time. That concern came to a head as the date for key stage 3 testing approached. It was clear that union members had criticisms to make about the national curriculum on educational grounds.

Since then the detail of the testing and assessment procedures has been reviewed (see below). Circulars set out advice on the statutory assessment of pupils at ages 7, 11 and 14 and Circular 2/98 attempts to reduce the bureaucratic burden on teachers further; paragraphs 21 and 22 of that document relate specifically to the curriculum.

The DfEE announced in 1995 that marking and administration of national tests for 11–14-year-olds would be tightened up following allegations that some schools opened test packs early, coached children or allowed them extra time. In 1998, owing to continuing problems, it was announced that "spot checks" would be made. Assessment arrangements are made by Order (e.g. the Education (National Curriculum) (Key Stage 1 Assessment Arrangements) (England) Order 1999 (SI No 1236)).

Some attempt has been made to reduce the administrative burden on teachers (see Circular 2/98 above); however, the emphasis is still on the provision of accurate information to interested parties. See for example the Education (School Performance Information) (England) Regulations 1996 (SI No 2577) and Circular 15/96, which provided for the publication of the first primary school performance tables in March 1997.

The Qualifications and Curriculum Authority

Section 21 of the Education Act 1997 established the Qualifications and Curriculum Authority (QCA). The property, rights and liabilities of the School Curriculum and Assessment Authority (SCAA) were transferred to the QCA under the Education (Qualifications and Curriculum Authority and Qualifications, Curriculum and Assessment Authority for Wales) (Transfer of Property and Designation of Staff) Order 1997 (SI No 2172). Further provision was made for the assumption of assessment responsibilities in, for example, the Education (National Curriculum) (Assessment Arrangements for Key Stages 1, 2 and 3) (Amendment) Order 1997 (SI No 2176).

The SCAA had previously been created from a merger of the National Curriculum Council and the School Assessment and Examinations Authority (see above).

Review of the curriculum

Sir Ron Dearing, chairman of the SCAA, was asked by the government to review the national curriculum. The Final Report reaffirmed that the national curriculum and its assessment and testing was the key to raising educational standards. However, it concluded that urgent action was needed to reduce the statutorily required content of its programmes of study and to make it less prescriptive and complex. A closely co-ordinated review of all the statutory curriculum Orders was put in hand, the aim being to:

- simplify and clarify the programmes of study;
- reduce the volume of material to be taught;
- reduce prescription so as to give more scope for professional judgement; and
- ensure that the Orders are written in a way which offers maximum support to the classroom teacher.

It was recommended, *inter alia*, that there should be no changes to the national curriculum for five years. The Technology Order was suspended for key stage 4. Testing was to be made simpler and there was to be a general "slimming down" of the curriculum to make it more manageable. Sir Ron Dearing announced (see *The Times*, 6 January 1994) that:

> The proposals also involve less prescription in what is laid down, less finicky detail in the arrangements for judging a pupil's progress and less division of subjects into statutory compartments.

In primary schools there was to be more free time to concentrate on the basics of English and mathematics. It is questionable to what extent these suggestions have been acted upon, although there has been an increased emphasis on literacy and numeracy (see below). Some critics say this was achieved by further prescription.

Following Dearing, in secondary schools some subjects were to become voluntary from the age of 14 and short courses were to be introduced in languages and technology. It has been suggested that pupils are finding it difficult to attain the highest grades as a result of undertaking short courses. There was some disappointment that the "unwieldy" ten-point assessment scale was retained, although it was "improved".

Attainment targets and programmes of study

The Secretary of State has published a number of Orders relating to attainment targets and programmes of study which are to apply. Orders are revised in batches: for example, in relation to some of the foundation subjects the following Orders apply:

- Education (National Curriculum) (Attainment Targets and Programmes of Study in History) Order 1998 (SI No 1988)
- Education (National Curriculum) (Attainment Targets and Programmes of Study in Geography) Order 1998 (SI No 1989)
- Education (National Curriculum) (Attainment Targets and Programmes of Study in Art) Order 1998 (SI No 1990)

- Education (National Curriculum) (Attainment Targets and Programmes of Study in Music) Order 1998 (SI No 1991)
- Education (National Curriculum) (Attainment Targets and Programmes of Study in Physical Education) Order 1998 (SI No 1987).

Literacy and numeracy

In 1998 the government, following on from Dearing, decided to place further emphasis on certain aspects of the curriculum which had been causing concern. Part of the daily timetable was to be designated specifically for the teaching of literacy (from Autumn 1998) and then numeracy (from Autumn 1999). This is to be achieved by suspending the attainment targets and programmes of study Orders in the foundation subjects at Key Stages 1 and 2. The requirement to follow the DfEE' s guidelines on literacy and numeracy are, at present, a matter of policy and are not statutory requirements. Some head teachers have indicated an inability if not an unwillingness, to comply with the policy. Any such refusal is likely to result in warnings from Ofsted. Head teachers are also to be set targets which will apply to the English results of 11-year-olds in 2000. Further target-setting will follow although there may be disputes if consultation between schools and LEAs on targets runs into difficulties.

Religious worship and education

Collective worship

Section 25 of the Education Act 1944 stated that, unless a pupil's parent requests that he or she be wholly or partly excused from attendance at religious worship in the school, the school day in every county and voluntary school should begin with collective worship on the part of all the pupils in attendance at the school and the arrangements made should provide for a "single act of worship", unless the school premises were unsuitable so as to make it impracticable to assemble the pupils for that purpose. A survey in 1985 found that only 6% of maintained secondary schools "… came close to obeying the 1944 Education Act's requirement that each day shall begin with collective worship involving all pupils" (*Times Educational Supplement*, 20 December 1985).

In passing the ERA 1988, it was recognised that there was a need to remove the provision for an act of worship from the beginning of the school day. It was also regarded as necessary to allow worship in separate groups. Section 6(1) stated: "all pupils in attendance at a maintained school shall on each school day take part in an act of collective worship ...". Section 7(1) provided: "In the case of a county school the collective worship shall be wholly or mainly of a broadly Christian character."

The nature of religious worship was considered in *R* v *Secretary of State for Education, ex parte R and D* [1994] ELR 495. It was held that the view that the 1988 Act permitted non-Christian elements in collective worship was correct as long as these did not deprive it of its "broadly Christian character". The court also noted:

> clearly Parliament contemplated that children from non-Christian families should be able to take part in collective worship even though these would generally reflect the broad traditions of Christian belief.

The provisions of the ERA 1998 were replaced by sections 385–388 of the Education Act 1996. Section 70 of and Schedule 20 to SSFA 1998 retain the requirement to provide such a daily act of collective worship. In 1998, it was reported that 70% of schools do not comply with the law but that few parents complain. The circumstances in which a pupil may be excused from attendance are set out in section 71 of SSFA 1998.

Religious education

Under section 25(2) of the 1944 Act, the only compulsory subject was religious instruction, which became in effect religious education.

Religious education is part of the basic curriculum under section 352(1)(a) of the Education Act 1996. Section 375 of that Act retained the requirement that such education should be "broadly Christian". Schedule 19 to SSFA 1998 sets out the required provision in respect of religious education.

Advisory councils

Under the ERA 1988, each LEA established a Standing Advisory Council on Religious Education (SACRE) to advise on collective worship and religious education. Section 391 of the Education Act 1996 (as amended by SSFA 1998) sets out the functions of advisory councils and section 390 the constitution of such bodies. Any new syllabus must recognise the fact that religion in this country is in the main Christian whilst taking into account the teaching and practices of the other principal religions represented in Great Britain, as required by section 8 of ERA 1988 and section 375 of the Education Act 1996.

Section 397 of the Act makes provision for public access to SACREs and agreed syllabus conferences and for public access to agendas for, reports for and the minutes of those meetings. Similar provision is made for committees and subcommittees of SACREs and conferences with special provision in relation to specified confidential information.

It is possible for teachers to opt out of religious education and worship. There is specific provision that teachers should not be discriminated against, now found in section 59 of SSFA 1998; however, there are exceptional provisions in relation to foundation and voluntary schools with a religious character, set out in section 60 of SSFA 1998. Under section 71 of that Act, parents may still withdraw their children from religious worship and/or education.

The Education Act 1993 charged Ofsted with the responsibility of inspecting the provision of collective worship as a part of the regular inspection pattern. Inspections also report on the provision of religious education. In June 1995, the chief school's inspector reported that one in three schools was failing to provide specific religious education for 14–16 year-olds: "in many schools the subject has become diluted with general humanities and social studies" (*The Times*, 29 June 1995).

Sex education

Under section 47 of the Education (No 2) Act 1986 governing bodies had specific responsibility in relation to sex education which they had a discretion to include or exclude in the curriculum. They had an obligation to ensure if it was included that due regard was given to moral considerations and family life.

DFE Circular 5/94, *Education Act 1993: Sex Education in Schools* provided guidance on the nature of sex education. The principles in *Gillick* v *West Norfolk and Wisbech Area Health Authority* [1986] AC 112 relating to contraception are also of interest.

Sections 403–405 of the Education Act 1996 now apply. Section 403 deals with the manner of provision and section 404 provides for policy statements. Section 241 of the Education Act 1993 gave parents a right to withdraw their child from sex education. They could do so wholly or partly and the school had to comply with the request.

However, withdrawal from sex education which forms any part of the national curriculum was not allowed.

Complaints could be made by parents about the provision of sex education under section 23 of the ERA 1988, but this has now been replaced by the provisions in the Education Act 1996 relating to complaints (see below).

See further Chapter 12 on the "freedom" which teachers have in relation to 'controversial' areas of the curriculum.

Vocational education

A new form of General National Vocational Qualification (GNVQ) launched in 1993 was piloted in schools as an alternative to more traditional examinations. Part 1 GNVQs in three subjects (business, health and social care, and manufacturing) have been designed to allow for closer integration and more work-based education for certain groups of young people aged over 14.

Detailed information on syllabuses is published from time to time and Circular 4/97 lists qualifications and syllabuses that have been approved under section 400 of the Education Act 1996.

Section 560 of the 1996 Act has been amended by section 112 of SSFA 1998 to allow for extended work experience for Key Stage 4 pupils. See further the Education (National Curriculum) (Exceptions at Key Stage 4) Regulations 1998 (SI No 2021).

Political education

Section 406 of the Education Act 1996 deals with the question of "political indoctrination" which is forbidden in schools. Section 407 sets out a duty to secure the balanced treatment of political issues.

Careers education

Circular 5/97 gives guidance on the effect of the provision in sections 43–45 of the Education Act 1997 for careers education in "publicly funded secondary schools". Schools have to allow careers service staff to provide careers education at school and must work with the careers service to ensure that pupils have access to up-to-date information and reference materials on careers.

Nursery schools

Although there is no prescribed curriculum applicable to nursery education, "baseline assessment" at Key Stage 1 is likely to have an effect on the activities of nursery schools.

In September 1995, the SCAA produced a 12-page report setting out guidelines on what children should be able to achieve by the age of 5 years. Children were expected to count to ten, write their name in upper and lower case letters, recognise a circle and understand simple number concepts. The guidance suggested that under-fives should be given an introduction to religion and that they should be taught the difference between right and wrong. The SCAA reported on a variety of "entry assessment schemes" and baseline assessment at Key Stage 1 was pioneered in Birmingham. The scheme was introduced nationally from Autumn 1998 in accordance with the provisions of section 16 of the Education Act 1997, the Education (Baseline Assessment) (England) Regulations 1998 (SI No 1551) and Circular 6/98.

Curricular complaints

The right to complain about the carrying out of duties and the exercise of powers concerning the curriculum and the provision of information formerly contained in section 23 of ERA 1988 was replaced by the Education Act 1996. The LEA is under a duty to establish complaints procedures where a school has or proposes to act unreasonably (Education Act 1996, s409). This complaints procedure is separate from that contained in sections 496 and 497 of the 1996 Act. Under section 39 of the SSFA 1998, governing bodies will be expected to establish complaints procedures, but only in so far as there is no statutory provision for such complaints.

Chapter 9

Employment and Training

Employment and Training

The employers

As with the providers of education, it is difficult to say with certainty who the employers are in the state education context. Responsibilities vary as between governing bodies, LEAs and the Secretary of State. In *National Union of Teachers* v *Governing Body of St Mary's Church of England (Aided) Junior School* [1997] IRLR 242 (see below), the governors were specifically identified as having responsibility for employment, notwithstanding that the responsibility for the provision of education is shared.

Section 54 of and Schedule 16 to SSFA 1998 regulate the staffing of community, voluntary controlled and community special schools. Section 55 of and Schedule 17 to SSFA 1998 have effect in relation to the staffing of foundation, voluntary aided and foundation special schools. If at any time a school under either provision does not have a delegated budget because of suspension, then the LEA will take over the powers of the governing body; for example, under section 54(3) the numbers of teaching and non-teaching staff to be employed at the school shall be a matter for the LEA.

The Schedules set out in detail the procedures to be followed in respect of both teaching and non-teaching staff. It is of interest that in Schedule 16 reference is made to the employment of staff "otherwise than under a contract of employment with the local education authority" (see also Chapter 4).

The governing body should notify the LEA of such appointments, but the LEA has no power to veto an appointment other than on grounds of qualifications. The LEA may give the governing body advice as to staffing.

In voluntary aided schools the governors had full control of staffing under the provisions of section 45 of the ERA 1988. This is preserved as long as there is a delegated budget under Schedule 17. As above, advice on staffing may be given by the LEA. In the Schedules a clear distinction is made between the appointment of head and deputy head teachers, other teachers and non-teaching staff.

Transfer of undertakings

Problems can arise when, for example, a private school is sold and new owners do not wish to retain the services of some or all of the previous members of staff. This potential difficulty was recognised in the "commercial" sphere and so the Transfer of Undertakings (Protection of Employment) Regulations 1981 (SI No 1794) were drafted to protect employees on transfer of a business by effectively preserving their continuity of employment. Thus, if the new employers wished to terminate their employment there was some possibility, subject to the other provisions of the Employment Protection (Consolidation) Act 1978 and latterly the Employment Rights Act 1996, that those employees could bring actions for unfair dismissal against the new owners. However, any venture which was not a commercial or business venture was specifically excluded.

This caused some difficulties for schools, especially those which were overtly non-profit making such as schools with charitable status. In *Woodcock* v *Committee of the Friends School* [1987] IRLR 98, a Quaker school with charitable status was held to be an 'undertaking' which was not in the nature of a commercial venture for the purposes of regulation 2 of the 1981 Regulations. The Regulations did not therefore apply and teachers who had been employed by the school immediately before its sale had to bring their claims for compensation for unfair dismissal against the committee which had managed the school rather than the new owners.

Section 75 of ERA 1988 made specific provision for the transfer of staff to schools which acquired grant-maintained status. The operation of that section was discussed in *Pickwell* v *Lincolnshire County Council* [1992] 91 LGR 509. The member of staff involved here was a catering assistant who had been employed at a school maintained by the LEA. In 1990, the board of governors applied for grant-maintained status under the 1988 Act. The transfer took place in January 1991. A decision had been made that the catering would be contracted out to a catering firm. The applicant chose redundancy and a question arose over who was responsible for the redundancy payments. The council had ceased to employ her from 31 December 1990 and section 75 of ERA 1988 provided that the governors should effectively step into the LEA's shoes. However, section 75 did not apply to those members of staff whose contracts had been terminated before the transfer. The Employment Appeal Tribunal held that this had not happened in the applicant's case. The position was regarded as unclear and the matter was remitted to an Industrial Tribunal for further consideration. It was stated that:

The appeal tribunal members were troubled by the circumstances of the case which were unlikely to be unique. It seemed unfair that the governors of a grant-maintained school whose budget was limited should have to make redundancy payments to staff who for 20 years or more had given faithful service to the county council. It was an essential lesson from the case that all governors in similar circumstances should take professional advice and enter into discussion with local authorities before the transfer date.

In *National Union of Teachers* v *Governing Body of St Mary's Church of England (Aided) Junior School* (above), a junior school was closed with the approval of the Secretary of State in 1992. A new school was opened with a temporary governing body. The applicants in this case had unsuccessfully applied for posts at the new school and were made redundant.

The applicants had been former employees of the original school and applied for unfair dismissal. At first instance, it was held that the 1981 Regulations did not apply because the school was not an undertaking in the nature of a commercial venture as per the *Woodcock* case above. However, the Court of Appeal allowed the teacher's appeal on the basis that Council Directive 77/187/EEC, known as the "Acquired Rights" Directive, also protects the rights of employees on transfer of a business. The Directive was applicable in this case as the school governors were held to be "an emanation of the state".

Reference was made to *Foster* v *British Gas plc* [1991] 2 AC 306, in which the test of whether a body was an organ of the state was also considered. However, Schiemann LJ felt that it was inappropriate to apply the test as laid down in *Foster* as if it were a definition section. The basis of the decision was that education was a public service. Yet the nature of the school is still a relevant consideration, per Schiemann LJ:

> Voluntary schools chose of their own volition to come within the state system ... once within the system, they were subject to a considerable degree of control and influence by the Secretary of State for Education and the local education authority.

The extent to which the 1981 Regulations and the Acquired Rights Directive applies in relation to schools is of particular concern when there are changes of status such as those anticipated by the SSFA 1998.

The case brought by the National Union of Teachers does seem to have clarified the position in terms of the role of schools in the state sector. With the intended demise of grant-maintained schools, the opportunity for confusion on this point seems to have lessened, although it may be argued that the status of CTCs is still anomalous. It is interesting to note that section 81 of SSFA 1998 allows for the modification of employment law under certain circumstances by the Secretary of State as it applies to schools during financial delegation.

It is also the case that the application of the 1981 Regulations in employment law generally is far from settled: see, for example, *Wilson v St. Helen's Borough Council; Meade v British Fuels* [1998] *The Times*, 30 October and *Cornwall County Care v Brightman* [1998] *The Times*, 10 March.

In *Lawrence v Regent Office Care Ltd,* [1998] *The Times*, 24 November it was held that Article 119, Treaty of Rome did not protect the rights of school dinner staff who had formerly been employed by a local authority and had subsequently transferred to private employers. They could not seek equality of pay with those still employed by that authority even where they could show their work was of equal value. The purpose of Article 119, it was said, was to avoid sex discrimination and it could not be applied more widely.

Teacher qualifications

The Teaching and Higher Education Act 1998 (THEA 1998) created, *inter alia,* a General Teaching Council for England (GTC) (a separate GTC for Wales is provided for). This organisation is considered by some members of the teaching profession to be much needed. Regulation of the profession has been *ad hoc* and is subject to further review. The GTC is intended to advise the Secretary of State on such matters as recruitment to the teaching profession and the training, development and career management of teachers. Entry into the profession is subject to guidance; however, the suitability of those who work with children and young persons is still heavily dependent on training providers satisfying themselves as to the suitability of applicants and making the appropriate checks (see below).

Eligibility for registration as a teacher is subject to statutory provision (see below). The Education (Teachers) Regulations 1993 (SI No 543), as amended by the Education (Teachers) (Amendment) (No 2) Regulations 1997 (SI No 2679), set out the types of teachers recognised for the purposes of employment in the state sector. The previous categories of teachers recognised by the 1993 Regulations (i.e. qualified teachers, overseas trained teachers and licensed teachers) are revoked except for transitional provisions.

The Education (School Teachers' Pay and Conditions) Order 1998 (SI No 903), *inter alia,* allows for the appointment of "unqualified teachers". Such teachers may be appointed to provide specialist teaching on an *ad hoc* basis for example, or may be student teachers. At the other extreme, the Order allows for recognition of "Advanced Skills Teachers".

In Schedule 16 to SSFA 1998 reference to "staff qualification requirements" refers to:

(a) qualifications
(b) registration
(c) health and physical capacity
(d) fitness on educational grounds or in any other respect.

Further details relating to (a) above are set out in Circular 2/99, Statutory Approval of Qualifications under Section 400 of the Education Act 1996. Circular 4/99, Physical and Mental Fitness to Teach of Teachers and New Entrants to Initial Teacher Training relates to (c) above.

In *Hampson* v *Department of Education and Science* [1991] 1 AC 171, the House of Lords held that a refusal by the Secretary of State to grant qualified teacher status to a Hong Kong trained teacher on the ground that her qualification was not comparable with specified UK qualifications could be indirect discrimination under the Race Relations Act 1976, and if so that decision could not be rendered lawful by showing that the decision had been taken in pursuance of a statutory instrument. The regulations in issue here were the Education (Teachers) Regulations 1982 (SI No 106). It was held that:

> ... almost every discretionary decision, such as that which was involved in the appointment, promotion and dismissal of individuals in ... the public sector of the teaching profession, was taken against a statutory background which imposed a duty on someone ...

The European Communities (Recognition of Professional Qualifications) (Second General System) Regulations 1996 (SI No 2374) are also useful in this context.

Registration may be refused if a person is prohibited from being employed as a teacher as a result of a direction given by the Secretary of State under section 218 of ERA 1988, is disqualified from employment by virtue of section 470 or 471 of the Education Act 1996, subject to similar provisions in Scotland and Northern Ireland, has failed to complete the necessary induction period or is the subject of a disciplinary order under Schedule 2 of THEA 1998.

Teacher training

Access to the teaching profession is regulated by teacher training providers. Circulars 10/95 and 11/95 both provide guidance; Circular 11/95 specifically gives advice to teacher training institutions about reporting misconduct by students and prospective students. Such persons may be subsequently barred by the Secretary of State from seeking employment as a teacher. Information about convictions may be obtained under the Police Act 1997.

The new programmes introduced by the 1997 Regulations are the graduate teacher and the registered teacher programmes. The programmes will allow a person who is not a qualified teacher to teach at a school maintained by an LEA, except a PRU, if he or she is authorised to do so. Authorisations to teach will be granted by the Teacher Training Authority (TTA). A person who is a graduate or registered teacher may acquire qualified teacher status if assessed as meeting the appropriate standards. The training of qualified teachers not employed in maintained schools during their training could be considered and approved by the TTA.

The functions of the TTA, established by section 1 of the Education Act 1994, were extended by the Teacher Training Agency (Additional Functions) Order 1997 (SI No 2678) so that training and authorisation could be regulated by them in accordance with the new programmes.

The Teacher Training Agency (TTA) has between 8 and 12 members appointed by the Secretary of State. One of the most controversial features of the Education Act 1994 was the introduction of school centred initial teacher training (SCITT). School governing bodies were allowed, if accredited, to provide initial training courses for teachers themselves or to set up or join a consortium of schools providing such courses;they may provide the courses entirely themselves or may join forces with an institution of higher education. Provision of training is to be a matter for the GTC in due course.

The content of initial teacher training courses has been reviewed and from September 1998 a "national curriculum" for initial teacher training institutions was introduced (see Circular 4/98). Teacher training institutions are subject to inspection by Ofsted (see Chapter 11).

Proposals to increase the number of unqualified classroom assistants in schools have alarmed some parts of the teaching profession and their training requirements are yet to be established.

The appointment process

Schedules 16 and 17 to SSFA 1998 set out in detail the appointment process to be followed by governing bodies. All appointments must be handled with care so as to avoid complaints on the basis of sex or race discrimination or allegations of ultra vires or breaches of natural justice.

In *Board of Governors of St Matthias Church of England School* v *Crizzle* [1993] IRLR 472, the governors of a Church of England school advertised for a head who was a committed, communicant Christian. The applicant was a Roman Catholic, Asian, non-communicant member. The applicant claimed that the advertisement was indirect discrimination against Asians. The Employment Appeal Tribunal held in this context that the needs of the governing body justified such an advertisement and in that sense it was objective, reasonable and legitimate.

In *University of Manchester* v *Jones* [1993] IRLR 2182 advertisements which contained a reference to the age of applicants were considered. In that case the applicant applied for a post at a university, but the principles are of universal application. The advertisement asked for "graduates aged 27–35". The applicant, a female, had graduated at age 41 and was 46 when she applied for the post. She claimed that the advertisement discriminated against women, not because "age discrimination" is unlawful but because it discriminates against women who are more likely because of family commitments to have graduated later in life. The Court of Appeal examined that proposition closely, but found there was little statistical evidence to support that argument. It was therefore held that there had been no discrimination.

In *R* v *Birmingham City Council, ex parte McKenna* [1991] *The Times*, 16 May, it was held that an interviewing panel constituted for the purpose of interviewing and appointing a head teacher should not operate with less than its full complement of members. In that case, a panel member attended the first meeting of the panel but could not attend the second meeting. The first meeting was attended by the applicant, who was not short-listed. The applicant claimed that the second meeting of the panel was unlawful. There was no suggestion that the panel could operate with depleted numbers; it was due only to meet two or three times so that there had been no thought of substitute members or other arrangements. It was held therefore that full attendance was required and as such the second meeting was improperly constituted. Interestingly, in this case no relief was granted as it was clear that the applicant would not have been invited to attend for a further interview in any event as five out of the six panel members had decided that the applicant would not go forward.

In *Bradford City Metropolitan Council* v *Arora* [1991] 2 WLR 1377, it was held that a Sikh woman who was unlawfully discriminated against on the ground of her race and sex when she applied for a job at a local authority college was entitled to exemplary damages in addition to the compensation that she received. The nature and extent of local authority duties in making appointments were considered in detail in the light of such cases as *Rookes* v *Barnard* [1964] AC 1129 and *Broome* v *Cassell Ltd* [1972] AC 1027.

Terms and conditions of teaching staff

The School Teachers' Pay and Conditions Act 1991 sets out in detail the terms and conditions of employment for head teachers, deputy head teachers and other teaching staff. The Act is supplemented by an annual Document and orders which address a number of issues including salary levels. The orders set out the responsibilities of all teachers, including head teachers.

The orders set out the "overriding requirements" of a head teachers employment. They are that the head teacher shall carry out his or her professional duties in accordance with and subject to:

- the provisions of the Education Acts
- orders and regulations made under those Acts
- any trust deed if a voluntary or former voluntary school
- any arrangements made under section 34 of ERA 1988 in respect of local management of schools.

See also the Education (Head Teachers) Regulations 1999 (SI No 1287).

In carrying out these professional duties there is an obligation on the head teacher to consult with the LEA, the governing body of the school, the staff and the parents where such consultation is appropriate. Such professional duties are as follows:

- Formulation of the school's aims and objectives
- Participation in the appointment of staff
- Management of staff, involving deployment, cover, allocation and the provision of information
- Liaison with staff unions and associations
- Curriculum matters according to the ERA 1988 (as amended) and the provision of collective worship
- Review of the work and organisation of the school
- Evaluation of the standards of teaching and learning
- Appraisal, training and development of staff
- Providing management information on the work and performance of staff
- Monitoring and recording pupil progress
- Formulating a policy on pastoral care
- Determining and ensuring matters relating to discipline

- Maintaining relations with parents, providing them with information, promoting relations with other bodies, advising and assisting governing bodies, liaison and co-operation with the LEA and with other school and educational establishments such as further education colleges.
- Allocation, controlling and accounting for resources
- Providing for the security and supervision of the premises
- Providing cover for absence by appointing deputy head teacher(s).
- Teaching where appropriate.

The head teacher's duties in relation to discipline are now specifically set out in section 61 of SSFA 1998. Head teachers are entitled to a daily break of reasonable length.

The TTA introduced an induction scheme for newly appointed head teachers. Section 18 of THEA 1998 provides for a professional qualification for head teachers which such persons will be expected to have or acquire. In 1998 it was announced that a dedicated training college for aspiring head teachers was to be established.

The 1991 Act sets out the conditions of employment for deputy head teachers. They are to play a major role under the direction of the head teacher in:

- formulating aims and objectives
- establishing policies
- managing staff and resources
- monitoring progress to achieve aims and objectives.

Further, a deputy head teacher must undertake any professional duties of the head teacher reasonably delegated to him or her by the head teacher. The role of the head teacher is to be undertaken in his or her absence. A break of reasonable length is also an entitlement for deputy heads.

The conditions of employment which apply to all teachers other than head teachers relate to:

- Professional duties
- Teaching
- Other activities
- Assessments and reports
- Appraisal
- Review: further training and development
- Educational methods
- Discipline, health and safety
- Staff meetings

- Cover
- Public examinations
- Management
- Administration.

Detailed provisions relating to working time are also covered except that these provisions do not apply to deputy head teachers. A full-time teacher is expected to work for 195 days per school year, 190 days of which are to be spent on teaching and other duties.

Teachers should be available for 1,265 hours per year; they should not be expected to undertake midday supervision and are entitled to a break of reasonable length. Teachers have traditionally been expected to work such additional hours as may be needed to enable them to discharge effectively their professional duties including, in particular, marking pupils' work, writing reports on pupils and preparation of lessons, teaching material and teaching programmes. The amount of time required for this purpose beyond the 1,265 hours depends upon the work needed to discharge a teacher's duties.

Some CTCs have experimented both with the length of the school year and the number of teaching days, advocating a return to the 200-day teaching requirement anticipated by the Education Act 1944, but this was met with opposition from the teacher associations. It is possible that schools in EAZs may experiment with the length of the school day.

On appointment, teachers will receive an appointment letter which will refer to appointment subject to terms and conditions as laid down. This will include not only those documents referred to above, but the standard terms and conditions in the "Burgundy Book" applicable to those in maintained schools.

Pay

The 1998 Document sets out pay scales and the assessment of appropriate salary points on the various scales, depending on the qualifications and experience of the teacher. Further provision is made in the Education (School Teachers' Pay and Conditions) (No 2) Order 1998 (SI No 1884).

The Secretary of State may designate certain schools as pilot schools for the introduction of performance-related pay having asked the School Teachers' Review Body to consider whether more could be done to attract good teachers to schools in difficult areas by introducing new incentives and utilising flexibility in the pay "spines". The School Teachers' Review Body's Fourth Report 1995 proposed and set out the criteria for performance-related pay for head teachers and deputies. The performance indicators are:

- year-on-year improvement in a school's examination or test results
- year-on-year improvement in pupil attendance
- evidence of sound financial management
- if there had been a recent Ofsted inspection, progress in meeting the requirements of the resulting action plan.

It remains to be seen if these criteria are adopted and they are currently under review by various teacher and other organisations.

The 1998 TPCO and Circular 9/98 provide for some flexibility. There are provisions for additional payments in respect of

- advanced skills teachers
- recognition of the head teacher's management role
- discretionary payments for out of hours activities.

Section 13 of SSFA 1998 allows for the disapplication of the Order in the case of schools in EAZs under the Act.

The teacher associations claim that there is disparity between male and female teachers in pay, but cases on equal pay have been limited to teachers in private schools and non-teaching staff. In *Ratcliffe v North Yorkshire County Council* [1995] 3 All ER 597, the applicants were school dinner ladies who had, as a result of the contracting out provisions of the Local Government Act 1988, been dismissed as redundant and re-employed at lower hourly rates. At an Industrial Tribunal hearing the dinner ladies were described as "a very economically vulnerable and dependent group". The women claimed that they had been discriminated against as they were paid less than male comparators under the provisions of the Equal Pay Act 1970. The House of Lords found that there was such discrimination, and it was, "the very kind of discrimination in relation to pay that the Act had sought to remove". The council had failed to show that the variation between male and female wages was owing to a material difference other than the difference of sex within section 1 of the Equal Pay Act 1970. See also *Lawrence v Regent Office Care Ltd* (above).

Non-teaching staff

As mentioned above, the SSFA 1998 distinguishes between the appointment of teaching staff and others. Schedules 16 and 17 set out in detail the procedures to be adopted and the information to be given in such appointments. In relation to Schedule 16, any recommendation for appointment must be forwarded to the LEA with details of the post, including hours to be worked, terms, pay etc.

Duties of care

In common with all employers, certain duties of care are owed specifically to employees. See further Chapter 7 and cases such as *Murphy* v *Bradford Metropolitan Borough Council* [1992] PIQR 68. In 1996, two cases were reportedly settled for sums approaching £100,000 where teachers has been assaulted by a pupil and a parent respectively. Also in 1996, a teacher who sustained multiple injuries in a car crash received £376,000 in the same year where the car was being used for a school trip as the school minibus had failed a safety check. In 1998, a head teacher received £150,000 for exposure to asbestos during inspections of the school boiler. Settlements are rarely accompanied by admissions of liability.

New duties of care are constantly under review by the courts (see e.g. *Spring* v *Guardian Assurance plc* [1995] 2 AC 296 at p 154 below with regard to references. One interesting case is that of *Walker* v *Northumberland County Council* [1995] IRLR 35 where it was held that a local authority employer that failed to relieve the pressure on an employee who had suffered one breakdown owing to pressure of work was in breach of its duty of care when he had a second breakdown. It was found that the employer had failed to take reasonable steps to avoid exposing the employee to a health-endangering workload. That case involved a social worker, but many teachers would find the comments relating to workload familiar. The employee's situation was summed up thus:·

> He had been trapped in a situation where on the one hand he was unable to control the increasing volume of stressful work and where on the other he was unable to persuade superior management to increase staff or give management guidance as to work distribution or prioritisation.

In 1998, a deputy head teacher reached a settlement with his LEA for £100,000 after he had suffered two nervous breakdowns and claimed he had been bullied by his head teacher, although the claim was denied.

The teacher associations are keen to monitor and challenge situations where teachers are perceived to have an excessive workload. See, for example, *Wandsworth London Borough Council* v *National*

Association of School Masters and Union of Women Teachers (above) in relation to the excessive workload of the national curriculum. The government have responded to some extent by, for example, reducing the bureaucratic burden on teachers through Circular 2/98.

Grievance and disciplinary procedures

In schools without a delegated budget, grievance and disciplinary procedures are usually drawn up by the LEA in consultation with the trade unions. Under the SSFA 1998, the governing bodies of schools with delegated budgets are required to establish disciplinary rules and procedures and grievance procedures, and they must take steps to make them known to the school staff.

Grievance procedures are usually referred to in the Statement of Terms and Conditions and are set out in detail in the documents which form the letter of appointment. Separate procedures are usually set out for head teachers and other teaching staff. Similar procedures may apply to non-teaching staff. Teachers' grievances can come from a variety of sources and can arise between members of staff and between members of staff and the head teacher. They can involve matters of little importance, but may often involve matters of fundamental importance and may call for the intervention of the governors and/or the LEA. It is common for there to be "informal" grievance procedures and a completely formal procedure where the informal procedure has failed or is inappropriate. The formal procedure usually gives recourse to a further, subsequent stage. The rules may allow for the parties concerned to be represented by a friend or a trade union representative.

The aim of disciplinary proceedings may be a relevant factor. Some governing bodies and/or LEAs are keen to repair any breakdown in discipline so that warnings, for example, do not remain on file long term. Such a procedure might involve:

- an oral warning, unrecorded and lapsing in six months;
- a meeting with a "friend" present, a record made and a warning letter which may last 12 months at the end of which the letter may be removed from the file;
- a final written warning lasting for two years which may be removed after this time; and
- a disciplinary panel which may decide on dismissal; the dismissal procedure is now set out in detail in the SSFA 1998 (see below).

Under the SSFA 1998, the Secretary of State retains the right to make rules relating to the conduct and discipline of staff and such rules may override those of the governing body. The threat of industrial action by teachers was considered in *R* v *South Tyneside Metropolitan Borough Council and the Governors of Hebburn Comprehensive School, ex parte Cram* [1998] COD 183, where the grievance concerned the proposed reinstatement of an excluded pupil.

The general position in grant-maintained schools was reviewed in *R* v *Secretary of State for Education, ex parte Prior* [1994] ELR 231.

Dismissal

The general law of employment applies to teachers and non-teaching staff in schools, although there are some specific statutory provisions which apply in relation to education. For a general overview see A Morris (1990), "Employment Law: Surveying the terrain", *Education and the Law* 1990, 2, 55–65.

It should be noted that the Industrial Tribunals Act 1996 has been amended by the Employment Rights (Dispute Resolution) Act 1998 so that Industrial Tribunals are now referred to as Employment Tribunals.

In 1995, the Chief Inspector of Schools announced that in 5,000 schools which had been inspected by Ofsted, 2% of teachers had been found to be very poor and that about 15,000 teachers needed to be removed on the basis of inadequacy. The need to establish a fast-track procedure for the removal of incompetent teachers was considered necessary and implemented under the SSFA 1998 (see below).

A preliminary consideration must be the grounds on which a teacher (or other member of staff) might be dismissed. It seems that the general law of employment is useful, in that to establish that a dismissal is fair an Industrial (or Employment) Tribunal (see below) must accept, on a balance of probabilities, that the dismissal was for one or more of the five reasons set out in the Employment Rights Act 1996. A dismissal can be fair if the employer can show that:

(a) the employee lacked capability or qualification for the job;
(b) the employee's conduct was unsatisfactory;
(c) the employee was redundant;
(d) continued employment would contravene statutory or other legal obligation; or
(e) some other substantial reason for dismissal.

In relation to (b) above, the types of conduct which may lead to a fair dismissal should be listed in the disciplinary procedure. Such acts might commonly include:

- theft or other forms of dishonesty
- violent, threatening or abusive behaviour
- persistent lateness
- unauthorised absenteeism
- disobedience of lawful instructions of the employer
- use/abuse of drugs or alcohol
- breach of good faith, such as revealing confidential information.

Although these apply in all cases, there are specific issues in relation to teachers. In many instances the governing bodies and/or LEA might be concerned about the example being set to young people, as in *Berrisford v Woodard Schools (Midland Division) Ltd* [1991] IRLR 247 (below).

Acts outside of school may therefore be relevant, although it could be argued that acts away from school premises should not be taken into account in all cases. As with all employees, summary dismissal will only be justified in cases of "gross misconduct".

In *Berrisford* v *Woodard Schools (Midland Division) Ltd* (above), an unmarried school matron in a private school was dismissed when she became pregnant. She told the headmaster that she had no immediate plans to marry. She claimed that she had been discriminated against on the grounds of gender. However, evidence was given that male colleagues in similar circumstances were given the choice of marrying, leaving or of giving up the relationship. It was held that the "objectionable conduct" being complained of was the example that was being given to the pupils, not the pregnancy itself, and so the argument that she was being discriminated against because her male colleagues could not get pregnant and suffer the same discrimination was rejected.

One of the main areas for concern is allegations of child abuse. Teachers were concerned when the Children Act 1989 came into force that they would have to deal with a spate of false allegations concerning child abuse. The Association of Teachers and Lecturers advised its members to:

> withdraw from any potentially dangerous or exposed situations, not to have any form of physical contact, including comforting, with pupils, and even to refuse to take part in activities where they might find themselves alone with one or two pupils. (*The Times,* 29 January 1993).

There has been some consideration given to "criminalising inappropriate relationships" between teachers and pupils even when they are both over the age of consent. This was rejected by Parliament, but guidance on the Secretary of State's powers and the Department's procedures in dealing with misconduct by teachers and others working with children and young persons is to be found in Circular 11/95.

Dismissal procedure

Schedule 16 to SSFA 1998 provides for governing bodies to notify the LEA when it is proposed to dismiss a teacher and to give the teacher notice of that dismissal within 14 days of the LEA being notified (in the case of community, voluntary and community special schools). The procedure in Schedule 17 in respect of foundation and voluntary aided schools differs slightly. There is provision for summary dismissal, suspension and appeals.

Those who feel that they have been discriminated against on the basis of gender, marital status, race or disability can make application to the Employment Tribunal for an initial determination of their case. They may do so either in relation to the employment, the termination of employment or the application for employment. Similarly, those who have been dismissed may approach the Employment Tribunal for a determination subject to any qualifying criteria being satisfied. Under section 38 of the Trade Union Reform and Employment Rights Act 1993, the power of Industrial Tribunals (as they then were) was extended to cover breaches of contract.

Under the provisions of the Employment Rights Act 1996, an employee must have been employed for a continuous period before gaining the protection of the Act in respect to unfair dismissal (although this has been considered discriminatory – see below). The qualifying period was two years until July 1999 when the period was reduced to one year.

There have been particular problems where teachers were employed on contracts which spanned the academic, but not the calendar, year. In *Ford* v *Warwickshire County Council* [1983] IRLR 126, the House of Lords held that a teacher who had been employed on a series of fixed-term contracts from September of one year to July of the next had continuous service from the time the first contract began in September 1971 to the end of the final contract in July 1979.

In *R* v *Secretary of State for Employment, ex parte Seymour-Smith* [1995] ICR 889, the two-year period was held to be indirect discrimination against women and incompatible with the principle of the Equal Treatment Directive 76/207/EEC. However, on appeal, the House of Lords felt that the matter should be referred back to the

European Court of Justice (see *R v Secretary of State for Employment, ex parte Seymour-Smith and Perez* [1997] 1 WLR 473). It remains to be seen if the reduction in the two year qualifying period to one year has resolved this issue.

Part-time staff

In *R v Secretary of State for Employment, ex parte Equal Opportunities Commission* [1995] 1 AC 1, the House of Lords held that the provisions of the Employment Protection (Consolidation) Act 1978 Act in respect of part-time employees were incompatible with European Community law. The government subsequently introduced the Employment Protection (Part-time Employees) Regulations 1995 (SI No 31) giving the same rights to part-time employees as their full-time counterparts had. In *Hammersmith and Fulham London Borough Council, ex parte Jesuthasan* [1998] *The Times*, 5 March it was held that male part-time employees were discriminated against and could rely on the *Equal Opportunities* case.

Withdrawal of recognition

The ultimate sanction available to the Secretary of State is to withdraw the recognition of an individual to teach and to place them on "List 99".

In *R v Secretary of State for Education, ex parte Standish* [1993] *The Times*, 15 November, it was held that in banning a teacher from further employment as such the Secretary of State should make express findings of fact and give reasons for his decision. In that case, the applicant for judicial review had been in possession or the author of certain obscene material and the Secretary of State ordered that he be debarred from teaching any child at a boarding school maintained by an LEA, a special school, a grant-maintained school or being employed by an LEA in a capacity other than as a teacher which would involve regular contact with children or young people under the age of 19. The direction was made under the Education (Teachers) Regulations 1989 (SI No 1319). The Secretary of State was asked to consider whether, in cases where the risk to pupils was of paramount concern, those Regulations as drafted were appropriate.

References

In *Spring* v *Guardian Assurance plc* [1995] 2 AC 296, the House of Lords held that an employer giving a reference regarding a former employee was under a duty to take reasonable care in its preparation and would be liable to the employee in negligence if it was inaccurate and the employee thereby suffered damage.

Retirement

Under national agreements teachers, male and female, may retire at 65. New arrangements were introduced in 1997 for early retirements with employers becoming liable for the extra cost of premature retirements (see Circular 15/97).

Discrimination was in issue in relation to retirement ages in *Bullock* v *Alice Ottley School* [1992] 91 LGR 32. A school had different retiring ages for teaching and domestic staff who retired at 60 and maintenance staff who retired at 65. This was held not to be a breach of the Sex Discrimination Act 1975. The school justified the difference by saying that it was difficult to recruit gardeners and other maintenance staff.

The meaning of "employment" for the purposes of pensions was considered by the House of Lords in *Preston* v *Wolverhampton Healthcare NHS Trust* [1998] *The Times*, 9 February. The termination of employment in the case of a teacher on fixed-term contracts was considered in *Hill* v *Pensions Agency* [1998] The Times, 20 July. The Teachers Pensions Regulations 1997 (SI No 3001) consolidate previous regulations with effect from February 1998 (although certain provisions came into effect previously). See also the Teachers' (Compensation for Redundancy and Premature Retirement) (Amendment) Regulations 1998 (SI No 2256).

Property rights

In *Hughes* v *Greenwich London Borough Council* [1994] 1 AC 170, the Court of Appeal considered the position where a headmaster occupied a house provided for him by the local authority on the campus of the boarding school where he was employed. It was held that it was unnecessary for there to be any term in his contract of employment specifically requiring him to reside there and no term could be implied. As such, Mr Hughes had become a secure tenant under the Housing Act 1985 and was not excluded from the right to buy provisions of that Act.

Benefits in kind

In *Pepper* v *Hart* [1993] AC 593, the taxation of benefits in kind were in issue, the benefits in this case being concessionary fees at a private school for members of staff. The taxpayers did not contest that they had received such benefits, but questioned the determination of the value of the benefits. The legislative provisions were said to be ambiguous and the House of Lords considered that in the circumstances it was appropriate to refer to *Hansard* in order to interpret the legislation.

Finance

Finance

Standard spending assessment (SSA)

The allocation of funds for education and other services by central to local government has been the subject of some controversy. The amount which the government allocates to local authorities based on what it believes that authority needs to run its services is the standard spending assessment (SSA). The SSAs are being frozen for three years from 1998 to provide local authorities with financial certainty, but it is hoped by many that during that time a review of the system will be undertaken. Some poorer LEAs receive less funding per pupil than more affluent areas under the present system.

The government has allocated extra funding for education from 1997/98 and in releasing these funds the government expects money to be used for particular purposes, for example, raising standards in schools. Section 3 of SSFA 1998 makes provision for the payment of grants to LEAs in respect of payments incurred in connection with the reductions in infant class sizes.

Given the increase in LEA responsibilities in SSFA 1998, some critics have commented that additional funding may not find its way into schools, despite an apparent extension of the system of financial delegation (see below). LEAs will have to fund EAZs, education development plans, school organisation committees, early years development partnerships, new school admissions procedures and the additional staff needed to implement these initiatives.

Local management of schools (LMS)

Traditionally, schools were financed on the basis of an "historic" budget (i.e. a budget based on the previous year's expenditure, adjusted where necessary). Schools could make savings, but the effect of doing so would probably be that the next year's budget would be cut, thereby removing any incentive to save. A number of pilot projects tested the idea of "financial delegation" and management consultants advised on the idea. According to Maclure:

> The funding of all the schools in a local authority area by means of a single
> formula is central to the strategy and ideology underlying the Act. It reduces
> the local authority's power to intervene in favour of one school rather than
> another, thereby limiting the scope for political intervention.

Under the ERA 1988, governing bodies were to take responsibility for
controlling budgets delegated to them. The distribution of funds was
to be essentially on a weighted, per capita basis. The delegation of
budgets was also to have important implications for staffing in that
governing bodies were to have more financial control over staffing.

LMS was phased in over a period of years and all county and
voluntary schools were eventually covered by it. Circular 7/88 set out
the intended aims of LMS:

- to enhance the powers of parents and governing bodies at the
  expense of the LEAs;
- to improve accountability for the use of finance and resources;
- to improve the efficiency with which resources are used in the
  education service;
- to provide a more equitable distribution to schools of available
  public funds; and
- to improve the quality of teaching and learning.

Schools which opted out (i.e. grant-maintained schools) had their own
system of funding via the Funding Agency for Schools.

The Education Act 1996 preserved the system of financial delegation and allowed for, *inter alia*, the modification of employment law
to reflect the role of governing bodies under LMS (see e.g. the
Education (Modification of Enactments Relating to Employment)
Order 1998 (SI No 218)).

In May 1998 a consultation paper, "Fair Funding: Improving delegation to schools" included the proposal that all schools should
receive control over funds previously retained by the LEAs, such as
funds for school repair and maintenance, school meals, curriculum
advice, library services, financial administration and supply cover. The
SSFA 1998 extends the system by giving all maintained schools greater
control over their budgets. Some commentators have said that the new
provisions effectively give all schools the freedom over their budgets
that grant-maintained schools had. If schools want to continue to use
LEA services, they will have to "opt in" rather than opt out.

Under section 45 of SSFA 1998 every maintained school shall have
a "budget share" allocated to it by the authority which maintains it. A
maintained school in this context is defined by reference to section 20
of that Act.

Financial schemes

Approval of schemes

Under section 48 of the SSFA 1998, every LEA is required to prepare a scheme for the financing of maintained schools. Such schemes must deal with matters as set out in the Act or in regulations to be made. Regulations will, it is suggested in section 48(2), require schemes to deal with:

- the carrying forward from one financial year to another surpluses and deficits arising in relation to schools' budget shares;
- amounts which may be charged against schools' budget shares;
- amounts which may be retained by school governing bodies and the purposes for which such amounts may be used;
- any conditions which may be applied, such as conditions prescribing financial controls and procedures;
- terms on which services or facilities are provided for the schools by the LEA.

In drawing up schemes the LEA shall take account of any guidance issued and shall consult the governing body and the head teacher of every school as defined in Schedule 14 to SSFA 1998. Such schemes are subject to the approval of the Secretary of State under Schedule 14. The Secretary of State may approve, give conditional approval or modify such schemes.

Imposition of schemes

After consulting the authority and any other persons "thought fit" the Secretary of State may impose a scheme on an authority where:

- the authority has failed to submit a scheme; or
- it appears to the Secretary of State that the scheme submitted does not accord with guidance given by him and cannot be made to do so by merely modifying it. Such a scheme will be treated as if made under section 48.

Publication

An approved scheme must be published on its coming into force and on any other occasions prescribed by the Secretary of State (Sched 14).

Variation of schemes

Where the LEA proposes to revise a scheme, the same consultative procedures as apply to the preparation of a scheme will apply. The Secretary of State may by direction revise the whole or part of a scheme having consulted the LEA and those persons thought fit. Where the LEA proposes to make variations to the scheme, it must consult and submit the proposed variation to the Secretary of State for approval.

Local schools budget

Under section 46 of SSFA 1998, an LEA's local schools budget for a financial year is the amount appropriated by the LEA for the purposes of meeting all expenditure of a class or description prescribed for the purposes of the section, which may include expenditure otherwise than in respect of schools.

Individual school's budget

The amount remaining after deducting from the local school's budget planned expenditure which may be deducted in accordance with regulations is to be known as the "individual school's budget". The Financing of Maintained Schools Regulations 1999 (SI No 101) specify what may be deducted from the local schools budget to arrive at the individual school's budget. Schedule 1 of the Regulations set out the following heads of deductions:

- expenditure supported by specific grants
- special educational needs provision
- school improvement measures
- access to education initiatives
- expenditure related to strategic management.

Under previous regulations, mandatory exceptions were to be left out of the determination of the amount available for allocation to individual schools. They included:

- all expenditure of a capital nature;
- repayment on loans to cover capital expenditure;
- expenditure falling to be taken into account in determining central government grants of a prescribed description; and
- such other items as may be prescribed.

Discretionary exceptions were the items which the LEA wished to except together with the mandatory exceptions. DES Circular 7/88 allowed LEAs to retain control of certain services where they could show that those services are more efficiently or effectively delivered centrally. Discretionary exceptions were divided into two groups: those subject to a limit of 10% (reducing to 7%) of the general schools budget, and those not subject to the limit. In the latter category fell the school meals service, dismissal and premature retirement costs, governors' insurance, grounds maintenance and cleaning. Items subject to the 10% (7%) limit included structural maintenance, premises insurance, pupil support, peripatetic teachers, statemented pupils, education psychologists, education welfare services, and school library services.

Certain discretionary items such as premature retirement compensation and dismissal costs were made mandatory exceptions from 1995/96.

Schools' budget share

Section 45 of SSFA 1998 provides that each maintained school is to have a budget share determined in accordance with sections 46 and 47 of the Act. The budget share is the amount allocated by the LEA in accordance with regulations to the school out of the individual school's budget for that financial year. Regulations will particularly address such issues as:

- the time when schools' budget shares are to be initially determined by LEAs;
- factors or criteria to be taken into account by LEAs or other requirements;
- the adjustments to be made in respect of permanently excluded pupils (see e.g. the Education (Amount to Follow Permanently Excluded Pupil) Regulations 1999 (SI No 495);
- provisions in respect of new schools;
- redetermining or making adjustments to budget shares to take account of matters arising during the financial year;
- requirements in respect of consultation to be carried out;
- the powers of the Secretary of State to authorise or redetermine budget shares.

Financial delegation

Section 49 of SSFA 1998 provides that every maintained school is to have a delegated budget. This means that the school's governing body has the right to manage the school's budget share. The LEA may not delegate to the school's governing body the power to spend any part of the authority's local schools budget subject to the provisions of section 49(4).

Where a school has a delegated budget, the LEA shall secure a sum equal to the school's budget share for that financial year (or part year) to be spent by the governing body (s 50). Sums will be provided to the governing body at such times and in such a manner as provided for in the scheme (s 50(2)). The governors may, subject to any stipulations in the scheme, spend the school's budget share in such a way as they think fit for the purposes of the school or for such purposes as may be prescribed. The governors are able to delegate to the head teacher powers of expenditure over any part of the delegated budget as is permitted by the scheme (s 50(6)).

Financial statements

Section 52 of SSFA 1998 provides that at the beginning of each financial year LEAs shall prepare a statement of planned expenditure and at the end of such a period shall provide a statement of planned expenditure applicable for that year, actual expenditure and any resources allocated to schools maintained by them during the course of the financial year. Such statements are to be published in a manner prescribed by the Education (Budget Statements and Supplementary Provisions) Regulations 1999 (SI No 486). Section 53 provides that these statements may be subject to verification by the Audit Commission.

Governors' liability

Governors are protected by section 50(7) of SSFA 1998 against personal liability in respect of any losses incurred by acting "in good faith" in their disposition of the school budget (see further below).

Suspension of financial delegation

Section 51 of and Schedule 15 to SSFA 1998 set out the circumstances in which financial delegation can be suspended. The LEA may suspend financial delegation where it appears to them that the governing body of a school which has a delegated budget:

- have been guilty of a substantial or persistent failure to comply with any delegation requirement or restriction, or
- not have been managing in a satisfactory manner the expenditure or appropriation of the delegated budget.

Not less than one month's notice should be given unless by reason of any gross incompetence or mismanagement the LEA feel it is necessary to give shorter notice or to suspend the delegated budget with immediate effect, also by notice. The notice must specify the grounds for the suspension. A copy of the notice must be given to the head teacher at the same time as the governing body and a copy must be sent to the Secretary of State to whom an appeal may be made. The LEA must review any suspension at the beginning of every financial year (unless imposed less than two months prior to the beginning of the financial year). An appeal can be made to the Secretary of State on a refusal to revoke a suspension. During any period of the suspension, the LEA may still allow the school governing body to spend such sums of the school's budget share as considered appropriate. The LEA may apply conditions as to the amount to be spent.

Governing bodies will be expected to develop their own school-based performance indicators. Additionally, under section 17 of SSFA 1998, where the LEA has intervened in a school "causing concern" then the right to a delegated budget may be suspended.

Deferment

Under Schedule 32 to SSFA 1998, a school which previously had its delegated budget suspended under section 117 of the Education Act 1996 (for mismanagement etc.) or section 28 of the School Inspections Act could have a delegated budget when that suspension was revoked.

Competitive tendering

Under the Local Government Act 1988, LEAs had to submit certain specified services to competitive tendering. School meals, grounds maintenance, cleaning and vehicle maintenance had to be put out to competitive tendering, while building maintenance was already subject to competitive tendering. Financial delegation schemes were affected by these arrangements.

Where the LEA had "contracted out" voluntarily, the governing body would be bound by the contract until renewal. Where the LEA had not yet published the specification of such services, schools were free to choose either the LEA arrangements or to make their own. The school could specify the standard of service required even if the LEA arrangements were chosen.

Where the LEA has published a specification, the school is bound by the contract until it expires, but where a contract is due for renewal the governing body could choose whether to stay with the LEA arrangements or make their own. Competitive tendering has certain staffing implications for non-teaching staff; see further Chapter 9 and cases such as *Ratcliffe* v *North Yorkshire County Council* [1995] 3 All ER 597.

Charging policies

Section 451 of the Education Act 1996 prohibits charging for the provision of education, although section 456 allows for the regulation of permitted charges and section 457 refers to remissions policies. The 1996 Act made it a statutory duty for all LEAs and the governing body of maintained schools to formulate and keep under review a policy on charges. The 1996 Act forbids charging for admission to the school and for all school curricular tuition, the exception being instrumental music tuition where that tuition does not form part of the national curriculum. Any other activities and optional extras may be charged for. Governors have a discretion over what charges they make. Charges can be made for school visits, both day and residential, provided that the trips fall partly outside school hours. No charge can be made for entry to public examinations where the pupil is being prepared for entry to that examination by the school, except that fees can be recovered from a parent where the pupil "fails without good reason to meet any examination requirement for that syllabus". The governing body must also formulate a remissions policy to set out the circumstances in which they would remit all or part of the charges.

Schedule 30 to SSFA 1998 makes certain minor amendments to the 1996 Act in respect of charging provisions.

Earmarked funding

Schools receive certain funds from various sources to be spent on school-focused activities and developments. Funds available in this way are not available for virement to other budget heads. There is provision, for example, for grants for partnership funding (see the Education (Partnership Grants) Regulations 1998 (SI No 1222)) and funding for "early excellence centres" (see the Education (Grants for Early Excellence Centres) (England) Regulations 1998 (SI No 1877)). Other schemes include finance for the education of travellers and displaced persons and "section 11" funding in respect of ethnic minorities provided for under section 11 of the Local Government Act 1966. Funds are available for raising standards under the SSFA, see Circular 13/98 The Standards Fund 1999–2000.

Education action zones (EAZs)

The purpose of an EAZ is to raise standards in a specific area. Such zones receive additional funding to, *inter alia*, pay higher salaries to "advanced skills teachers" (see Chapter 9).

The EAZ schemes will attract additional funding of £500,000 as a supplement to their budgets. The government announced in 1998 that £250 million was to be allocated to increase the number of EAZs.

Community use of schools

Schedule 13 to SSFA 1998 provides that the occupation and use of the premises of schools, both during and outside school hours, shall be under the control of the governing body subject to directions by the LEA, any relevant enactments and any transfer of control agreements entered into by the governing body. Schedule 13(1)(4) in relation to community schools and (3) in relation to foundation schools states that:

> … in exercising control of the occupation and use of the premises outside school hours the governing body shall have regard to the desirability of those premises being made available for community use.

Similar provision is made in respect of voluntary schools in Schedule 13(7), although rather more specific provision is made in respect of activities in these schools at weekends.

Funding Agency for Schools (FAS)

The financial relationships between LEAs and schools which opted out under the ERA 1988 resulted in considerable litigation. See, for example, *R v Department of Education and Science, ex parte Dudley Metropolitan Borough Council* [1991] 90 LGR 296; *R v Secretary of State for Education and Science, ex parte Birmingham City Council* [1992] RVR 218; and *R v Secretary of State for Wales, ex parte Gwent County Council* [1994] 34 RVR 214. Similar problems also occurred in relation to CTCs: see, for example, *R v Secretary of State for Education, ex parte Inner London Education Authority* [1990] COD 412.

The FAS was established under the Education Act 1993 and began to operate with effect from 1 April 1994. From that date, it assumed responsibility for distributing funds to all grant-maintained schools. It operated under the guidance of a board of between 10 and 15 members. The members included head teachers, school governors and education administrators.

The FAS's primary functions were:

- the calculation and payment of recurrent, special purpose and capital grants to grant-maintained schools and grant-maintained special schools under the 1993 (and subsequently the 1996) Education Act;
- the financial monitoring of grant-maintained schools, including value-for-money studies; and
- the provision of sufficient school places.

The FAS produced an Annual Report and also produced a Code of Conduct which was developed with the provisions of the Nolan report on Standards in Public Life in mind. The FAS also produced a corporate plan covering the period from April 1995 to March 1998 which set out its aims and objectives in detail. Regulations provided for the detailed financial provisions relating to grant-maintained schools (e.g. the Education (New Grant-maintained Schools) (Finance) Regulations 1998 (SI No 798) and the Education (Grant-maintained and Grant-maintained Special Schools) (Finance) Regulations 1998 (SI No 799)).

Section 132 of SSFA 1998 dissolved the FAS. Notwithstanding this, there is provision in Schedule 32 of SSFA 1998 for the continued operation of grants in relation to grant-maintained schools. Regulations will provide for the discharge of functions relating to these grants to be discharged by the Secretary of State or by LEAs. Litigation involving the

FAS has also continued: see, for example, *R v Funding Agency for Schools, ex parte Essex County Council* (1998, unreported, trans ref CO/597).

Assisted places

Since its introduction following the implementation of the Education Act 1980, about 70,000 children and their parents have received help with school fees, although not all the places in England were filled. The scheme aimed to enable pupils who might otherwise not be able to do so to benefit from education at independent schools. The scheme in England was based on a fixed number of places, unlike the scheme in Scotland which allocated the money to the schools to use as they thought fit.

The government announced in 1996 that the assisted places scheme would be expanded, and section 1 of the Education Act 1997, extended the scheme to schools providing only primary education.

Following the change of government in May 1997, the Education (Schools) Act 1997 abolished the scheme in England and Wales, and also made provision for the phasing out of the scheme in Scotland. Section 130 of SSFA 1998 makes provision for transfer assisted places (see also the Education (Assisted Places) (Amendment) Regulations 1998 (SI No 1726)). The resources to be saved were to be specifically applied to the reduction of class sizes. Independent schools meanwhile announced that they intended to fund a version of the assisted places scheme themselves.

In *R v Cobham Hall School, ex parte S* [1997] *The Times*, 13 December, it was held that decisions of independent schools participating in the assisted places scheme were susceptible to judicial review. The decision of the school in this case was to withdraw a pupil from her assisted place. It was submitted that the school was not a public body and was not therefore subject to judicial review (see further Chapter 3). However, it was held that the school in this instance was working within a statutory framework and was then in a similar position to that of a CTC. The case of *R v Governors of Haberdashers' Aske's Hatcham College Trust, ex parte Tyrell* [1995] COD 399 was relied upon, and the withdrawal of the place was found to be unlawful.

Financial assistance to non-maintained schools

Under section 128 of SSFA 1998, an LEA may assist any primary or secondary non-maintained school whether inside or outside their area make arrangements for pupils to be provided with primary or secondary education at such schools. Regulations may be made to specify the types of expenditure under this provision, but fees for education and for board and lodging, if provided, are specifically mentioned. Section 16(1)(c) of the Education Act 1996, which made similar provision, shall cease to have effect.

Section 458 of the 1996 Act, which relates to charges for board and lodging at boarding schools, is amended by Schedule 30 to SSFA 1998.

Grants and scholarships

Section 518 of the Education Act 1996 is substituted by section 129 of SSFA 1998. An LEA may pay such expenses of children attending community, foundation, voluntary or special schools as may be necessary to allow them to take part in any school activities, and they may grant scholarships, bursaries, exhibitions or other allowances in respect of persons over compulsory school age.

Regulations may make provision for LEAs to determine in each financial year to what extent they propose to exercise their power.

Rating

Section 78 of SSFA 1998 provides that for the purposes of rating under the Local Government Finance Act 1988, the occupier of a community, voluntary controlled or community special school, whereas the governing body of a foundation, voluntary aided or foundation special school is the occupier.

Value added tax (VAT)

The government has confirmed its intention not to extend VAT to school fees. The case of *Customs and Excise Commissioners* v *St Mary's Roman Catholic School* [1996] STC 1091 did concern the application of VAT to building work. The school was built some ten years before the playground was completed owing to planning complications, and the LEA no longer had funds for the project. The playground was built using funds raised by the school. The application of the rules on zero-rating depended on there being a "temporal link" between services provided in the course of construction. The interval in time in this case meant that the temporal link could not be established.

Teacher training

The TTA can identify subject shortages and allocate funds for bursaries to attract trainee teachers in those subjects. In 1998, the government announced the payment of incentives to graduates in certain subject areas to attract them to the teaching profession. Additional funding has also been made available for the training of aspiring head teachers. Under Schedule 30 to SSFA 1998 the grant for education support and training (the "Gest" scheme), provided for under section 484 of the Education Act 1996, is to be replaced by 'education standards grants'.

Financial incentives have been considered in respect of mature students so that, for example, career development loans may now be disregarded in the assessment of mandatory awards payable by LEAs to trainee teachers (see further the Education (Mandatory Awards) (Amendment) Regulations 1998 (SI No 162)).

Recoupment

Section 494 of the Education Act 1996 (as amended by Schedule 30 to SSFA 1998) provides for payments in respect of permanently excluded pupils where that pupil is subsequently educated by another authority. See also the Education (Amount to Follow Permanently Excluded Pupil) Regulations 1999 (SI No 495), referred to above.

Nursery education

The financing of nursery education has proved controversial in recent years, particularly with the introduction of the nursery voucher scheme under the Nursery Education and Grant-Maintained Schools Act 1996. The Nursery Education (England) Regulations 1998 (SI No 655) prescribe the matters which relate to the making of grants for nursery education including the authorities and persons to whom grants may be made, and the method of calculating the amount of grant to be paid.

Private Finance Initiative (PFI)

Recent governments have indicated that the PFI is to apply to education. PFI involves financial input from business, both local and national. The first commercial school development under the scheme was at Colfox School, Bridport, Dorset. The intention is that the school will offer leisure facilities to the public and vocational training. The PFI contract covers the building and the maintenance of the school for 30 years and is similar to PFI contracts in other sectors, e.g. the NHS where such contracts are more advanced than those in education. Further details relating to this and other PFI schemes in education are available from the Audit Commission in a Management Paper, "Taking the Initiative: a Framework for Purchasing under the Private Finance Initiative" (1998).

The impact of this initiative may be felt in the further and higher education sectors in the immediate future (see Chapter 14).

Transfer of property

Under the SSFA 1998 transfers of status will require transfer of staff and land. Detailed provisions are set out in sections 73–75. The Education Transfer Council will perform the functions of the Education Assets Board under Schedule 29. Transfers on discontinuance of schools are dealt with in section 76 and Schedule 22.

Section 77 and the School Standards and Framework Act 1998 (School Playing Fields) (Modification) (England) Regulations 1999 (SI No 1) address the problem of the disposal of school playing fields, one of the most valuable assets that a school is likely to have. Under the section there shall be no disposal of a playing field used by a maintained school for the purposes of that school or which have been used at any time within the previous ten years without the Secretary of State's consent. Similarly, changes of use also require such consent.

Inspections

Inspections

The legislative basis for inspections

Under section 77(2) of the Education Act 1944, the duty of the Secretary of State was set out in relation to inspection. The section stated that it was his duty to cause inspections to be made at such intervals as appeared to him to be appropriate and at such times as considered appropriate. Later, the statutory basis of inspections was regarded as unsatisfactory. Reform of the system of inspections carried out by Her Majesty's Inspectors (HMIs) was announced by the government in 1991. The Parent's Charter issued by the DES in that year promised that every state school would be inspected regularly and those who were to carry out the inspections would be approved by a national body which would ensure that the inspections were thorough. The Education (Schools) Act 1992 set out in detail the new inspection system. HMIs were retained in the short term to be replaced eventually by Her Majesty's Inspectorate of Schools. The 1992 Act was amended by the Education Act 1993 and then by the School Inspections Act 1996. The Education Act 1997 made some amendments to the 1996 Act and introduced the inspection of LEAs. In 1997, the detailed provisions contained in regulations were consolidated by Education (School Inspection) Regulations 1997 (SI No 1966).

The SSFA 1998, as its name suggests, devotes a proportion of its provisions to the raising of standards. Although most of the sections in that Act involve new powers, the bulk of the School Inspections Act 1996 remains in force with some further amendment.

Relevant institutions

Grant-maintained, independent schools (including CTCs) and PRUs were included under the relevant legislation. The scheme of inspections operates slightly differently in Wales. Voluntary schools differ in that inspection in relation to religious education still rests with governors.

Ofsted

The Office of Her Majesty's Chief Inspector of Schools (HMCI), a non-ministerial government department, was established in 1992 under the Education (Schools) Act 1992. The Act made HMCI responsible ultimately to Parliament and to the Secretary of State for Education. The School Inspections Act 1996 (the 1996 Act) provides that the Chief Inspector shall not be appointed for a term of more than five years (although he or she may be reappointed) and may be removed from office by Her Majesty on the ground of incapacity or misconduct.

The duties of the HCMI are now set out in the 1996 Act. They are set out as general and specific duties. The general duties are to keep the Secretary of State informed about:

- the quality of the education provided by schools (in England);
- the educational standards achieved in those schools;
- whether the financial resources made available to those schools are managed efficiently; and
- the spiritual, moral, social and cultural development of pupils at those schools.

When asked to do so by the Secretary of State, the Chief Inspector shall give advice to the Secretary of State on matters specified and shall inspect and report on a school or class of school specified by the Secretary of State. The specific duties are to:

- establish and maintain a register of inspectors;
- give guidance to such persons in respect of inspections and reports;
- review the system of inspections (including the standards of inspections);
- review the effect of legislation on inspections; and
- promote efficiency by encouraging competition in the provision of services by inspectors.

Section 2(6) of the 1996 Act provides that in exercising his or her functions, the Chief Inspector shall have regard to such aspects of government policy as the Secretary of State may direct.

The Chief Inspector shall make an annual report to the Secretary of State, who shall lay a copy of it before Parliament and may make other reports as he or she sees fit. Administrative support is provided through the Office for Standards in Education (Ofsted). There is a separate HMCI for Wales provided for in sections 4–6 of the 1996 Act.

Regular inspections took place on a four-year cycle in England and a five-year cycle in Wales originally, although in 1996 it was announced that schools would be inspected every six years unless there was evidence of underachievement (see the Education (School Inspection) (No 2) (Amendment) Regulations 1997 (SI No 995)). Weak schools would be inspected more frequently until they showed improvement. "Underachieving" schools include good schools which are considered to be coasting.

Inspectors of Schools

The Chief Inspector is assisted by Inspectors of Schools to whom functions of the Chief Inspector may be delegated. Inspectors of Schools may also conduct inspections (see below). Appointments to the post of Inspector of Schools is by order (see e.g. the Education (Inspectors of Schools in England) Order 1997 (SI No 2564)).

Registered inspectors

Under section 3 of the 1996 Act, the Chief Inspector may cause any school in England to be inspected. Under section 7, no person shall conduct an inspection unless he or she is registered as an inspector. The Chief Inspector will not register a person as an inspector unless he or she is satisfied that an individual is a fit and proper person for discharging the functions of a registered inspector and will be capable of conducting inspections competently and effectively (Sched 3 to the 1996 Act, as amended by the Education Act 1997).

Once applications are received, references are checked and an applicant may be offered a place on a training course. In deciding whether to accommodate an individual on such a course, qualifications and experience are taken into account together with the phase of education involved and geographical location. HMCI can then ensure that there are enough trained inspectors in the primary, secondary and other phases in different parts of the country so that the system works. On successful completion of training (see below) there is a formal invitation to register as an inspector.

The register states the phase of education the inspector is qualified to inspect, the length of time the registration will last plus any other conditions. One general condition is that the "Framework for Inspection" will be adhered to (the guidance issued by Ofsted).

In September 1992, it was reported that some 4,600 training places had been awarded. Of those, male applicants out-numbered female applicants by two to one, half were in the 40–49 age range, few were from ethnic minorities and the bulk of applications came from London and the South-East. Five lecturers had applied to be "lay members" (see below) alongside solicitors, policemen and others. The rejection of applications by three leading educationalists prompted a response from the first HMCI, Professor Stewart Sutherland, who stated that inspectors were required to have "an objective viewpoint".

Under section 8 of the 1996 Act (as amended), a person's name can be removed from the register if he or she:

- is no longer a fit and proper person;
- is no longer capable of conducting inspections competently and effectively;
- has failed to comply with a condition to which his registration was subject;
- has produced a report which is seriously misleading in whole or in part without reasonable explanation.

Section 9 provides that appeals can be made in respect of registration procedure. Schedule 2 makes further detailed provision in respect of the appeals procedure.

The general duties of the registered inspectors are to report on:

- the quality of education provided by schools;
- the educational standards achieved by those schools;
- whether the financial resources made available to the school are managed efficiently; and
- the spiritual, moral, social and cultural development of the pupils at those schools.

The specific duties of a registered inspector are to:

- conduct each inspection
- deploy team members
- complete satisfactorily a training course and be assessed in a range of competencies as a team member on a full inspection of a school
- tender for contracts
- chair meetings of parents and governors
- justify the judgements of each report
- be accountable for the final report.

Team members

Under Schedule 3 to the 1996 Act, every inspection shall be carried out by a registered inspector with the assistance of a team. Team members take part in inspections but are not "team leaders". They have expertise in a subject or an aspect of a school and will also have completed a training course. Team members may have teaching or inspection experience or may be financial or management experts. The registered inspectors determine the composition of a team to ensure that the team as a whole can cover everything in the Ofsted "Framework" subject to the detail of the specification of the individual school.

Lay members

Lay inspectors are those members of a team who have no personal experience in the management of any school or the provision of education in any school. They can be governors (but not of the school being inspected), and their primary function is not having business or financial expertise. They may be involved in looking at the general efficiency of the school, but they should not be confined to that aspect and should play a full part in the inspection team. Lay inspectors are meant to bring a commonsense view of a school and as such these inspectors can come from any walk of life.

At least one member of each inspection team should be a lay member. One controversial aspect relating to lay members is the possibility that, after appropriate training, they might become registered inspectors and lead teams. Critics have stated that they feel that such members may not have the requisite experience to form and lead teams.

Training

Schedule 3 to the 1996 Act makes detailed provision in respect of training. All inspectors must satisfactorily complete a course of training. Lay inspectors do not receive the same training as the other team members because of their different backgrounds and needs.

Intending registered inspectors must undergo a training course and monitoring. Training concentrates on the Ofsted Framework. The monitoring by HMIs enables HMCI to report to the Secretary of State on the performance of the system as a whole, but it is also used to consider applications for re-registration.

Impartiality

No inspection team member may have any connection with the school which might cast doubt on his or her ability to report impartially on the school. Anyone who has any connection with the school in question, is employed at the school, is a member of the school governing body or who is the proprietor of the school in the case of an independent school should not be included as part of the inspection team (Sched 3).

Pre-inspection procedure

First, Ofsted informs the school that they are in the inspection programme for a particular school year in the autumn term of the previous year. Secondly, Ofsted makes formal arrangements and writes to the school well in advance of the term planned for the inspection, explaining the arrangements in detail. The governors are asked to inform Ofsted of holidays and dates of any events which might hinder the inspection.

Thirdly, Ofsted consults the governors on the specification for each school. Coverage is comprehensive for all schools but the governors should inform Ofsted of any subjects offered outside the national curriculum, any foreign languages taught and any other facts which may require adjustment to the specification.

Fourthly, Ofsted invites tenders against the specification from at least two registered inspectors. There is no set rate for inspection. HMCI indicated that the fees for the inspection of a small primary school would be about £5,000, up to a maximum of £30,000 for a large secondary school, although these figures excluded VAT. Fifthly, Ofsted then awards the contract.

Sixthly, the registered inspector contacts the school and makes arrangements for any preparatory work and for the inspection itself. Detailed returns are made by the head teacher. The inspectors are required to ascertain to what extent the school's values, plans and procedures are expressed in clear policies and documentation. As a result the information demanded from the school includes:

- its aims and objectives
- its development plan
- the national curriculum development plan
- the written statement of the governors' consideration of the LEA curriculum policy

- curricular policy on matters such as sex and political education, special educational needs, equal opportunities, religious education and collective worship
- financial information
- the response to complaints concerning the national curriculum
- information about the most recent governors' annual report to parents and the numbers attending the annual parents meeting.

Seventhly, the governors inform the following that the school is to be inspected:

- parents of all registered pupils
- the LEA (if a maintained school)
- those who are the foundation governors if a voluntary school
- the local Training and Enterprise Council and representatives of the local business community (particularly employers of former pupils) if the school is a secondary school. The views of the business community can be sent to the registered inspector.

Eighthly, the registered inspector sends sealed questionnaires to parents via the school "pupil post". The school sends the sealed returns back to the registered inspector.

The governing body then arranges a meeting between the registered inspector and parents. Three weeks' notice must be given together with an explanatory statement by the registered inspector, both of which must be sent by pupil post.

Finally, the meeting takes place during which the registered inspector gathers views on a range of issues. No staff who have day-to-day responsibility for the school may attend. No governors may attend. The registered inspector may be monitored by the attendance of an HMI.

Inspections by Inspectors of Schools

Under section 12 of the 1996 Act, where HCMI is satisfied that it is not reasonably practicable to secure that the school is inspected by a suitable registered inspector, the inspection may be carried out by a member of the Inspectorate.

The inspection "Framework"

Ofsted has revised the inspection Framework and the *Handbook for the Inspection of Schools*. Further guidance on the use of the Framework was anticipated by section 2(3)(b) of the 1992 Act. Both the Framework and the Handbook were revised during 1995 and had to be adopted with effect from the summer term 1996. The aim of revisions to the Framework were said to be to:

- make the inspection process more manageable for schools and inspectors;
- make the Framework more applicable to nursery, special and primary schools;
- improve judgements on the quality of education provided by schools and on the achievements of pupils; and
- ensure that attention is paid to the school's own evaluation of its strengths and weaknesses.

Three separate versions of the Handbook have now been produced by Ofsted. They cover:

- nursery, primary and middle schools which are deemed to be primary;
- secondary schools and middle schools which are deemed to be secondary; and
- special schools.

The "Guidance on Inspection Requirements" in the Handbook sets out how inspection evidence is to be gathered by:

- review of documentary evidence;
- observation of lessons and other activities;
- talking with pupils;
- sampling pupils' work;
- discussion with the staff, the appropriate authority and others involved in the work of the school.

The Inspection Schedule sets out the structure of the inspection report. In the context of the characteristics of the school the team must consider the "Outcomes" of the school by looking at the educational standards achieved. This must be approached by looking at:

- attitudes, behaviour and personal development
- attainment and progress
- attendance.

Contributory factors which must be taken into account are grouped under two headings:

- Provision, including:
  - the curriculum and assessment
  - pupils' spiritual, moral, social and cultural development
  - teaching
  - support, guidance and pupils' welfare
  - partnership with parents and the community.
- Management, including:
  - staffing, accommodation and learning resources
  - leadership and management
  - the efficiency of the school.

Of particular interest to the education lawyer are those areas which involve consideration of some legal requirements. For example, under the heading of "support, guidance and pupils' welfare" arrangements for child protection should be considered, as should any health and safety matters. Health and safety is of interest, as it is conceded in the guidance that it is unlikely that there will be an expert on hand. Health and safety is not audited, but inspectors must report on what they see. The guidance states that "Controlling health and safety risks is an essential part of educational provision" (p 98 of the Handbook for secondary schools). Subject inspectors such as those in technology have a special responsibility to look at health and safety.

Other areas where "legal checks" are in effect carried out are:

- the implementation of the national curriculum
- the provision of religious education and collective worship (not in voluntary schools)
- statements on sex education
- equal opportunities
- special educational needs.

There are detailed references to legal requirements in relation to equal opportunities where it is required that inspectors should evaluate "how far the school complies with the relevant legislation, including the Education Act (1944), the Sex Discrimination Act (1975), the Race Relations Act (1976), the Education Act (1981), the Education Act (1986), the Children Act (1989), the Education Reform Act (1988) and subsequent case law." (p 112 of the Handbook for secondary schools). Similar requirements are mentioned in respect of statutory provision relating to special educational needs.

It remains to be seen how effective inspection teams can be in this regard without lawyers as a part of the team, although as mentioned above some lay members of teams were acknowledged to come from the legal profession and the police.

There is no requirement to inform the authorities of any breaches of the law unless they relate to the welfare of any pupil, but references to alleged breaches of the civil and criminal law in the report and any summary could have profound effects for the school and the LEA or other authority. Many teachers are opposed to the system of inspections; however, it remains an offence to wilfully obstruct inspections and inspectors have a right of entry and a power to inspect documents under sections 2(8) and 3(3) of the 1996 Act.

Post-inspection procedure

Under section 15 of the 1996 Act the total period allowed for the inspection and the preparation of the report shall not exceed three months.

The registered inspector discusses the findings of the team with the head teacher and members of the school's senior management team (i.e. heads of departments). The registered inspector then discusses the findings with the governing body at a special meeting. It is made clear to the governors that there will be no debate with them at this stage. The object is to share with them the outcomes of the inspection and to clarify matters through response to questions.

Previously, inspectors were to make it clear that the report's findings are not negotiable when arranging this meeting and that the judgements in the report would not be modified as a result. Under the new Framework, the emphasis is very much on the importance of feedback; however, ultimately judgements cannot be negotiated, although factual errors can be corrected.

The registered inspector then produces the report and a summary of the report is sent without delay to the Secretary of State and the appropriate authority for the school. Copies and a summary are sent to the Chief Inspector, the governors, the head teacher and those who appoint the foundation governors in a voluntary school. In the Framework documents the emphasis is on the clarity of the report, which should be in clear language not using "educational jargon".

The "appropriate authority" make arrangements for the parents of every registered pupil to be sent a copy of the summary report and for the report and summary to be seen by any member of the public who asks to see it. Photocopies should be made available subject to charging arrangements, although that charge should not exceed the cost of supply.

If the report indicates that "special measures" should be taken, then the appropriate authority should consider the report and draw up an action plan. Action plans should be finalised. Specific dates should be identified for action on each item. The plan could be a full development plan and include wider issues than those mentioned in the report; however, attention must be drawn to those items which are being considered as a result of the report.

The governors' annual report to parents must include a statement indicating the progress being made in implementing the action plan. The Deregulation (Provision of School Action Plans) Order 1997 (SI No 1142) reduced the burden on the appropriate authority to ensure that every parent had a copy of the action plan.

Religious education

Under Schedule 30 to SSFA 1998 (para 199), section 23 of the 1996 Act is amended. It is the duty of the governing body of any voluntary or foundation school which has been designated under section 69(3) of SSFA 1998 by the Secretary of State as having a religious character to secure that denominational education and the content of the school's collective worship are inspected. Inspections may be carried out by such persons as set out in section 23 of the 1996 Act, who need not be registered inspectors. The detail of reports including publication is set out in Schedule 4 to the 1996 Act.

Intervention in "failing schools"

Under the Education Act 1993, schools which were considered to be failing were made the subject of "Education Associations" appointed by the Secretary of State such as the Hackney Downs School which was ultimately closed.

In *R v Secretary of State for Education and Employment, ex parte Morris* [1996] ELR 198 a challenge was made to the decision to close the school. It was held that in the particular circumstances of that case the decision had not been unlawful.

Sections 14–19 of SSFA 1998 replace the regime for failing schools introduced by the Education Act 1993. Intervention in the running of schools which are to any extent failing may be taken in three circumstances:

- where the school is subject to a formal warning,
- where the school has serious weaknesses,
- where the school requires special measures.

A warning notice may be given where the LEA are satisfied that:

- the standards of performance of pupils at the school are unacceptably low and are likely to remain so unless the authority exercise their powers under either or both of sections 16 and 17, or
- there has been a serious breakdown in the way the school is managed or governed which is prejudicing, or is likely to prejudice, such standards of performance, or
- the safety of pupils or staff of the school is threatened, whether by a breakdown of discipline or otherwise.

In such circumstances the LEA may give a warning notice to the governing body of a maintained school and a copy of it to the head teacher. The governing body must previously have been warned of the matters complained of and have been given a reasonable opportunity to remedy them to the LEA's satisfaction. If the governing body fail to secure compliance with the notice, then notice may be given of the LEA's intention to exercise its powers under sections 16 and 17.

Action may also be taken where a report of an inspection of the school has been made under Part 1 of the School Inspections Act 1996 and the person making the report has stated in it that in his or her opinion the school has "serious weaknesses". Action may be taken, as under the previous legislation, where an inspection report has been made and the person making that report states that in his or her opinion special measures are required to be taken in respect of that school.

Under section 16, the LEA can appoint additional governors to the governing body. Under section 17, the LEA can suspend the right to a delegated budget. These powers are based on existing powers in the School Inspections Act 1996.

Two new powers are that the Secretary of State will be able to appoint additional governors under section 18 where the school requires special measures, and may nominate one of the additional governors to be the chairman. The Secretary of State has power to pay such governors. Under section 19, a school requiring special measures may be closed. This power replaces the use of education associations and references to such associations are now omitted by Schedule 30 to SSFA 1998 (para 200).

Under the Education Act 1993 and subsequent legislation, special measures can be taken in relation to certain schools where there is evidence of some or all of the following:

- low attainment and poor progress in the subjects of the curriculum by the majority of pupils
- regular disruptive behaviour, breakdown of discipline or high levels of exclusions
- significant levels of racial tension or harassment
- poor attendance or high levels of truancy
- unsatisfactory teaching
- failure to implement the national curriculum
- poor provision for pupils' spiritual, moral, social and cultural development
- pupils at physical or emotional risk from other pupils or adults in the school
- "abrasive and confrontational" relationships between staff and pupils
- ineffectiveness of senior managers, head teacher or governors
- loss of confidence in the head teacher by staff, parents or governors
- high levels of staff turnover, demoralisation of staff
- poor management and inefficient use of resources, including finance
- poor value for money.

See further Annex 1, Part 1 of The Framework in the *Ofsted Handbook for Secondary Schools 1995.*

Ofsted should be made aware of the need for special measures before the content of the report is made known to the school, although the head teacher may be informed orally. In the event of a pupil or pupils being seriously at risk, the head teacher and any other appropriate authority must be informed immediately. The form of words to be used in the report is given in the Handbook. A draft report must be sent to Ofsted; the judgment of HMCI will be awaited. HMI from Ofsted will consider the draft report and advise HMCI. If HMCI agrees that the school requires special measures, the registered inspector must include this in his or her report and again the appropriate form of words are given in the Handbook.

Under section 134 of SSFA 1998, reports of inspections may be published electronically. It is provided that such reports shall be treated as privileged for the purposes of the law of defamation unless the publication is shown to be made with malice.

Clearly the aim of the SSFA 1998 is to deal with failing schools without the necessity of waiting for an inspection report, although it seems likely that many interventions will be based on the outcome of Ofsted reports.

External complaints adjudicator

The appointment of an external complaints adjudicator was anticipated by the government in July 1997 in the White Paper, "Excellence in Schools". The Ofsted Complaints Ajudicator (OCA) acts as an impartial referee where individuals or institutions feel that Ofsted has handled their complaint poorly, treated them badly or where they consider that Ofsted's conclusions in the matter are unfair in the light of the relevant evidence. The service is free to the complainant. Written confirmation will be required from Ofsted that their complaints procedure has been exhausted before the OCA will look at a case. Certain matters are excluded from consideration, such as complaints from Ofsted staff, complaints from contractors about the award of contracts or matters which are before the courts or under consideration by the Parliamentary Commissioner for Administration (PCA). Complaints will be investigated rather than decisions reviewed; professional judgements cannot be altered but redress, in the form of recommendations, may include financial compensation. Those dissatisfied with a decision of the OCA may ask their MP to refer the case to the PCA.

Inspection of LEAs

Section 38 of the Education Act 1997 provides for the inspection of LEAs and sections 39–41 make further provision in relation to those inspections. The inspection is a review of the way in which the LEA are performing any function of theirs, of whatever nature, which relates to the provision of education for specified categories of schools. Inspectors have similar rights of entry and access to information as they do in the inspection of schools. Details relating to the publication of reports and action plans are set out in the Education (Publication of Local Education Authority Inspection Reports) Regulations 1998 (SI No 880).

Section 8 of SSFA 1998 has introduced a new power in the form of a new section 497A of the Education Act 1996, section 497 having repealed section 99 Education Act 1944. Section 497A applies to any function of an LEA which relates to the provision of education for children of compulsory school age or for persons above or below that age who are registered as pupils at schools maintained by the LEA. The power in section 497A is exercisable only where the Secretary of State is satisfied that the LEA are failing in any respect to perform any function to which this section applies to an adequate standard (or at all). Section 477A(3) empowers the Secretary of State to direct an LEA officer to secure that any function to which the section applies is performed in such a way as to achieve such objectives as are set out in the direction. Such directions may be carried out on behalf of the LEA by the person specified at the LEA's expense and directions to perform other functions may be given if the Secretary of State considers it expedient. Under section 497A(4), a person specified in a direction will have the same powers of entry and inspection as available under the School Inspections Act 1996 but in respect of the LEA's premises, documents and records.

Education action zones (EAZs)

Under sections 10–13 of SSFA 1998, the Secretary of State is empowered by order, where he or she considers it expedient to do so, with a view to improving standards in the provision of education at any particular maintained schools, to provide for those schools to constitute collectively an education action zone (EAZ). No order will be capable of being made unless the governing body of the schools consent. Under section 11 an Education Action Forum may be created by the Secretary of State, which will be a body corporate. One person appointed by each of the governing bodies of the participating schools will be a member of the Forum unless a school chooses not to make such an appointment. One or two persons will be appointed by the Secretary of State. An Education Action Forum shall have as its main object "the improvement of standards in the provision of education at each of the participating schools". The Forum will be able to discharged any "prescribed" function of the governing body. A pay and conditions order under the School Teachers' Pay and Conditions Act 1991 may be disapplied in relation to a school which is a member of an EAZ. The national curriculum may be varied in such zones and there is likely to be experiment with the length of the school day and school holidays. Although schools in an EAZ need not be failing as such, the first 25 zones are in areas of low educational performance. Most will be led by LEAs, but several will be led by businesses. Each zone has to attract private sponsorship of £250,000 with the government providing an extra £750,000 a year. Most of the sponsorship will be in the form of services or equipment. See further Chapter 10 on funding EAZs.

Beacon schools

It is intended that schools which perform well in inspections will attract additional funding of up to £50,000 per year to pass on their methods to other schools and teachers.

Nursery schools

Section 10 of the 1996 Act listed schools to be covered by the Act and nursery schools maintained by the LEA were included in that list. The SSFA 1998 sets out detailed provision for the inspection of nursery schools in section 122 and Schedule 26. A separate system of inspections and registration of nursery education inspectors exists. Schedule 28 to SSFA 1998 also makes amendments to the 1996 Act in respect of nursery education. Ofsted updated the relevant Handbook on the inspection of nursery education (also covering the private, voluntary and independent sectors) in 1998. An interesting case on the registration and inspection of nursery provision is that of *Windrush Microsystems (trading as Rainbow Daycare and Nursery School)* v *Norfolk County Council* (1998, unreported). Details of the case are available through ELAS.

Independent schools

Until 1979, independent schools could describe themselves as 'recognised as efficient by the Department of Education'. When that system was abolished, independent schools associations developed their own inspection systems and the creation of Ofsted provided the impetus for further review of those systems.

Ofsted produced two documents relating to the inspection of independent schools. One set out HMI procedures for the inspection of independent schools for two different purposes: first, registration (and re-registration), and secondly, the school or an aspect of its work. The second document sets out the structure of an inspection which is similar to that set out in the Framework for the inspection of other schools. See further "Inspecting Independent Schools: HMI Methods and Procedures". October 1993 and "Inspecting Independent Schools, A Framework", September 1994.

A number of bodies have had the power to inspect independent schools, including Ofsted, the Independent Schools Council (ISC) and the Headmasters' and Headmistresses' Conference (HMC). In 1995, ISC and HMC asked Ofsted to examine their inspection systems and to make recommendations.

The result is that these inspections will merge and take on the characteristics of Ofsted inspections, and from 2000 independent schools will be inspected according to the same criteria as Ofsted inspections with a six-yearly cycle and compulsory publication of reports. Financial and manpower restrictions have made it difficult for Ofsted to routinely inspect independent schools and it seems likely that Ofsted will delegate its role not only in inspections, but also in re-registration visits.

Local authority inspection services

Ofsted inspections originally did not offer advice as such, so LEAs retained their advisory services, although they were compelled to put those services on a semi-independent "agency" footing from 1992. Under section 14 of the 1992 Act, LEAs could maintain inspection services to obtain information about schools maintained by themselves if it was not reasonably practicable to obtain the information in any other way. Ofsted has subsequently announced that it will act as an advisory service for LEAs, the DfEE, the TTA and the QCA as part of its extended remit.

Under section 24 of the 1996 Act, any LEA may provide a school inspection service for the schools within their area. Such a service may extend to schools which are not maintained by them.

Teacher training institutions

Under the Education Act 1994, it was a condition which could be imposed on funding that teacher training institutions should allow for inspection conducted by Ofsted. Some of these inspections have proved controversial and legal action has been threatened. The funding implications of a poor Ofsted report are considerable. One difficulty in bringing legal action subsequent to an inspection is the case of R v *Higher Education Funding Council, ex parte Institute of Dental Surgery* [1994] 1 All ER 651 and the principles of "academic peer review". The introduction of the external complaints adjudicator may have prevented legal action in the short term, with the outstanding disputes being dealt with under the complaints system. Section 20 of THEA 1998 amends the Education Act 1994 and relevant parts of the School Inspections Act 1996 with respect to inspections of teacher training institutions.

Chapter 12

Freedom of Speech and Information

Freedom of Speech and Information

Defamation

Defamation is an area of law which is of increasing importance to those in the teaching profession, not least of all because of the high profile that education has been given by the major political parties. Teachers, especially those in senior management, may well be called upon to make statements about important and contentious matters such as school admissions and transport provision to the media. Such statements should be made with the utmost care. Similarly, statements made within the confines of the school (i.e. to parents, governors and pupils) are subject to the requirement of care. It is often head teachers who seem to bear the most responsibility for care and accuracy in the making of statements. The general law of defamation applies; there are no rules which are education-specific. The dearth of recent cases probably has more to do with the high cost of bringing actions in defamation rather than the probity of the teaching profession and others. The Defamation Act 1996 made some amendments to both procedural and substantive aspects of the law.

The basics are still very important. Defamation is a tort which protects a person from untrue imputations which harms his or her reputation in the eyes of others. Untrue statements which do not cause harm may be injurious or malicious falsehoods. The classic definition of defamation in *Sim v Stretch* [1936] 2 All ER 1237 is that defamation "consists of the publication of material which reflects on a person's reputation so as to lower the plaintiff in the estimation of right-thinking members of society generally". Another part of the test is that the defamatory statement would tend to cause the plaintiff to be shunned or avoided (see *Youssoupoff v Metro-Goldwyn-Mayer Pictures Ltd* [1934] 50 TLR 581). It is no defence to an action that there was no intention to defame. There are two important matters to be further considered in any case: whether there has been publication and the capacity to sue the defendant.

Publication

The defamatory matter must be communicated to some person other than the plaintiff (or claimant under the CPR). It is not enough that the plaintiff feels insulted by what is said or written: it must have the potential to affect the reputation of the plaintiff in the eyes of others. In school, a statement made in front of a class of pupils has the potential to be defamatory, whereas a statement made to a pupil on his or her own does not. Care must be taken, therefore, to see that defamatory remarks if they are made are not published. There are difficulties where conversations are overheard. Generally the rule is that where publication could have been reasonably anticipated there can be liability, for example where a teacher is called in to see the head alone but the door is left open or where a letter is sent which may be opened by a third party (e.g. a secretary). In such a case if the letter is marked "Private and Confidential" the opening of it by a third party would probably be regarded as an unauthorised act and publication would be deemed not to have taken place. A letter which is dictated to a secretary is regarded as privileged, and as long as there was no malice in the statement no publication will have taken place (*Bryanston Finance Co Ltd* v *de Vries* [1975] QB 703).

Each separate publication gives rise to a new cause of action.

Capacity to sue

Statements made about a class of persons cannot usually lead to an action, so that an allegation that all teachers were incompetent would not be actionable. If the statement referred to a small, identifiable group, such as teachers in a particular school, then each teacher might be able to bring a separate action.

In *Derbyshire County Council* v *Times Newspapers* [1993] AC 534, it was held by the House of Lords that it would be contrary to the public interest to allow democratically elected public bodies to sue in defamation. Such bodies should be open to "uninhibited public criticism ... the threat of civil actions for defamation would place an undesirable fetter on the freedom of speech ...". The position of central government departments was also considered, it being acknowledged that this was an area where private citizens had greater rights than public institutions.

Types of defamation and defences

Libel

Libel is a statement in a permanent form. It includes printed or written statements, words daubed on a wall, spoken words in a play, film, television or radio programme, and can include representations by way of effigy or statue. Libel is actionable *per se* without any proof of damage.

In *Gillick* v *British Broadcasting Corporation* [1995] *The Times*, 20 October, a case arose concerning the campaigner, Victoria Gillick. In a television discussion concerning, *inter alia,* a previous court case involving Mrs Gillick and her concerns about contraceptive advice and sex education generally (see below) words were used which (the Court of Appeal held) suggested that Mrs Gillick was morally responsible for the deaths of two young girls. The Court of Appeal was satisfied that the words used would have been likely to affect Mrs Gillick "adversely in the estimation of reasonable persons generally". Neill LJ summarised the relevant principles; of particular interest are his comments on the nature of "reasonable persons":

> The hypothetical reader or viewer was not naive but he was not unduly suspicious. He could read between the lines. He could read in an implication more readily than a lawyer and might indulge in a certain amount of loose thinking. But he must be treated as a man who was not avid for scandal and someone who did not, and should not, select one bad meaning where other non-defamatory meanings were available.

It is generally agreed that electronically stored information can form the basis of an action in libel because of the degree of permanence involved in storing information in computer memories or the printing of such information. Some change in the law is likely to be prompted by the use of the Internet.

As yet this area of the law is essentially unregulated and, with the increasing use of the Internet and the sending of information by E-mail in particular, many academic institutions are already experiencing difficulties. Some schools and universities have felt it necessary to prevent access to some information available on the Internet. In 1998, the Association of Teachers and Lecturers expressed fears in the light of government policy to ensure that all schools are linked to the Internet as part of the "national grid for learning" initiative. Andrew Charlesworth, in "Code makers on the ether enigma" *The Times Higher Education Supplement,* 10 November 1995 said:

> The simple fact is that in electronic publishing there are myriad pieces of British legislation which must be taken into account, including those

concerning liability for content of publications, covering such topics as defamation, obscenity, blasphemy and provisions with regard to sex discrimination and advertising standards.

Slander

Slander is a statement in a transitory form, for example word of mouth or even a gesture. It is only actionable *per se* in limited circumstances, i.e. where there is imputation:

- of a criminal offence punishable by imprisonment, e.g. to call a pupil a thief (see *Ormiston* v *Great Western Railway* [1917] 1 KB 598)
- of some contagious or infectious disease including sexually transmitted diseases
- that a girl or woman is 'unchaste'
- of unfitness or incompetence in the plaintiff's work.

Section 2 of the Defamation Act 1952 provides that:

> In any action for slander in respect of words calculated to disparage the plaintiff in any office, profession, calling, trade or business held or carried on by him at the time of publication, it shall not be necessary to allege or prove special damage whether or not the words are spoken of the plaintiff in the way of his office, profession, calling, trade or business.

In *Jones* v *Jones* [1916] 2 AC 481, a headmaster claimed that he had been slandered by allegations of adultery. No special damage had been suffered and it was found that the words were not spoken of him "in the way of his calling". His action failed. Since the amendment to the common law by section 2, it may be easier to show that imputations relating to a teacher's personal life are calculated to disparage him in the way of his calling. Vulgar abuse which is intended as "mere insult" is not defamatory (*Parkins* v *Scott* [1862] 1 H & C153).

Defences

There are numerous defences available in defamation actions.

Truth

It is not necessary to prove literal truth but that the substance of a statement is true.

Fair comment on a matter of public interest

The defendant must prove that the statements were honest, based on facts that were true and there must be no malice. They must be in the form of an opinion rather than statements of fact.

There appear to have been some problems in some LEAs connected with balloting of parents with regard to change of status. A case mentioned in *The Times Educational Supplement*, 10 November 1995 told of a Birmingham-based head teacher who had successfully sued for libel and had received an undisclosed sum in the High Court. The action was brought against the city council and a former vice-chair of education. The vice-chair had written to parents on council notepaper at the time of a ballot alleging the head had let student numbers fall and that there had been wastage of money by mismanagement. One factor which seems to have influenced the decision was the nature of the attack on the head teacher, who is reported to have said:

> It is true to say at the time Birmingham attacked quite bitterly any attempt to opt out of local authority control. But I was the only head teacher who came under personal attack.

Consent
In the school context this may involve giving permission to say or do something in the school magazine or school play, for example.

Privilege
Absolute privilege only applies to certain documents and statements in court proceedings. Teachers may have to give evidence in court cases and as such these statements would be privileged.

Qualified privilege covers reports made in the execution of public or private duty provided that they have been made without malice and with an honest belief in their truth. The defence could be used in cases concerning reports on teachers, statements in testimonials or references, reports on children, reports given to courts and in any circumstances where there is a duty to impart information (see below).

Section 134 of the SSFA amended the School Inspections Act 1996 by inserting a specific reference to the defence in relation to Ofsted reports, as there were concerns about the naming of individual teachers in those reports. The section now provides that "For the purposes of the law of defamation any report published by the Chief Inspector ... shall be privileged unless the publication is shown to be made with malice". The section also provides for publication by electronic means.

The defence could also be used by parents if they were making complaint about the implementation of the national curriculum and in the writing of letters to the LEA or head, for example, as long as the report etc. has been written in good faith there will be no action even if there is false statement which could be defamatory. Malice can be evidenced not only by personal spite, but also for example, by the showing of the report to a wider audience than was strictly necessary.

In *Hume* v *Marshall* [1877] 37 LT 711, letters to the headmaster and the governors concerning the drunkenness of the plaintiff, an assistant master at the school, were held to be made in good faith and without malice. They were therefore privileged.

In *Ripper* v *Rate* [1919] *The Times*, 17 January, the letters of the defendant to the Surrey Education Committee alleging cruelty by a headmaster were held to be privileged and there was no evidence of malice. The headmaster's action therefore failed. A similar case was decided in the House of Lords (see *Reeve* v *Widderson* [1929] *The Times*, 24 April). However, in *Goslett* v *Garment* [1897] 13 TLR 391 bona fide statements made about a former teacher were held not be privileged as he had left the school and the head was under no duty to make any comments.

Offer of amends

This is where the defendant offers to publish a correction or apology and takes steps to retrieve copies of the offending statement. This defence is only available in certain limited circumstances (e.g. where there has been an "innocent" publication of words which might be defamatory).

Unintentional publication

Under the 1996 Defamation Act, a defendant who was not the author, editor or publisher, who took reasonable care and who had no reason to know or believe that he or she was contributing to the publication of a defamatory statement can use the defence of unintentional publication.

References

The position with regard to references was given special attention in *Spring* v *Guardian Assurance plc* [1995] 2 AC 296 where the House of Lords considered the duty of care owed by employers to employees in the writing of references (see also Chapter 9). In that case Mr Spring had brought an action in malicious falsehood, breach of contract and negligence when an unsatisfactory reference was written about him which effectively brought to an end his career in insurance. The writer of the reference believed in the truth of certain allegations made in the reference, but failed to investigate the truth or otherwise of those allegations. The action in malicious falsehood failed and there was found to be no malice. Similarly the action in contract failed.

The House of Lords considered the reference to be defamatory but stated that there would have been a defence of qualified privilege if a defamation action had been brought. Such a defence could only have been defeated by the existence of malice, which could not be proved. In the circumstances, the only cause of action which remained was in negligence and there was found to be a duty of care under the principles of negligent mis-statement as set out in *Hedley Byrne* v *Heller* [1964] AC 465. An employer who provided a reference to a prospective employer of an employee would owe a duty of care in its preparation.

It is possible not to provide a reference at all, but merely certify employment details in appropriate cases. The *Spring* case does leave open certain questions, for example whether a former employee is owed the same duty of care, whether any person providing a reference owes the duty of care and whether future employers may sue on the basis of "glowing" references which prove to be unfounded.

Although teaching is one of the professions in which a rehabilitated person must disclose spent convictions if asked to do so, under the Rehabilitation of Offenders Act 1974 a writer of references need not disclose spent convictions, even if asked to do so. If he does so disclose the information, it must be factually correct.

Schools also prepare references in respect of pupils and, although these will be subject to the general law on defamation, much may depend on whether pupils ever see their references. The implementation of the Data Protection Act 1998 (see below) will mean that pupils may have a right to see these references.

Copyright and data protection

The Copyright, Designs and Patents Act 1988 now sets out the law relating to copyright, the right to which is automatic and does not have to be registered. Copyright is normally vested in a qualified person under the Act and is based on the protection of original material in a recorded form. Where, however, work is produced by an employee in the course of his or her employment, the copyright will belong to the employer unless there is some prior agreement to the contrary. Anyone who is not the owner of copyright must obtain prior approval before copying material or giving a public performance of protected material.

Under the Copyright Act 1911, work was protected for 50 years after the author's death. This period, known as the PMA (*post mortem auctoris*), was extended with effect from 1 July 1995 by an EEC directive.

There are some concessions to users, for example where the material is copied for research or private study. These concessions are based on the defence of "fair dealing" (see below). Copying by means of a reprographic process is restricted under sections 32 and 36 of the 1988 Act, although limited multiple copies can be made. Examination boards retain copyright in examination papers, although it may be possible to reproduce questions for examination purposes. Copyright licences may be issued by the Copyright Licensing Agency (CLA) which covers, for example, off-air recording of certain educational programmes, Ordnance Survey maps and public performances of certain pieces of music and other sound recordings. Agreements between local authorities and the CLA allow for copies to be made from books and journals.

In *British Broadcasting Corporation* v *British Satellite Broadcasting Ltd* [1991] *The Times*, 22 January it was held that since the 1988 Act the monopoly in broadcast material had been eroded by allowing the use of broadcast material subject to the defence of fair dealing and an accompanying acknowledgement. It was reported that "the CLA has succeeded in making education at all levels pay for their volumes of copyright photocopying" (*The Times*, 9 June 1994).

It was reported in 1993 that an investigator on behalf of the CLA had enrolled for a course at a college to prove that the college was illegally photocopying material and incorporating that material into course notes. The chief executive of the CLA said in *The Guardian*, 16 March 1993:

> Making unauthorised copies of copyright works is much like any form of theft ... Universities and colleges that make copies and fail to take out a licence are indicating their indifference to honouring either the intellectual property rights of their own staff or the rights of other academic establishments.

Universities and colleges appear to be having continuing problems with respect to copyright.

Under the Data Protection Act 1984, schools should be registered with the Data Protection Registrar as data users. The Act protects information kept on computer, but information which is stored for a short period is exempt. It has always been considered that pupil references were exempt from the Act because they are usually stored electronically for less than two months. They are then printed out and may be computerised again if needed later in the admissions process. Under the Data Protection Act 1998, amendments required to implement the Data Protection Directive are likely to take effect in 1999. Rights of access will be extended to manual records. References will therefore no longer be confidential and university admissions officers fear that references will become anodyne. Under section 30(2) of the 1998 Act, it is possible for regulations to be made exempting health, social service and education records from some of the requirements of the Act.

The data recorded must be accurate and disclosed only for certain purposes. A case on the "usc" of data under the Act is *R* v *Brown (Gregory)* [1996] 1 AC 543.

Individual pupil information

Section 22 of the Education Reform Act 1988 sets out the right of parents to receive reports on their child's progress and assessment. The Education (School Records) Regulations 1989 (SI No 1261) provided for parents (and pupils in certain circumstances) to see the pupil's curricular record. They may point out any inaccuracies in writing and the governing body must then either amend the record or leave the document intact and append the comments. Certain information is exempt from disclosure under the Regulations, such as references for further and higher education, statements of any special educational needs and statements in any court proceedings. Detailed provision is made by way of other regulations in respect of information relating to individual pupils; see for example the Education (Individual Pupils' Achievements) (Information) (Amendment) Regulations 1997 (SI No 1368) and 1998 (SI No 877)). These, together with Circulars 1/97 (primary schools) and 2/97 (secondary schools), set out what is to be included in the report to parents provided for, *inter alia,* by the Parent's Charter. The report must be sent to parents at least once a year. Reports should also be prepared at the end of the pupil's school career and if there is a change of school. The report must include information about:

- national curriculum tests at ages 7, 11 and 14 together with a comparison with national test results
- results in any public examinations
- achievements in any other subjects

- general progress and attendance record
- a contact person and information about making an appointment to go into the school to discuss the report.

The SSFA 1998 amends the Education Act 1996 and inserts section 537A, which allows for individual pupil information to be collated and published without reference to the pupil's name, see also the Education (Individual Performance Information) (Identification of Individual Pupils) Regulations 1998 (SI No 1834).

General school information

Information provided to government

Under the Education (School Performance Information) (England) Regulations 1996 (SI No 2577), head teachers and governing bodies were obliged to provide the Secretary of State with information about the results of statutory national curriculum assessments. The Regulations were amended by the Education (School Performance Information) (Amendment) Regulations 1997 (SI No 2060) to include information on GNVQ results.

The Education (School Performance Information) Regulations 1998 (SI No 1929) and the Education (School Performance Information) (England) (Amendment) Regulations 1998 (SI No 3260) ... make further provision for information to be provided to the Secretary of State via LEAs (in the case of maintained schools) in a prescribed format.

In November 1992, information comparing the examination results of all local schools, including grant-maintained schools, CTCs and some independent schools, was published in every area of England. Since 1993, all independent schools and colleges in the new further education sector were included. Circular 15/96 set out the information to be included in the first primary school performance tables to be published in March 1997. The information contained in the so-called "league tables" includes:

- examination results, including success in vocational examinations as well as GCSE and A Level
- information about the school
- truancy, including national averages.

There have been allegations that schools have manipulated their ranking by, for example, removing truants and disruptive children so that they do not feature in the overall picture.

Work has been undertaken by the DfEE to determine how the tables might reflect the "value-added" element in schools. Many schools criticised their "rating" on the basis that the tables did not adequately reflect the lack of resources, catchment area etc. The new value-added methods have been criticised as statistically flawed and part of the new system was abandoned by the DfEE in late 1998.

Information to parents

School prospectuses

Under the Education (School Information) Regulations 1998 (SI No 2526), the information which is to be contained in the school prospectus is set out. This information must include:

- the names of the head and the chair of governors and information on how to contact them
- the classification of the school
- admissions information
- arrangements for visits
- provision for special educational needs
- ethos and values of the school
- religious affiliations, if any
- attainments of pupils and destinations of pupils
- a summary of absences.

Circulars 7/98 (primary schools) and 8/98 (secondary schools) deal further with the content of school prospectuses.

Admissions

As part of the admissions process parents will need to make informed decisions when applying for a school place for their children. The published admissions criteria must therefore be clear, fair and objective (see further Circular 12/98). This is especially important in the light of the *R v Greenwich London Borough Council, ex parte Governors of John Ball Primary School* [1990] 88 LGR 589, which provided for the equal treatment of parents applying for places from inside and beyond the LEA boundary, and *R v Rotherham Metropolitan Borough Council, ex parte Clark* [1998] 96 LGR 214, in which it was held that arrangements must be in place for all parents to express a preference if they wished to do so. Publication of information about admissions is required by section 92 of SSFA 1998. Every autumn the DfEE collects data from all admissions authorities about admission appeals lodged, the number withdrawn, the number settled before going to appeal and the number heard and their outcomes. The draft Freedom of Information Bill proposes to allow parents access to detailed information about admissions, e.g. why a child was refused admission. This information, although unlikely to be free, will assist parents in the preparation of admission appeals.

Meetings with parents

Under section 43 of SSFA 1998, each maintained school must hold an annual parents' meeting to provide an opportunity for discussion of:

- the governors' report
- the discharge of the head teacher, governing body and LEA's functions in relation to the school
- the aims and values of the school
- how the spiritual, moral, cultural, mental and physical development of pupils is to be promoted at the school
- how pupils are to be prepared for adult life
- standards of educational achievement
- how discipline, behaviour and well-being of the pupils is to be promoted.

The police and other authorities

The police may not enter school premises without invitation, except in relation to the possession of offensive weapons, although they may enter under a warrant. Confidential records kept by schools fall within the category of excluded material under the Police and Criminal Evidence Act 1984 and are exempt from compulsory disclosure during searches for evidence. Children may be interviewed by the police on school premises under the provisions of the Code of Practice on the 1984 Act. A responsible adult must be present. The police must be informed if the school is aware of controlled drugs on the school premises, either for use or supply.

Staff may also be interviewed. In *DPP v G* [1997] *The Times*, 24 November, it was held that a head teacher was not a person "charged with the duty of investigating offences or charging offenders" under section 67(9) of the 1984 Act. Consequently, when the head interviewed a teacher about an alleged assault on a pupil, the head was not required to administer a caution before questioning.

Particular care should be taken in investigating circumstances which may lead to permanent exclusion (see further Chapter 5). Care should be taken when alleging the commission of a criminal offence when excluding a pupil. In *R v Cardinal Newman's School, Birmingham, ex parte S* [1998] COD 283 the dangers inherent in identification evidence in an exclusion appeal were emphasised. in *R v London Borough of Camden and the Governors of the Hampstead School, ex parte H* [1996] ELR 360, it was held that the governors had to make "reasonably thorough and balanced" enquiries into the incident that led to the head teacher's decision to permanently exclude a pupil.

Schools may be asked to prepare a report for court. As mentioned above, such reports are covered by qualified privilege. Parents may see the contents of such reports. Care should be taken in giving evidence in court; the law relating to contempt applies generally. In *R v Derbyshire County Council, ex parte The Times Supplements Ltd* [1991] COD 129 it was found that the council had deliberately tried to mislead the court as to the true reasons for decisions made by its education committee. The court found that the council had acted vindictively or in bad faith in its dealings relating to certain newspaper advertisements and that they had failed to give any 'educational reasons' for their decisions.

In *R v Higgins* [1996] 1 FLR 137, it was held that where a defendant in a criminal trial sought access to the school records of a witness the local authority was under a duty to claim public interest immunity. It would then be a matter for the trial judge to conduct a balancing exercise to ascertain whether the public interest in keeping such information confidential outweighed the public interest in seeing that justice be done.

There was some concern that schools might find themselves in a difficult position following the implementation of the Asylum and Immigration Act 1996, which requires employers to check the immigration status of prospective employees. Teachers' associations announced that they were not prepared to supply immigration information. A spokesperson was reported in *The Times Educational Supplement*, 10 November 1995 as saying:

> It's clearly not desirable for schools to act as immigration officers. The information a person is required to give to enrol in a school has no bearing on immigration status; the only checking that schools and local authorities are required to do is to check that the child is living in the correct catchment area.

Information relating to child protection, especially in the light of any abuse, must be reported to the head teacher under the guidance in DES Circular 4/88, as amended.

Schools are required as a matter of course to submit various returns to the LEA, the Secretary of State and Registered Inspectors of Ofsted. Inter-agency information is often required, for example in relation to child protection, and the government announced plans in 1998 to increase this inter-agency involvement. Care must be taken in identifying those thought to pose a threat to young children. In *S* v *Newham London Borough Council* [1998] *The Times*, 5 March, it was held that a local authority was not immune from an action in defamation in respect of information which identified a social worker as such a person. Similarly, care must be taken in the sharing of such information. In *Re V (Minors) (Sexual abuse: Disclosure)* [1998] *The Times*, 9 October, it was held that there was no general duty on local authorities to inform others of the identity of those found guilty of child abuse in care or other family proceedings. This duty in relation to schools must be balanced against the duties imposed by "List 99" and other child protection procedures (see further Chapter 9).

Sex education

Sex education is part of the basic curriculum under the Education Act 1996. Effectively the subject has become compulsory for those receiving secondary education. Parents can withdraw pupils from sex education unless it is being received as part of the national curriculum.

The Education (School Information) Regulations 1994 (SI No 1412) stated that the governors must give information about the manner and context of sex education. DFE Circular 5/94 set out how sex education might be approached, including the introduction of topics such as HIV and AIDS. Age and maturity of the pupils are key factors in the content of sex education. The circular warns teachers not to trespass on the rights and responsibilities of parents. Care must be taken in giving contraceptive information or advice on abortion, for example. In *Gillick* v *West Norfolk and Wisbech Area Health Authority* [1985] AC 112, Mrs Gillick challenged the rights of general practitioners to give under-age girls contraceptive advice. Giving such advice without parental consent may cause difficulties in a school situation.

References to homosexuality may be affected by section 28 of the Local Government Act 1988, which forbids local authorities from promoting the teaching in any maintained school the acceptability of homosexuality as part of a family relationship. Care must be taken not to offend or to encourage experimentation.

Political education

The Education Act 1996 forbids any political bias in the curriculum. Where politics are discussed, either within the school or as part of extra curricular activities, a balanced view must be taken. The national curriculum guidance documents suggest that politics should be part of the cross-curricular themes, particularly on citizenship where it is necessary to look at "democracy in action". The duties of the governing body under the SSFA now include a reference to "citizenship" and the preparation of pupils for the adult world.

Religious education and worship

The ERA 1988 stated that the act of collective worship should be "wholly or mainly of a broadly Christian character". In voluntary schools the character of such worship is to be determined by governing bodies. Not all acts of worship have to be broadly Christian in character, as long as most of them are. This would appear to be a pragmatic view based on the recognition that there might be problems in multi-ethnic schools. Parents can withdraw pupils from this type of collective worship and this would allow for participation in another type of worship. The involvement of SACRE in the formulation of local syllabuses allows for local needs to be met (see also *R* v *Secretary of State for Education, ex parte R and D* [1994] ELR 495). The Human Rights Act 1998 enshrines the European Convention on Human Rights into UK law, although it will not be implemented until 2000 or later. Part of the Act protects the right to education in conformity with parents' religious and philosophical convictions.

Discrimination

The governing body and/or the LEA have responsibility to ensure that there is equality of opportunity, which means in effect that they must guard against sex and race discrimination as set out under the provisions of the Sex Discrimination Act 1975 and the Race Relations Act 1976. Disability statements have to be prepared by LEAs (see the Education (Disability Statements for Local Education Authorities) (England) Regulations 1997 (SI No 1625). Circular 3/97 also gives guidance on the implications of the Disability Discrimination Act 1995 for schools and LEAs in England.

Confidential information

In 1994, following a review of procedure, teachers were asked to inform head teachers if they became aware that under-age pupils were sexually active. The general secretary of the NASUWT, Nigel de Gruchy, said in *The Times,* 23 April 1994:

> If teachers are forced by law to report pupils to their parents it would destroy any relationship of trust. It is akin to a priest being forced to inform the police of things he has heard in the confessional.

The area of "confidences" is clearly a difficult one. Following the exchange referred to above, three teacher associations asked a QC for an Opinion. He considered that it is largely down to the individual teacher to decide whether to respect individual pupil confidences in the light of what is best for the child. This would be subject to any express statement from the head that he or she should be told of such matters, in which case the head should be informed. The head then has to decide, on the basis of his or her professional judgement, what should be done with that information.

Certain information, such as examination results, may be regarded as confidential until the official release date and time. In 1995 it was reported that a teacher had resigned as a high school's examination co-ordinator after pupils heard about their A Level results a day before the official release date. The leak of information was denounced as "totally unacceptable" by the headmaster and the governors (*The Times,* 23 August 1995).

Obscenity

In addition to concerns over the content of the Internet, as mentioned above, there may be problems with more traditional material such as books. A protracted police enquiry in 1997 was conducted into a library book held at a university which was allegedly pornographic. It was decided not to prosecute, but only after a lengthy campaign against the perceived "censorship" by a number of educational institutions across the world.

Chapter 13

Special Educational Needs

Special Educational Needs

The relevant legislation

Until the Education Act 1993 the legislation which applied to special educational needs was the Education Act 1981.

The 1981 Act was based, at least in part, on the recommendations of the Warnock Report 1978, *Special Educational Needs: Report of the Committee of Enquiry into the* Education of Handicapped Children and Young People (DES). In 1987 a House of Commons Select Committee concluded:

> that the lack of specific resources has restricted implementation of the 1981 Act. A commitment of extra resources is needed if significant further progress is to be made. *Special Educational Needs: Implementation of the Education Act 1981* (1987).

One commentator has noted that: "The plain fact was that, by 1990, the Education Act of 1981 was not perceived as working effectively." C. Dyer. 'The Code of Practice through LEA eyes', *British Journal of Special Education*, Vol 22 No 2 June 1995.'

The 1981 Act was replaced by the 1993 Act which was itself replaced by the 1996 Education Act. The law in this area remains constantly under review and further legislative reform is likely, a 1997 Green paper, *Excellence for all Children*, sets out specific proposals for further reform. Although many of the principles have remained the same throughout the legislation certain transitional provisions have caused problems.

In *R v Secretary of State for Education ex parte Skitt* [1995] COD 270, a dispute arose concerning transitional provisions relating to closure of schools. Another case concerning closure of a special needs schools was *R v Lambeth Borough Council, ex parte N,* [1996] ELR 299, although that concerned an alleged lack of consultation with parents. The emphasis on mainstream schooling for children with special educational needs anticipated by the Green Paper is likely to lead to more closures of special schools and some will become foundation special schools under the SSFA.

The introduction of the Special Educational Needs Tribunal has had an impact on case law, although many cases are now being dealt with initially at a local level the operation of the Tribunal and its decisions are generating reported cases mainly by way of judicial review, (see below and Chapter 3 generally).

The legislation is supplemented not only by regulations but also by a Code of Practice. The Code was required by section 157 of the 1993 Act which set out the purposes of the Code and the process of consultation of approval by Parliament. The Code was published by the DFE in May 1994 and came into effect on 1 September 1994: see further the Education (Special Educational Needs Code of Practice) (Appointed Day) Order 1994 (SI No 1414) and Circular 6/94, *The Organization of Special Education Provision*. Sections 313 and 314 of the 1996 Education Act provide for the Code and its revision under the most recent legislation.

Special educational needs

Under section 312 of the 1996 Act, a child has special educational needs if he or she has a 'learning difficulty' which calls for special educational provision to be made for him. Usually a child is one who has not attained the age of 19 and is a registered pupil at a school. The needs of children aged under 2 and from 2–5 are also considered by the Act. A child will have a learning difficulty if:

- he has significantly greater difficulty in learning than the majority of children of his age;
- he has a disability which prevents or hinders him from using educational facilities generally provided for pupils of his age within the area of the LEA; or
- he is under 5 years of age and is or is likely to fall into one of the above categories if special educational provision were not made for him.

It is estimated that one in five children will have a learning difficulty at some stage of their schooling. One in fifty will have a complex learning difficulty requiring special educational provision to be made through a statement to be drawn up by the LEA.

The nature of a 'learning difficulty' was considered in some detail in *R v Secretary of State, ex parte C* [1996] ELR 93, where it was held that "not every difficulty in learning was a learning difficulty". The child in this case had been able to overcome her learning difficulties and as a result it was decided that special educational provision was not needed. See page 230 below on gifted children and special educational needs.

There is also some overlap with disruptive pupil behaviour and the behaviour support plans anticipated by the SSFA are likely to address special educational needs and related issues. In relation to pupils with disabilities there may be some overlap with the provisions of the National Health Service and Community Care Act 1990 which requires general assessments of special needs (see *R* v *Berkshire County Council, ex parte P* [1997] BMLR 71).

It remains to be seen what a 'learning difficulty' is. Most LEAs have categories which qualify the term such as 'moderate' or 'severe'. *The Times Educational Supplement*, 3 November 1995 reported that many LEAs have already introduced tight new definitions of need to restrict the number of requests for statements. Requests rose from 153,000 in 1991 to 233,000 in 1998. The Green Paper aims to reduce the number of statements by a third. The Secretary of State for Education has called the present system for issuing statements 'bureaucratic and wasteful'.

It is important to distinguish between those cases which involve special educational needs and other types of case. The most confusing situation is possibly that illustrated by *R* v *East Sussex County Council, ex parte Tandy* [1998] 2 WLR 884. That case concerned 'special education provision' in relation to a 'sick' pupil. The pupil suffered from myalgic encephalomyelitis (ME) which meant that she found it difficult to attend school. The case, which went to the House of Lords, concerned the level of home tuition she could expect under the provisions of section 298, Education Act 1993 which was substantially re-enacted in section 19, Education Act 1996. Although the pupil in that case had been 'statemented' at an earlier stage at the time of the case there was no such statement of special educational needs in effect and as such whilst the case may well be about 'special education provision', it is not a case about 'special educational needs provision'.

Similarly, cases such as *Christmas* v *Hampshire County Council* [1998] ELR 1 and *Phelps* v *Hillingdon London Borough Council* [1999] 1 WLR 500 on duties of care (and breaches of such duties) lie outside the law on special educational needs even though the conditions which are the subjects of those cases, particularly dyslexia, may be the subject of a statement of special educational needs. The relationship between the 'negligence' cases and the special educational needs regime was considered in the composite appeals of *E* v *Dorset County Council and others*, [1995] 3 WLR 152, see further Chapter 7.

The Government announced in 1998 that dyslexia will be a priority for schools and extra funding has been made available to assist with 'early intervention'. The link between disruptive pupils and those with special educational needs (as mentioned above) is likely to become increasingly important with research into 'school phobia' and 'attention deficit disorder'. Some disruptive children may have special educational needs whereas others may not.

Statements

A statement sets out a description of the child's educational needs and the additional provision that must be made to meet those needs. LEAs, schools and parents are bound by the statement.

Identification and assessment

Under the legislation the responsibility is placed on LEAs to ensure that they identify those for whom they are responsible who have special educational needs. In practice this will usually involve initial identification by the school or the parents who will then inform the LEA. In *R v Hampshire County Council, ex parte W* [1994] *The Times*, 9 June it was held that a local authority may decide that a request from a parent for a statement of special educational needs was made unreasonably. In doing so the test to be applied by the authority was not the high standard of the public law test of unreasonableness but "was rather a straightforward factual test based on all the material before it."

Under section 329 of the 1996 Act the local authority must comply with a formal request from a parent if it considers that an assessment would be appropriate and no assessment had been carried out in the previous six months.

In *C v Lambeth London Borough Council*, [1999] *The Times*, 27 May it was held that a LEA could take into account the fact that a child's needs were being addressed by private education. As he was making good progress a statutory assessment was not justified.

A 'parent' in this context is defined in section 576, Education Act 1996 and may include a foster parent following the decision in *Fairpo v Humberside County Council* [1997] 1 All ER 183, although that decision related to rights of appeal.

In the Code of Practice the emphasis was placed on the school in accordance with the general principle of the early identification of special educational needs. The 1996 Act sets out a staged process of monitoring and assessment of children experiencing learning difficulties.

The first three stages focus on the work schools should do:

Stage 1: class or subject teachers identify or register a child's special educational needs and the school's special needs co-ordinator should take 'initial action'. It is thought that baseline assessment and the emphasis on literacy and numeracy should assist with the early identification of special educational needs.

Stage 2: The co-ordinator together with the teachers draw up an 'action plan' for the child as a result of information gathered.

Stage 3: The teachers may then be supported by specialists from outside the school and a new action plan will be drawn up.

At *Stage 4* the LEA become involved, carrying out assessments which may be multi-disciplinary in nature and then, only at *Stage 5* will the LEA consider a need for a statement which, if made, will be monitored and reviewed.

Schedule 26 of the 1996 Act sets out the notice procedure. The notice must be served on the parents and certain other persons including the head teacher of his school. Information should be given about the procedure of the assessment, the parents' rights to make representations and the person who can be contacted at the LEA. The LEA must then give notice in writing of its decision whether or not to assess the child, in most cases giving reasons. This should be done within six weeks of the notice being served.

Failure to identify special educational needs may lead to an action in negligence as in *Phelps* v *London Borough of Hillingdon* (above) where a pupil's dyslexia remained undiagnosed. Although the pupil was referred to a psychologist the matter was not taken further and the statementing process was not undertaken. On appeal it was held that no duty was owed by the psychologist to individual pupils in negligence.

The type of assessment

Although parents could request an assessment they could not dictate the type of assessment considered appropriate by them or believed to be in the child's best interests. In *R* v *Surrey County Council, ex parte G and H* [1995] COD 50 the children had been seen at the Dyslexia Institute and it had been recommended to the parents that they should make a request to the local authority that the children be assessed as the children had exhibited some features of dyslexia. The Council refused the request on the basis that the children were not suffering from sufficiently serious or significant problems to warrant a full assessment. It was held that the parents could not dictate the nature and scope of the assessment. The authority were only under a duty to make an assessment where they thought or had reason to believe that the child had special educational needs.

However, the duty was a continuing one and either on the basis of its own judgement or on the basis of further evidence the authority could make a full assessment.

However, the Education (Special Educational Needs) Regulations 1994 (SI No 1047) made further provision in respect of 'advice' which should be sought when making an assessment. This includes the wishes of the parent and the child. Written advice should be sought from 'experts' though there are likely to be some disputes about disclosure, see below.

The assessment must be carried out within the prescribed period, i.e 10 weeks from the service of the notice unless it is impracticable to do so.

Making the statement

In R v *Isle of Wight County Council, ex parte RS and AS* [1993] 1 FLR 634, it was held that having made a draft statement of special educational needs a local authority was not obliged to go on to make a final statement. A local education authority could make the decision not to make and maintain a statement of special educational needs up to the time of issue of the final statement.

In *R v Secretary of State for Education and Science, ex parte E* [1992] FLR 377 it was held that where a statement was made each of the learning difficulties specified had to be provided for. E had difficulty with literacy and numeracy skills. The numeracy difficulties had been included in the statement but no special educational needs provision was made for them. The Council argued that they were included in the statement merely to make it comprehensive. Nolan J. considered that:

> The case could not be dismissed on the basis that the local education authority expressed themselves badly or made a mistake in filling in the form. The statement was no ordinary form.

The judge's decision was upheld in the Court of Appeal where Balcombe LJ thought that an analogy made by the judge to a medical diagnosis and a prescription, with reference to the statement of special educational needs and subsequent provision was 'entirely apt'.

The format of the statement was set out in the 1994 Regulations.

There are now six parts to the statement with up to eight appendices which can include the representations made etc..

The parts of the statement are as follows:

I. Introduction
II. Special Educational Needs
III. Special Educational Provision
IV. Placement
V. Non-Educational Needs
VI. Non-Educational Provision
VII. Other Arrangements.

A copy of the proposed statement must be served on the parents and the parents may express a preference as to the school to be named in the statement. This will be one of the matters that will not be specified until the final statement is made. The LEA may not make that statement until it has considered representations concerning it.

It was established in *L v Clarke* [1998] ELR 129 that section 324(3)(a), Education Act 1996 (and the 1994 Regulations) required a high degree of specificity in the making of the statement. Some flexibility was possible but there would have to be no doubt as to what was required for the child.

A school need not be named in the statement. The argument that section 324, Education Act 1996 implicitly required the naming of a school was rejected by the Court of Appeal in the composite appeals of *Richardson v Solihull Metropolitan Borough Council, White v Ealing London Borough Council and Hereford and Worcester County Council, ex parte Lane* [1998] *The Times*, 10 April. This was partly on the basis that it was clear from section 319 of the Act that provision could be made otherwise than at school.

The copy of the statement must be served within eight weeks of the service of the proposed statement.

Excluding statements

In *R v Cumbria County Council, ex parte NAB* [1995] COD 180 it was held that under the 1981 Act there was a wide discretion available to the local authority to exclude categories of children who would automatically not be statemented. In this case the local authority had a policy of statementing children in various situations for example, children with blindness, deafness, mental handicap, low developmental (or intelligence) quotient and specified learning difficulties. Children in other categories had their special educational needs left to be determined by their schools. In this case the mother had made representations on the matter to the local authority and they had been listened to, but there was nothing irrational or unlawful in having such a policy.

Named persons

The 1993 Act attempted to clarify the role of the 'named person' to whom the statement must refer although the concept of the named person was introduced in the 1981 Act. One commentator has written that:

> ... most LEAs ignored it or simply gave parents the name of the person responsible for their child's assessment. K. Simmons *British Journal of Special Education* Vol. 22 No 2 June 1995.

The 1996 Act reflects the 1981 and 1993 Acts in that the LEA is under a duty when finalising a statement to give notice in writing the name of a person with whom contact may be made for information and advice about the child's special educational needs. The Code of Practice, to which local authorities must 'have regard' makes it clear that such persons are expected to be independent, however the LEA appoints the 'named person' and is not bound to accept the suggestion of the parent so it remains to be seen how independent the named person is in any given case.

Post-statement procedure

Under section 328(5), Education Act 1996 statements should be reviewed annually and, subject to the parents' right to make representations, the LEA may amend or cease to maintain the statement. The 1994 Regulations set out the procedure for review, making separate provision for those pupils who will not attain the age of 14 in the school year and those who will. Notice(s) must be served and meetings arranged to discuss the child's progress. Amendments may be made to the statement. A local authority may be able to divest itself of responsibility when the pupil reaches 16, see *R v Oxfordshire County Council, ex parte B* (below).

Under the 1981 Act, the parents of a statemented child had a right of appeal to an appeal committee or the Secretary of State. Under the 1993 Act the appeal lay to the Special Educational Needs Tribunal.

Special educational needs provision

Under section 312 of the 1996 Act, special educational provision is educational provision which is additional to, or otherwise different from, the education provision made generally for children of his age maintained by the local authority (other than special schools) in their area. Under section of the 1996 Act any arrangements made must be kept 'under review'.

Special needs pupils can attend schools in either the maintained (including grant-maintained schools), or independent sectors. Under section 316(1) Education Act 1996 there is a presumption that a special needs pupil will attend a mainstream school rather than a special school, this is in line with current government policy and was confirmed in *Jules* v *Wandsworth London Borough Council* [1998] ELR 243.

The first grant-maintained special school was opened in September 1994 and the complexities of funding such provision became apparent in *R* v *London Borough of Hillingdon, ex parte Governing Body of Queensmead School* [1997] ELR 331, see below.

Under section 347 of the 1996 Education Act, independent schools may be approved as schools suitable for the admission of children for whom statements of special educational needs are maintained. The curriculum must be broadly based and balanced in such schools and there are requirements in respect of volunteers, school premises and the number of pupils, see further the Education (Special Educational Needs) (Approval of Independent Schools) Regulations 1994 (SI No 651) and the Education (Special Educational Needs) (Approval of Independent Schools) (Amendment) Regulations 1998 (SI No 417). Withdrawal of approval requires consultation with the proprietor concerned unless there are special circumstances, see *R* v *Secretary of State for Education and Employment, ex parte McCarthy,* [1996] *The Times,* 24 July.

Many LEAs have a policy of educating children with special needs in 'mainstream' schools, see for example *R* v *Newham London Borough Council, ex parte R* [1994] COD 472 where it was held that to have such a policy was not unlawful. Under the legislation integration of pupils is a requirement subject to the wishes of the parents. Section 316 of the 1996 Act states that a child with special educational needs should be educated in a school which is not a special school unless that is incompatible with the wishes of the parent and providing that certain prescribed conditions were fulfilled. These conditions are that education in a mainstream school would be compatible with:

- the special educational provision which his needs call for
- the pupils with whom he will be receiving efficient education
- the efficient use of resources.

The duty is confined, subject to certain conditions, to securing that they are educated at an ordinary rather than a special school unless that it is incompatible with the wishes of the parents.

The operation of 'parental preference' in relation to special educational needs provision has caused much difficulty and is a process quite distinct in many respects from that of parental preference generally. In *Catchpole* v *Buckinghamshire County Council,* [1998] COD 279 Thorpe LJ stated that, "Parental preference had a part to play in what was appropriate and might be the decisive factor where there was parity of costs and facilities. But parental preference might be ill-informed or capricious." In *Crane* v *Lancashire County Council* [1997] 3 FCR 587, it was held that the LEA did not have to conduct a balancing exercise between the suitability of the school and the parental wishes before naming a school in the statement, "the suitability of a school was a question of fact not fairness".

What 'facts' the LEA may take into account has been the subject of some dispute and inevitably has led to problems concerning disclosure.

In *R* v *Secretary of State for Education, ex parte S* [1995] 2 FCR 225 it was held that the Secretary of State for Education was entitled to make a decision as to the provision for special educational needs. This might involve a process of consultation and any advice which was given during the course of that consultation did not have to be disclosed to interested parties unless new material was discovered as a result. Russell LJ stated in the Court of Appeal that:

> The concept of fairness did not normally require disclosure. If it did then there should be disclosure but that would only arise in the most exceptional cases ...

Peter Gibson LJ in the same case concurred but also said that:

> ... the Secretary of State had conceded that considerations of fairness necessitated disclosure notwithstanding the fact that the 1981 Act said nothing about it.

In *White* v *Ealing London Borough Council, Richardson* v *Solihull Metropolitan Borough Council* and *Hereford and Worcester County Council, ex parte Lane* [1998] *The Times*, 10 April, it was held that where a school was under consideration on appeal to the Tribunal and that school had not been suggested by either of the parties, in the interests of the parties and the child's welfare, the Tribunal should inform the parties so that representations might be made.

The main difficulties have concerned the taking into account of resources when identifying a suitable school, as further discussed below. Provision of any facilities which are regarded as 'surplus' to those regarded as sufficient to meet the identified special educational needs is likely to be challenged on the basis of lack of resources, see *Hackney London Borough Council, ex parte Silyadin*, [1998] *The Times*, 17 September where the provision of a boarding place was considered as 'surplus' to the needs of the child.

In *L v Kent County Council*, [1998] ELR 140 an error of law was disclosed when the LEA named a school in the statement which used methods incompatible to those the child had received at a former school. The school proposed by the parents would have used compatible methods.

Non-educational provision

It is possible for a statement of special educational needs to include references to non-educational provision. In *C v Special Educational Needs Tribunal*, [1997] ELR 390 the statement referred to occupational therapy and physiotherapy in Part 5 of the statement. It was contended that those matters should have been referred to in Part 3 of the statement given the expertise of the school in question. It was held that there was no ground for interfering with the structure of the statement in the circumstances of the case. A statement of special educational needs might specify the provision of transport from home to school. In *R v Hereford and Worcester City Council, ex parte P*, [1992] *The Times*, 13 March it was held that such a statement would not be deficient in failing to specify a maximum time for that journey. The case was considered in the light of section 55 of the Education Act 1944 as amended and the conclusion reached was that:

> Non-stressful transport was … a non-educational provision which had to be specified in the statement of special educational needs … the regulations did not require that the statement should spell out in terms that the transport had to be non-stressful.

In *R v Havering London Borough Council, ex parte K*, [1998] 96 LGR 325, it was held that a decision not to provide financial assistance for transport to a special school outside the LEA area had been reached unlawfully as the LEA had taken into account its own view that the child could have been suitably educated locally. That was an extraneous consideration.

In *R v Lambeth London Borough Council, ex parte M*, [1995] *The Times*, 9 May it was held that the provision of a lift at a mainstream primary school to enable a disabled pupil to use rooms on the first floor could not be regarded as a provision for an educational need in the context of the local authority's statement of special educational needs. It was a matter which related to the pupil's mobility rather than her educational needs. However, the case was referred back to the Council for a re-assessment of the child's educational and non-educational special needs.

A policy must include:

- information about the school's special educational provision;
- information about the school's policies for the identification, assessment and provision for all pupils with special needs;
- information about the school's staffing policy and partnerships with bodies beyond the school.

Under the legislation and the Code of Practice on the identification and assessment of special educational needs governing bodies must 'use their best endeavours' to see that appropriate provision is made for pupils with special educational needs. The governing body must:

- secure that the necessary provision is made;
- secure that where the responsible person has been informed by the LEA that a pupil has special needs that those needs are made known to those who are likely to teach that pupil. The responsible person may be a governor or head teacher;
- consult with the LEA concerning special needs provision;
- ensure that all the activities of the school are open to pupils with special needs as far as that is practicable;
- report on the implementation of the school's policy for special needs pupils in the annual governors' report to parents.

The report must include information of the success of the school's policy, any significant changes to it and any consultation with the LEA.

Resource implications

Making a statement

In determining what constitutes appropriate special needs provision in any case, the LEA is obliged to consider what would be the efficient use of resources in considering parental preference. This is similar to the requirement in all cases of parental preference but in special needs cases, the impact on resources is likely to be considerable and the emphasis on this aspect is much more pronounced. The concept of parental preference was considered in *B* v *Special Educational Needs Tribunal,* [1998] *The Times,* 26 March. It was held that the Tribunal should have considered the financial resources of both the LEA which had made the statement and the resources of the neighbouring LEA in which the preferred school was located.

In *R* v *Cheshire County Council, ex parte C,* [1996] *The Times,* 8 August, a school nominated as appropriate for a child could be funded partly by the LEA and partly privately so that the cost to the LEA was no more than the cost of a local school. It was held that the decision as to whether the school was appropriate had to be made on educational and not financial grounds.

Maintaining the statement

Funding in respect of maintained schools may come from the LEA and elsewhere. Section 322 of the 1996 Act provides that where any health authority or local authority could help in the exercise of the LEA's functions, the LEA may request help from that authority.

However, having made a statement of special educational needs, the obligation to pay for that provision cannot be delegated. In *R* v *Harrow London Borough Council, ex parte M* [1997] 3 FCR 761, it was held that a failure on the part of a health authority to provide resources could include special educational needs.

In *R* v *Brent and Harrow Health Authority, ex parte Harrow London Borough Council* [1997] FCR 765, it was held that a health authority was not prevented from rationing resources set aside to assist LEAs in providing for those with special educational needs.

In *R* v *Oxfordshire County Council, ex parte P,* [1996] ELR 153 it was held that schools could use part of their delegated budgets to pay for any shortfall although should a school fail to do so or withdraw previous funding, the duty remains with the LEA to maintain any statement of special educational needs.

The Education (Grant-maintained Special Schools) (Finance) Regulations 1994 (SI No 2111) provided for the determination by the Funding Agency for Schools of amounts of grant for grant-maintained special schools in England which were formerly maintained special schools. The 1994 Regulations have been superseded by the Education (Grant-maintained and Grant-maintained Special Schools) (Finance) Regulations 1998 (SI No 799). Despite the financing arrangements for grant-maintained schools, the responsibility for funding for special educational needs rested with the LEA.

In *R v London Borough of Hillingdon, ex parte Governing Body of Queensmead School* (above) the issue was whether the governing body of a grant-maintained school were obliged to make up the shortfall in LEA provision out of its own funds. It was held that there could be such an obligation although the LEA in this case ultimately restored the funding in question. The fact that there had been a lack of consultation was commented on by the court. In the interest of fairness, consultation should be a matter of course unless there was an unexpected and urgent necessity to reduce the budget.

Pupils aged over 16

In *R v Dorset County Council, ex parte G* [1995] ELR 109 December, the LEA in accordance with its obligation under the Education Act 1981, section 7, arranged provision for the special needs of G. G was educated at a residential school which only catered for pupils up to the age of 16. The authority paid his school fees until the end of the summer term 1994 which was just before his sixteenth birthday. Since that date the local authority had taken the view that their responsibilities under the statement came to an end and that funding was then the responsibility of the Further Education Funding Council (FEFC) (*see further* Chapter 14). The effect of the Further and Higher Education Act 1992 was considered in detail. It was considered that the 1992 Act contained none of the 'statutory scaffolding' for pupils aged over 16 which was found in the 1981 Act for children of compulsory school age. The court ultimately concluded that the Council's reponsibility for G did not come to an end when he reached 16 although there was a duty on the FEFC to consider what, if any, responsibility it had for the education of G. Under the 1992 Act the FEFC only had a duty to pay for a child's schooling were it was impracticable to compel an LEA to do its duty or if a statement was amended to exclude provision at a school but the FEFC was satisfied that there was a duty on them under section 4(3) of the 1992 Act. There was no breach of the duty on the FEFC in this case.

Following the case of G (above) the DfEE issued a Circular Letter 1/96 to provide clarification of the respective roles of LEAs, FE colleges and the FEFC. However, the case of G was distinguished on its facts in *R v Oxfordshire County Council, ex parte B* [1997] 1 FCR 69. In *R v Further Education Funding Council, ex parte Parkinson*

[1997] 2 FCR 67 it was held that the duty to make provision under section 4 Further and Higher Education Act 1992 had to be 'tailor-made' to the needs of the pupil.

Special Educational Needs Tribunal

The 1981 Act set out methods of appeal under that Act which had to be exhausted before judicial review could be sought.

This was made clear in *R* v *Salford City Council, ex parte L* [1992] *The Times*, 17 April where it was confirmed that:

> The principle of judicial review should not supplant the normal statutory appellate procedure was not in doubt.

In *R* v *Clwyd County Council, ex parte A* [1994] 1 FCR 334 the rights of appeal were clearly identified, there was an appeal to an appeal committee of the local education authority or to the Secretary of State. The ERA 1988 had amended the 1981 Act which, "brought the applicant a choice of avenues of appeal … and there was no inconsistency and repugnance between the two."

Appeals to appeal committees necessarily had to be subject to the rules of natural justice and the principles of ultra vires, see for example *R* v *Camden London Borough Council, ex parte S* [1991] LGR 513 where the appeal committee procedure was flawed.

The Special Educational Needs Tribunal was established by section 177, Education Act 1993. The constitution and procedure of the Tribunal is now set out in sections 333–336 Education Act 1996 and the Special Educational Needs Tribunal Regulations 1995 (SI No 3113). The legislation covers five aspects:

1. Membership of the Tribunal and establishing Tribunals to exercise the jurisdiction;
2. Provisions for the making of an appeal to the Tribunal and reply from the local authority;
3. Preparation for the hearing;
4. The determination of the appeal;
5. Additional powers of the Tribunal.

In the appeals of *E* v *Dorset County Council, Christmas* v *Hampshire* and *Keating* v *London Borough of Bromley* (above) it had been stated in the Court of Appeal that:

> The appropriate remedy lay through the appeal structure set out in the legislation and by way of judicial review.

The House of Lords considered that:

> ... there was no legal or commonsense principle which required one to deny a common law duty of care just because there was a statutory scheme which addressed the same problem.

The jurisdiction of the Tribunal was not an issue for consideration in these cases nor was it considered as part of a wider discussion. It remains to be seen if the courts will take the same view when they have regard to the jurisdiction of the Tribunal in such cases.

In *R v Special Educational Needs Tribunal, ex parte South Glamorgan County Council* [1996] ELR 326, the Court of Appeal confirmed that a challenge to a decision of the Tribunal should be by appeal to the High Court under Order 55 of the Rules of the Supreme Court rather than by way of judicial review.

In *Simon v Special Educational Needs Tribunal* [1996] 1 WLR 382, it was held that a child had no right of appeal to the High Court against a decision of the Tribunal; such an appeal could only be brought by parents of the child concerned or the LEA. The situation in this case was that the mother of a child with special needs sought to challenge the decision of the local authority to send her son to an ordinary maintained school and not an independent special school. The matter was heard by the Tribunal and thereafter an appeal was launched in the High Court. An appeal from the Tribunal lay to the High Court under the provisions of section 181 of the 1993 Act which added the Special Educational Needs Tribunal to the list of those to which section 11 of the Tribunals and Enquiries Act 1992 applied. Under the legislation the appeal procedure is as follows:

- a notice of appeal is signed by the parent, naming the child and the authority whose decision is disputed;
- the authority replies to the notice;
- the appeal might be withdrawn by the parent.

The references in the Act to the appeal procedure refer to parents or the local authority. Persons other than the parties may attend although the Act allows neither party to call more than two witnesses to be examined orally. In the light of this the courts concluded that there could only be two parties to an appeal, the parents and the local authority. In the Simon case it was stated that: the court had no jurisdiction to hear an appeal brought by a child.

This would be so even in this case where the child was applying through his mother as next friend. Although the court held that it had no jurisdiction in this matter a number of other procedural and evidential points in relation to it were considered for example, whether it would be appropriate to bring an appeal by way of case stated. It was held that this would be appropriate.

A member of the Independent Panel for Special Education Advice, John Wright, was quoted in the Times Educational Supplement, 25 August 1995 as saying that:

> The routes to legal challenge have been closed down enormously. If it's only parents who qualify for legal aid who can challenge, then obviously that is bad for individual children.

This was especially unfortunate as Mr. Wright felt that the judges had been the friends of children with special needs.

In the same article N. Pyke reported that following a review of legal aid and tribunals the Special Educational Needs Tribunal was opposed to the availability of legal aid in any case and that the Tribunal was under pressure to, for example, complete cases in half a day.

Special needs and the national curriculum

In ERA 1988, section 1 the duty to comply with the national curriculum refers to all pupils. There was a general power under section 17 of that Act to modify the national curriculum or exempt pupils from all or part of the national curriculum. The position is preserved by the Education Act 1996. Specific provision is made in respect of educational provision in statements and for such temporary exceptions as may be necessary.

Ofsted and special needs

In the Ofsted guidance on the inspection of secondary schools it was stated that:

> Inspectors will need to check that the school has regard to the 1994 Code of Practice on the identification and assessment of special educational need and to the earlier relevant sections of the 1993, 1988 and 1981 Education Acts.

There then follows a checklist of matters to be considered. Throughout the guidance there is reference to special needs pupils and staffing, attainment and action plans for example are all part of the inspection process.

In September 1998 the DfEE produced guidance on action planning after Ofsted inspections in special schools, *Effective Action Planning after Inspection: Planning improvement in special schools.*

Gifted children

One question which remains open is to what extent are children with high levels of intelligence within the category of those with 'special educational needs. 'According to one article (A Gardiner "Time to nuture the talents of tomorrow, *The Times,* 4 October 1993) the 1944 Education Act was never fully implemented in that the requirement to provide education according to a child's age, ability and aptitude has been ignored in repect of 'gifted' children. The author claimed that: "the intellectually gifted [are] the only group of children who do have their potential met as of right."

It has also been suggested that such children will have their needs met by 'masterclasses' in schools and the use of selective places under the SSFA. Those selective places are only available in certain subjects and there remains a question as to how children will be selected for those places.

The relationship between special needs and gifted children has been considered in case law. In *R v Secretary of State for Education, ex parte C* [1996] ELR 93 it was held by Schiemann J. that the Secretary of State was entitled to conclude that a child whose high intelligence enabled her to overcome learning difficulties which stemmed from short term auditory memory problems did not have special educational needs. Her needs could be met in an ordinary maintained school.

In *R v Cumbria County Council, ex parte NAB* (above), it was held that it was lawful for the local authority to have a policy of excluding certain children from 'statementing'. Such a policy might include children whose intelligence was too high for them to qualify.

In *R v Portsmouth City Council, ex parte Faludy* [1998] *The Times*, 17 September, it was held that a highly intelligent pupil who had gained a place at Cambridge University at 15 years of age despite being severely dyslexic and dyspraxic need not be assessed by the LEA in respect of his special educational needs. There was no power or duty under the 1996 Act to make such an assessment in respect of higher education provision. In general terms it was accepted that the fact that a child was of above average intelligence did not mean that the child could not have special educational needs.

Chapter 14

Further and Higher Education

Further and Higher Education

The further and higher education sectors

The Further and Higher Education Act 1992 received the Royal Assent on 6 March 1992. In the autumn of 1992, colleges were incorporated and further education corporations came into being which were eligible to receive transitional funding. 1 April 1993 became known as 'vesting day' when the corporations became fully independent. Colleges acquired a separate legal identity and staff and assets were transferred from the LEA. Governing bodies were able to employ their own staff, own land and buildings and enter into contracts. Local authorities were not compensated for the loss of assets as they were felt to have been provided for the public good. Adult education was divided into vocational and non-vocational, the LEA retained the funding of the latter.

The further education sector now comprises:

- 'general' further education colleges
- tertiary colleges
- sixth form colleges
- agricultural and horticultural colleges
- art, design and performing arts colleges
- certain specialist designated colleges.

Private colleges remain outside the state sector.

Since the implementation of the ERA 1988, polytechnics became self-governing, having previously been under LEA control, and following the 1992 Act the bifurcated system of universities and polytechnics was abolished, the latter becoming universities. Section 77(1) of the 1992 Act confers power on the Privy Council to authorise the title 'university' to any institution within the higher education sector.

The naming of some institutions has caused problems. The Business Names Act 1985 may apply to colleges and universities but in *London College of Science and Technology Ltd* v *Islington London Borough Council* [1997] ELR 162 it was held that each case has to be considered on an individual basis as the 1985 Act might not apply to all educational establishments.

The Teaching and Higher Education Act 1998 (THEA), sections 39 and 40, prohibit the use of the title 'university' unless authorised by an Act, Royal Charter or approved by the Privy Council.

The Education (Listed Bodies) (Amendment) Order 1998 (SI No 876) adds to the list of bodies under the ERA 1988 which are recognised as providing courses in preparation for a degree. Such degrees are recognised awards. It is an offence to grant, offer to grant or offer any invitation in relation to unrecognised awards.

Funding

Funding councils

The Higher Education Funding Council (HEFC) and the Further Education Funding Council (FEFC) allocate funds in their respective sectors. The 1992 Act sets out their respective functions in detail with some minor amendment in THEA.

Higher education funding

The HEFC allocates money on the basis of student numbers and special initiatives. Student numbers may include those who are not receiving tuition according to *O'Connor v Chief Adjudication Officer* [1999], *The Times*, 11 March. It was held that a student who took leave of absence for a year to study at home was a full-time student although that case was heard in the context of social security legislation. Extra funding is available for rewarding research activities and quality teaching programmes. In *R v Higher Education Funding Council, ex parte Institute of Dental Surgery* [1994] 1 All ER 651, the Institute applied for judicial review of a decision of the Funding Council. The Council had appointed a panel to assess the quality of research undertaken at universities. Research ratings are linked to funding and the Institute received a lower rating in this exercise than it had in previous years. A cut of some £270,000 in the research grant allocated to the Institute resulted. The Chief Executive of the HEFC refused to give reasons for the lower rating and would not allow an appeal unless it could be shown that the rating had been based on erroneous information. The application for judicial review was dismissed in the High Court. It was held that there was no duty to give reasons for decisions generally. Such a duty arose only in certain situations, for example where there were issues of personal liberty. Other situations would be where the decision appears aberrant. There must be prima facie evidence that something has gone wrong. According to Sedley J:

> It follows that this class does not include decisions which are in themselves challengeable by reference only to the reasons for them. A pure exercise of academic judgment is such a decision.

It has been confirmed in a Report of Quality Assessment 1992–92, (HEFC) which examined nearly 1,000 assessments by the HEFC in individual university departments that, unsurprisingly, those universities which receive the most funding achieve academic excellence and vice versa, the difficulty being that under this formula the rich institutions become richer and the others, particularly the former polytechnics attract less funding.

The charitable status of higher education corporations is dealt with by way of an amendment to the ERA 1988 set out in section 41, THEA.

Further education funding

The further education colleges are said to play an important part in the government's strategy for training and education, including the commitment to 'lifelong learning' and the 'New Deal'. As such colleges have been asked to increase places by more than 400,000 by 2002. Colleges are guaranteed only 90% of their funding year-on-year and must bid for the rest. Since colleges gained their independence from local authorities, colleges receive funds based on the number of students they recruit and retain. Under-recruitment leads to financial penalties. Rural colleges are said to suffer particularly because of this national funding formula.

Under the FEFC, governing bodies are responsible for:

- efficient financial planning and other management controls to safeguard public funds;
- efficient and economic management of all resources, spending capital assets, equipment and staff;
- ensuring that finances are taken into account when reaching decisions.

Governors may be removed for fraud or malpractice. In 1994 college governors at a tertiary college faced removal from office over the purchase of a nightclub and hotel. An investigation found no evidence of fraud but concluded there was:

> abundant evidence of inadequate financial control, failure to observe due procedures, an absence of openness and a determination of the governing

body to stifle any questioning of executive decision-making. *The Times,* 18 November 1994.

In 1995 it was announced that at least 48 further education colleges were in financial difficulties. The Public Accounts Committee report, *Managing to be Independent,* said that the position of governors was not clear when a college had financial difficulties and that some governors had taken out indemnity insurance to protect their personal wealth. The FEFC told the Committee that it could not give an absolute assurance that no governor would ever face financial jeopardy. It was reported that: "A court case was needed to test how far governors might be held to account." *The Times,* 10 August 1995.

The Report also concluded a set of guidelines from the DfEE and the Welsh Office was urgently needed on the extent of liability of governors, not only in further education but also in grant-maintained schools and universities. One commentator thought that governors' liability fell somewhere between the respective liabilities in charity law on one hand and company law on the other and that: "Governors of further education colleges sit uncomfortably between these twin peaks of legislation". *See* J Graystone, "Debts and Governors – Courting Disaster", *TES* 3 November 1995.

Severe financial problems arose at one college in particular following incorporation. A dispute between Coventry City Council and Coventry City College which was settled in late 1995. The college was in debt to the local authority at the time of incorporation and the council was seeking repayment of the debt. The details of the settlement have been made public and the reasons for settlement are of interest. In the *Times Educational Supplement,* 10 November 1995 it was reported that:

> As the wrangle developed, the council suing the college for repayment, the City Council found itself neck-deep in waters still uncharted since incorporation in 1993. The framing of legislation removing colleges from council control left the question of liability for previously acquired debts open to different legal interpretations as both parties discovered. Contradictory legal views also emerged over the implications of the college becoming insolvent if the debt were enforced and whether the FEFC would then be liable for the money owed. The uncertainty prompted the city council's lawyers to advise their clients to settle.

The college was to pay back just over £1 million over a 10-15 year period and return a car park and other land to the council.

In 1998 the Public Accounts Committee expressed continuing concern about the performance of colleges and urged the FEFC to help the worst performing colleges by identifying strategies for success and setting challenging targets. The use of 'whistleblowing' policies has also been suggested as a way of identifying abuse and misman-agement of funds. The FEFC have considered the possibility of nomi-nating their own governors.

Information about the academic performance of further education institutions is required under Education (Further Education Institutions Information) (England) Regulations 1995 (SI No 2065) as amended by the Education Institutions Information (England) (Amendment) Regulations 1997 (SI No 2173), Circular 8/97 and the Education (Further Education Institutions Information) (England) (Amendment) Regulations 1998 (SI No 2220).

The charitable status of further education corporations is dealt with in section 41 THEA.

European funding

Colleges and universities may now be able to benefit from European sources of funding. The administration of these funds has been the subject of litigation, see *R* v *Birmingham City Council, ex parte Birmingham College of Food and Sutton Coldfield College* and *R* v *Cheshire County Council, ex parte Halton College*, [1995] COD 107 where challenges were made in respect of the administration of funds distributed from the European Social Fund (ESF) which was estab-lished under Article 123 of the Treaty of Rome. The question which arose in these cases was one of 'specificity' i.e. the way in which the funds were applied. All applications under European law failed but the application in respect of the Birmingham College was allowed on the basis of domestic law.

Private finance

The Private Finance Initiative (PFI) introduced by the Government in 1992 to promote partnership between the private and public sectors was launched in education in 1995. Education schemes have been regarded as unattractive by construction firms as they involve a low capital cost: some firms will only consider schemes in excess of £30 million. As a result there have been initiatives to combine proposals. A scheme to buy student halls of residence and construct new university buildings worth over £500 million was reported to have received private financial backing in 1998.

Income generation

Both further and higher education corporations may have assets at their disposal to enable them to generate their own income and this is understandably encouraged by the government. Raising income from conferences and use of accommodation during vacations is commonplace and has taken many institutions in to the commercial sphere. As indicated above, governing bodies must take care when investing and also when divesting the institution of land or other property. *In re University of Westminster* [1998] *The Times*, 1 September, the Lands Tribunal refused to remove restrictive covenants affecting land of which the university was the freehold owner.

In *Nahum v Royal Holloway and Bedford New College* [1998] *The Times*, 19 November, a dispute arose concerning the payment of commission relating to the sale of a painting by Constable.

Employment

The changes in the legal framework of further and higher education have had an enormous impact on the contracts of employees, particularly teaching staff.

Terms and conditions

In further education, colleges and polytechnics staff who had been employed by LEAs could either stay on their 'old' contracts or they could change to new contracts with less favourable terms and conditions. A 'one-off' financial incentive was given to staff who agreed to change to the new contracts. Not all employees took the opportunity to change and as a result some staff remain on the old local authority contracts known as 'silver book' contracts after the document in which their terms and conditions can be found. Although the terms of these contracts are generally more favourable, there have been no salary increases for two years. Staff taking up new appointments, including promotions, were placed on the new contracts. This alleged 'imposition' of the new contracts had fuelled a long running dispute between lecturers' associations and the employers.

In the 'new' universities the conditions of service are decided from time to time by the board of governors. The most contentious areas even in 'agreed' contracts are hours of work and exclusivity. The nature of the job of lecturers is such that staff are usually required as a matter of contract to work such hours as are reasonably necessary to fulfil the duties and responsibilities of the post. Formal scheduled teaching responsibilities are subject to a maximum depending on the grade of lectureship which usually relates to a weekly or yearly basis. A common provision is that lecturers should be available for teaching purposes on 260 days a year (see further below). These hours of working do not apply in all subjects, for example those involved in teacher education might be specifically excluded from these provisions, especially if they are involved in school-centred initial teacher training. The teaching year will not normally exceed a stated period, commonly 38 weeks of which two weeks will be spent on teaching related administration.

In further education the employers have common representative bodies, the most notable being the College Employers Forum (CEF). Some associations have negotiated a new contract with the CEF but others remain opposed to the new contracts. Some colleges have withdrawn from the CEF, one Principal announced in 1995 that instead of paying the annual fee to CEF (which ranges from £3,500–8,000) he would be looking at alternative personnel and legal services from independent solicitors. For this and other reasons there is no one voice to represent colleges.

Contracts of employment in higher education are also now a matter for negotiation between the lecturers associations and the universities although the 'old' universities do have charters which still apply and which may still affect employment matters. Under the ERA 1988, the University Commissioners were given the role of securing the statutes of each 'qualifying institution' under that part of the Act. Section 206 of the 1988 Act excluded the jurisdiction of university 'visitors' in certain matters, see below. The duties of these Commissioners were extended to 1 January 1995 by the Education (University Commissioners) Order 1993 (SI No 3056).

Employment disputes

Many of the employment related matters which come before the courts are common to those in teaching generally with the exception of the role of visitors in universities which is discussed below. Employment matters often concern those members of staff other than teaching staff. In *Leicester University Student's Union* v *Mahomed*, [1995] IRLR 292, an employee of a student's union claimed unfair dismissal and racial discrimination. In that case the procedure before industrial tribunals was in issue. It was decided that establishing the two-year qualifying period in unfair dismissal cases generally was a pre-condition to a finding of unfair dismissal and was not a factor which determined the jurisdiction of the tribunal to hear the facts.

The question of transfer of undertakings was considered in *Kenny* v *South Manchester College* [1993] IRLR 265, where the terms and conditions of staff transferred from an LEA to a College had to be protected under the Transfer of Undertakings (Protection of Employment) Regulations 1981 (SI No 1794). The staff in this case were employed to teach in a prison.

In *Sunderland Polytechnic* v *Evans* [1993] IRLR 196, a lecturer took part in a half-day stoppage as a part of industrial action. A whole day's pay was deducted from her salary. It was held that the industrial tribunal had no jurisdiction to determine the lawfulness or otherwise of the deduction. The question of what constitutes a 'day's' pay has been a matter of some conjecture. As there is a general requirement in most lecturing contracts to teach over a certain number of days per year, commonly 260 the question is whether a day's pay is 1/260 or 1/365. See further, J Pointing, 'What is the value of a day's work', *Education and the Law* 1995 7(1) 13–15.

Part-time staff

In the further education sector there has been some disquiet among members of the teaching staff that part-time members of staff are being encouraged to register with Education Lecturing Services which is working with colleges to provide part-time staff for 'assignments' on a self-employed basis.

The hourly rate paid to such lecturers is generally lower than that paid by the colleges themselves and 'self employed' status removes the employment protection only recently extended in the case of part-time employees. Some colleges will only recruit part-time staff in this way.

In *Cast* v *Croydon College* [1998] *The Times*, 26 March a manager of the college's information centre was refused permission to work part-time and job-share on return from maternity leave. The case was remitted to the industrial tribunal, the Court of Appeal having found that the college had erred in law in its consideration of the case.

The academic year

In most colleges and universities the nature of the academic year is changing so that as a result of the introduction of 'modular' courses staff will have to work on a 'semester' basis, often two fifteen-week semesters a year. Some professional associations have raised doubts about the educational value of such a system and concern about the possible impact on contracts and workload. One Chief Executive of a lecturers' association said that under this system:

> The spring term is a chaotic hotchpotch including two periods of teaching, an examination period and an inter-semester break in which assessments are marked. *The Times,* 27 July 1995.

Exclusivity

Exclusivity relates to external work undertaken by members of the teaching staff. Whilst universities like to appear to be supportive of external activities which support a lecturer's professional activities lecturers are as a general rule required to seek prior approval for participation in external work. Obligations exist in relation to patents, inventions, confidentiality and copyright which form part of the contractual arrangements. Some posts will also carry a 'post-termination' restriction clause.

Security of tenure

University lecturers traditionally had 'security of tenure' in that they could only be dismissed for 'good cause', the meaning of which was set out in the university's charter. The meaning of this phrase has caused considerable difficulty. The ERA 1988 removed security of tenure from university teachers (see *R v Lord President of the Privy Council ex parte Page,* below). In that case the phrase was coupled with a requirement that the lecturer was appointed subject to the terms of that appointment including notice periods. The House of Lords held that there had been no error of fact or law in Mr. Page's dismissal without proof of 'good cause'.

The dismissal of a probationary lecturer was considered, in the context of Northern Ireland's academic tenure provisions, in *Deman v Queen's University of Belfast* [1997] ELR 431.

Student grants and loans

Local authorities make mandatory awards for students undertaking first degrees and other designated courses. Those grants traditionally covered the full cost of tuition fees at universities and colleges within the 'state' sector however the position has altered under the THEA

1998 (see below). Section 22 of the 1998 Act sets out the basis for the new arrangements for giving financial support to students. Parents and 'home' students (see below) in certain circumstances must pay £1000 per academic year in tuition fees. Formerly tuition fees were paid by LEAs and there was no related means testing. There is now a sliding scale of contributions. The maintenance grant is likely to be phased out and the Education (Student Support) Regulations 1998 (SI No 1884) provide for loans for eligible students in respect of maintenance with effect from 1 September 1998. Pending revision of the system maintenance grants will continue to be means-tested with access to loans as a means of topping-up grants, the value of which has decreased in real terms. Other grants are awarded on a discretionary basis.

Types of student

Universities and colleges classify students as 'home' or 'overseas' students and charge different fees accordingly. To qualify as a home student three years residence in this country is required. The home student category will now include nationals of the European Union.

In *Kent* v *University College London* [1992] 156 LG Rev 1003, it was held that a student who was seeking to challenge the decision of a college that he did not satisfy the criteria for entry to the college as a 'home student' should have brought his case as an application for judicial review. His case had been brought in the Chancery Division as a matter of private law. The Court of Appeal held that this was inappropriate and the matter was one of public rather than private law (see further Chapter 3). The case concerned the Education (Fees and Awards) Regulations 1983 (SI No 973). The student had been born in Singapore but had come England in 1988 with a view to settling here permanently. His parents and other family members already lived here. The College took the view that he had come to England mainly or primarily to complete his education and to continue on to university. The College took the view that at the time of his application in 1991, when he had been resident in England for three years, he still did not qualify for 'home' student status and he was to be charged the higher fees demanded of 'overseas' students. The Court of Appeal considered the question:

> It was now too late to let the matter go with the possibility of proceedings in the Divisional Court. The Court had heard the appeal although it came from a judge before whom the matter should never have been put.

In the event the appeal of the college against a finding that the student should pay 'home' students fees was dismissed because there had been no cross-examination of the deponent, evidence having been heard on affidavit. As such there could be no basis for doubting the student's good faith. See also *Orphanos* v *Queen Mary College* [1985] 2 WLR 703 where the issue of fees and racial discrimination was considered in the case of a student from Cyprus.

The Education (Fees and Awards) Regulations 1997 (SI No 1972) provided that differentiation which might otherwise be unlawful under the Race Relations Act 1976 shall be lawful.

Means testing

The payment of mandatory awards for maintenance has been subject to a means test. The system is now regulated by the Education (Mandatory Awards) Regulations 1998 (SI No 1166) made under the Education Act 1962. Reforms will be made to allow for the fact that student loans are now available for maintenance (see below).

The responsibility for determining eligibility for mandatory awards depends on the 'belonging regulations'. LEAs are only responsible for awards to students who are ordinarily resident in the area of that LEA, see the Education (Areas to which Pupils and Students Belong) Regulations 1996 (SI No 615), Circular 1/96 and the Education (Areas to which Pupils and Students Belong) (Amendment) Regulations 1997 (SI No 597).

In the case of most students the means-test is on the basis of their parents' income. In the case of mature students this will be on their own income, if any.

The regulations make allowance for Career Development Loans which may now be disregarded in assessing entitlement to a maintenance grant. An 'older students' allowance is also payable to students aged over 26 in certain circumstances. 'Income' may not include money acquired by a wife from her husband under the presumption of advancement as in *R* v *Harrow London Borough Council, ex parte Coker* [1989] COD 439.

Discretionary grants

Discretionary grants and awards may be made by local authorities and it would seem that it is not unlawful for local authorities to have general policies in respect of such grants. The problem with such cases is that it would seem to 'fetter' the discretion of the council by making such a policy, something which is frowned upon generally in administrative law but which is not unlawful. In *British Oxygen Co Ltd* v *Board of Trade* [1971] AC 610 Lord Reid said:

> What the authority must not do is to refuse to listen at all. But a Ministry or large authority may have had to deal already with a multitude of similar applications and then they will almost certainly have evolved a policy ... There can be no objection to that ...

In *R* v *Shropshire County Council, ex parte Jones* [1997] COD 116, a student began a higher education course with the benefit of a mandatory grant. He was unable to continue with his studies because of his mother's illness. Following her death he wished to resume his studies and was told he could only be considered for a discretionary award. This was refused mainly due to local authority expenditure cuts. It was held that the decision to refuse him a grant should be quashed, the LEA had operated a rigid policy and had not given weight to the partial completion of the course by the student.

In *R* v *Southwark London Borough Council, ex parte Udu* [1996] ELR 390, it was held that the LEA could have a policy to refuse grants to students attending private institutions or post-graduate courses. This was so even though it meant that those educational opportunities were lost to prospective students who could not arrange alternative funds.

The Court of Appeal felt that the decision of the LEA was a political decision which could not be interfered with by the courts.

In *R* v *Bexley London Borough Council, ex parte Jones* [1995] COD 393, the applicant having taken a first degree applied for a grant to read for a second degree in medicine. As a result the applicant was only eligible to receive a discretionary award. The Council had a policy of not awarding discretionary grants for such purposes however it was held that the formulation of the Council's policy admitted no exceptions. The local authority had effectively disabled itself from considering individual cases.

In *R* v *Warwickshire County Council, ex parte Collymore* [1995] COD 52, the applicant was informed that she would be refused a discretionary grant to study at the College of Law as a matter of policy. She was invited to apply to have this decision reviewed but her application was still rejected. On application for judicial review it was held that the policy had been applied in an over rigid manner and the local authority had failed to give proper consideration to the application.

In *R* v *Warwickshire County Council, ex parte Williams,* [1995] COD 182, the decision to refuse the applicant a discretionary grant had been reconsidered in the light of the Collymore case, above. However it was held that the refusal in this case was reasonable, Parliament having given the task of distributing 'public bounty' to local authorities they could exclude recipients who had access to alternative sources of funding.

Both of these cases were considered in *R v Buckinghamshire County Council, ex parte Sharma* and *R v Wiltshire County Council, ex parte Lakhbir Kaur* [1998] COD 182 where it was held that a policy which included 'exceptional circumstances' did not have to be defined.

Student loans

The Education (Student Loans) Act 1990 was passed to allow students to borrow money from a central fund to assist them with maintenance. The Students Loans Company was set up by the government to administer the system and distribute funds.

The Education (Student Loans) (Amendment) Regulations 1998 (SI No 1676) increased the maximum amounts which may be lent to students.

The Education (Student Loans) (Amendment) Regulations 1997 (SI No 2919) were made to provide that the condition that students should be settled in the UK to be eligible for a student loan should not apply to students who began their courses before 1 August 1997. Both of the above sets of regulations were revoked by the Education (Student Loans) Regulations 1998 (SI No 2110) in consequence of the Education (Student Loans) Act 1998. The 1998 Act made provision for the transfer of student loans to the private sector, prescribed terms and conditions for loans and dealt with the administration of public sector loans.

The 1990 Act, the Education (Student Loans) Act 1996 and the Education (Student Loans) Act 1998 were all repealed by THEA 1998. THEA implements new arrangements for loans and provides for further 'sales' of loans to the private sector.

Freedom of speech

In *R v University of Liverpool, ex parte Caesar-Gordon* [1991] 1 QB 124, the university imposed conditions on a meeting to be held where it was considered that those conditions were necessary to ensure good order. Section 43 of the Education (No 2) Act 1986 required the University to take such steps as are reasonably practicable to ensure that freedom of speech within the law is secured for members, students and employees of the establishment and for visiting speakers.

In *Webb* v *O'Doherty* [1991] 3 Admin. LR 731, a student's union passed various resolutions on matters relating to the Gulf war and spent money on a campaign against the war. It was held that campaigning, in the sense of seeking to influence public opinion on political matters, was not a charitable activity. Accordingly, the funds of a student's union which was an educational charity could not be used for the campaign.

Section 202(2) of the ERA 1988 stated that the University Commissioners (see above) shall have regard to the need [inter alia] to ensure that academic staff have freedom within the law to question and test received wisdom and put forward new ideas and controversial or unpopular opinions without placing themselves in jeopardy of losing their jobs or any privileges which they may have at their institutions. This principle is preserved in the Education Act 1993 and the Further and Higher Education Act 1992 section 68.

The jurisdiction of visitors

'Visitors' regulate the internal affairs of universities and are appointed in accordance with the statutes and other instruments which govern the constitution of the university. The nature and extent of the jurisdiction of visitors has been considered by the courts regularly over the centuries, see for example, *Philips* v *Bury* [1694] Holt KB 715 and *R* v *Chancellor of Cambridge University* [1723] 1 Str. 557. Visitors have a role in two main areas, the disciplining of students and the dismissal of members of staff. See now the jurisdiction of visitors since the ERA 1988 and the inter-relationship with University Commissioners, above.

Members of staff

In *Thomas* v *University of Bradford* [1985] 3 WLR 248, a lecturer who had been dismissed claimed that the university had dismissed her in breach of the statutes, charter, ordinances and regulations which formed part of her contract of service. The university claimed that the dismissal was a matter entirely within the exclusive jurisdiction of the university visitor. On an application for judicial review it was held that this was not so. The dispute was not concerned with academic suitability, the awarding of degrees, admission to courses or any other 'purely domestic matters'. The university was not seeking to dismiss her for 'good cause' see above and hence since the only question was whether the procedures had been adhered to the court was competent to decide that question.

Similarly in *R v Lord President of the Privy Council, ex parte Page*, [1992] 2 WLR 1112, the House of Lords held that the decision of a university visitor was not amenable to challenge by judicial review on the ground of error of law or fact. Mr. Page had argued that he could only be dismissed for 'good cause'. The university had simply relied on the notice period in his contract of employment and dismissed him on the basis of redundancy. The locus classicus of the law on visitors was held to be the decision of Chief Justice Holt in *Philips v Bury* (above) which had been repeatedly applied for the last 300 years (most recently in the Thomas case above). Lord Browne-Wilkinson stated that:

> Judicial review would, however, lie in cases where the visitor had acted outside his jurisdiction in the narrow sense or abused his powers or acted in breach of the rules of natural justice.

The reluctance of the courts to interfere with the jurisdiction of visitors was confirmed in *R v University of Nottingham, ex parte Ktorides* [1998] COD 26.

Students

The courts will as a general rule refuse to investigate matters of an academic nature as in *R v HM The Queen in Council, ex parte Vijayatunga* [1989] 3 WLR 13. The student in this case claimed that the examiners who had been appointed to examine her PhD thesis were not suitably qualified. It was held this was purely a matter of academic judgement in which the court should not interfere and therefore a committee of the Privy Council acting for the Queen as visitor of the University of London were entitled to decline to investigate the student's claims and that decision was not subject to judicial review.

A somewhat unique situation arose in respect of the Inns of Court and the Council of Legal Education. In *R v Council of Legal Education, ex parte Halstead* [1994] *The Independent* 9 August it was held that where judges of the High Court were visitors their jurisdiction was in the alternative. In that case their Lordships decided to sit in their capacity as judges of the Divisional Court. The case concerned applications made by the applicant and others for admission to the Inns of Court School of Law which had been refused. The application for judicial review of the decision was rejected but their Lordships made it clear that they had chosen to hear the case as judges rather than as visitors because of the availability of legal aid for such proceedings and the more extensive appeals available.

The jurisdictional point was also taken in *R v Council of Legal Education, ex parte Joseph* [1994] COD 318, but not considered. The applicant sought judicial review of the Council's failure to certify completion of the course and competence. The view of the court was that on the merits the appeal was hopeless and that the appeal should never have been brought.

In *R v Her Majesty's Judges Sitting as Visitors to the Honourable Society of the Middle Temple, ex parte Bullock* [1996] ELR 349, the role of the Visitor was considered in detail and in the context of the Courts and Legal Services Act 1990.

In the new universities and further education colleges the disciplinary bodies will be the governing body or committees created by the governors. The Quality Assurance Agency announced in 1998 that it was working with students and institutions to draw up a code of practice on disciplinary matters generally in order to establish a more consistent approach across the further and higher education sectors.

In *R v Manchester Metropolitan University, ex parte Nolan* [1993] *The Independent*, 15 July, it was held that any procedural deficiency in proceedings was likely to result in the benefit being given to students or members of staff in the event of a dispute. In that case a student had been found guilty of cheating in an examination by a disciplinary body. It was subsequently found that the decision of that body was made when not all the relevant information was before them and so it was set aside.

It is important that any internal procedures are exhausted before reference is made to the courts. Even then the courts may be reluctant to intervene. In *R v Liverpool John Moores University, ex parte Hayes*, [1998] ELR 261, it was held that only an internal committee of the university could decide on eligibility for a degree, the court could not intervene with the academic judgment of that committee and the student was bound to use the internal appeals process.

A similar view was taken in *M v London Guildhall University*, [1998] ELR 149. The High Court would not act as a court of appeal from the university examiners.

Admissions

The question of admission to courses rarely comes before the courts; it being regarded, as mentioned above as a 'domestic matter' and for each individual university to determine. In Scotland in 1995 a student lost his challenge in the courts when he was refused a place to read medicine. The only concern of the courts was to see, "... whether the university had acted illegally by imposing an undisclosed condition for admission", *The Times*, 23 August 1995. No such illegality was found in that case.

In *Moran* v *University of Salford* [1993] *The Times*, 23 November, the applicant had been offered a place at a university and had accepted, that offer was subsequently withdrawn. It was held that there was a strong case that there was a contractual relationship in such circumstances but that in the facts of this case there would be no interlocutory mandatory injunction.

There are likely to be a number of admissions related issues which become the focus of litigation over the next few years. Fears have been expressed that universities and colleges will not be able to accommodate disabled students in breach of the Disability Discrimination Act 1995. The information which is provided in admissions documents is also likely to come under scrutiny with regard to Data Protection (as mentioned in Chapter 12). The Universities and Colleges Admissions Service (UCAS) has been urged to ensure prospective students declare any criminal convictions in the interests of the safety of other students.

Governing bodies

As mentioned above there are concerns about governing bodies and the personal liability of governors in financial matters. Just as that dimension is unclear it is also true to say that the appointment and role of governing bodies in higher education generally is unclear.

Although Instruments and Articles of Government for both further and higher education institutions are mentioned in the 1992 Act, the Nolan Committee on Standards in Public Life was reportedly told that universities were operating "closed" and "incestuous" processes for the appointment of governing body members which raised important questions about accountability. They tended to operate as a closed book and forthcoming vacancies were not advertised. Some institutions have responded positively to this criticism.

Student unions

The Education Act 1994 provides, in Part II, that governing bodies of
further and higher education institutions must ensure that a student
union complies with a number of requirements. Section 20 of the Act
defines student unions, section 22 sets out the requirements. The Act is
not limited to student unions in universities. The governing body must
take such steps as reasonably practicable to ensure that the union
operates fairly and democratically and that it is accountable for its
finances. The union should have a written constitution and students
should have a right not to be a member. Details should be given of any
external organisation to which the union is affiliated. Provision should
also be made in respect of complaints against the student's union. See
further, W Hinds, 'The Education Act 1994 – the student union provisions', *Education and the Law* 7(3) 133–145.

Extracts from the AMA/ACC Code of Practice on Procedure (Revised December 1994 by D Ruebain)

Lay Members of Appeal Committees

3. (a) The Education Act requires Authorities and governing bodies to advertise for lay members, in accordance with regulations made by the Secretary of State for Education, and requires Authorities and governing bodies to consider appointing to appeals panels any persons who have responded to such advertisements.

   (b) For county, voluntary controlled and maintained special schools, neither a member of the Authority, nor an employee, may be appointed as a lay member. For voluntary aided and special agreement schools, neither a governor of the school, nor a person appointed to a list drawn up by the maintaining Authority, nor an employee of the maintaining Authority may be appointed as a lay member.

   (c) A person is eligible to be a lay member of an appeal committee if s/he is a person without personal experience in the management of any school or the provision of any education in any school otherwise than as a governor or in any other voluntary capacity. In addition, every lay member appointed by an Authority must not have, or must not at any time have had, any connection with the Authority in question or with any person who is a member of or employed by that Authority of a kind which might reasonably be taken to raise doubts about her/his ability to act impartially in relation to the Authority. With respect to lay members appointed by governing bodies, that person must not have, or at any time have had, any connection with the school in question or with any person who is a member of, or employed by, the governing body of that school of a kind which might reasonably be taken to raise doubts about her/his ability to act impartially in relation to the school.

   (d) It is for each Authority and governing body to determine whether a particular person is eligible to be a lay member. Where there is a doubt, Authorities and governing bodies should err or the side of caution and not appoint.

Size of Appeal Committee

4. (a)   The Act requires that appeal committees shall consist of three, five or seven persons. Experience has shown that too large a number can be daunting to parents and pupils and impartiality and informality can probably be best secured by a committee of three. Particular care needs to be taken in cases where one or more members drop out in the course of an appeal and where there are a number of appeals to be heard. The appeal can proceed by agreement if three or five members remain.

   (b)   Under no circumstances can an appeal continue if the number of committee members drops below three at any stage during the appeal. In the *Camden Case* ... the three member committee, having considered an appeal, adjourned for four days to conclude a number of remaining appeals. One of the original three members was unable to attend the second meeting and her place had been taken by a new member. The Court confirmed in the clearest terms that the same three members had to attend throughout and make a decision.

   (c)   It could be helpful to convene a hearing with five members to provide for the situation where one member might have to withdraw because of a conflict of interest which had not been appreciated until immediately before the appeal. In those circumstances one other member must also drop out, in order to ensure that the relevant number is three. Care should be taken to ensure that the composition of the committee remains in accordance with statutory requirements.

Conduct of Proceedings

General

15. In all cases the conduct of proceedings is largely at the discretion of the appeal committee itself and, as suggested previously, should be based on fairness coupled with informality. Informality is unlikely to be assisted by the tape recording of the proceedings, a practice which should be avoided. Sufficient time must be allowed for each party to put its case. The committee, should ensure that parents and pupils are given the opportunity to comment on relevant information obtained from the Authority or governing body. Care must be taken to ensure that no party attending the hearing is present alone with the appeal committee in the absence of the others. Suggested methods of proceedings in the case of various types of appeal are set out below. The order of proceedings should preferably be notified in advance to the parties. If the appeal committee wish at the hearing to vary the notified procedure, they should only do so after hearing the view of all parties present and entitled to make representations. In the case of admission appeals it should be remem-

bered that Forbes J in the *South Glamorgan Case* ... suggested that it would be preferable for the Authority to present its case first ... It is usually helpful if the Chair or clerk of the committee makes a statement opening the appeal explaining the procedure to be followed in the hearing.

Admission Appeals

16. (a) In an admission appeal the order of the hearing should be as follows:
     - the case for the Authority (or governing body);
     - questioning by the parents;
     - the case for the parents;
     - questioning by the Authority (or governing body);
     - summing up by the Authority (or governing body);
     - summing up by the parent.

    (b) The committee may ask questions at any time if they require clarification of what is being said or if they need more information in order to reach their decision.

    (c) This procedure may have to be adapted in multiple appeals ...

Exclusion and Reinstatement Appeals

17. (a) In an exclusion appeal in respect of a county, voluntary controlled or maintained special school, the order of hearing should be as follows;
     - the case for the Authority;
     - questioning by the parent or pupil;
     - the case for the parent or pupil;
     - questioning by the Authority;
     - representations by the governing body;
     - questioning by the parent or pupil;
     - questioning by the Authority (if necessary);
     - summing up by the Authority;
     - summing up by the parent or pupil.

    (b) In an exclusion appeal in respect of a voluntary aided or special agreement school, the order of hearing should be as follows:
     - the case for the governing body;
     - questioning by the parent or pupil;
     - the case for the parent or pupil;
     - questioning by the governing body;
     - representations by the Authority;
     - questioning by the parent or pupil;
     - questioning by the governing body (if necessary);
     - summing up by the governing body;
     - summing up by the parent or pupil;

(c) In a reinstatement appeal in respect of a county, voluntary controlled or maintained special schools, the order of the hearing should be as follows:
- the case for the Authority;
- questioning by the governing body;
- the case for the governing body;
- questioning by the Authority;
- representations by the parent or pupil;
- questioning by the governing body;
- questioning by the Authority (if necessary);
- summing up by the Authority;
- summing up by the governing body.

(d) The principles behind the above procedures is that the respondent should start, the appellant should follow, and the third party should be confined to making representations or responding to questions. The committee may ask questions at any time if they require clarification of what is being said or if it needs more information in order to reach its decision.

(e) In cases which are known to be complex or particularly contentious and where witnesses as to fact are likely to be called, the Authority or governing body, in making arrangements for the appeal, should consider allowing the third party the right to take a full part in the proceedings. A full procedure for an exclusion appeal in respect of a county, voluntary controlled or maintained special school in such a case is as follows:
- the case for the Authority, with witnesses;
- questioning of the Authority and their witnesses by the parent or pupil and the governing body;
- the case for the parent or pupil, with witnesses;
- questioning of the parent or pupil and their witnesses by the Authority and the governing body;
- the case for the governing body, with witnesses;
- questioning of the governing body and their witnesses by the Authority and the parent or pupil;
- summing up by the Authority;
- summing up by the governing body;
- summing up by the parent or pupil.

(f) Full procedures in respect of exclusion appeals for voluntary aided and special agreement schools and reinstatement appeals should follow a similar form.

(g) The committee may adjourn any appeal in exceptional cases ... it is essential that no part of the proceedings takes place other than in the presence of all the committee members.

DfEE Guidance on the new schools admissions procedure

Legislation

The School Standards and Framework Act 1998 (and transitional regulations made under that Act) place restrictions on the circumstances in which an appeal committee can uphold an appeal for the admission of a child to an infant class at a school. The restrictions apply where the local education authority or governing body refuse to offer a place to the child on the grounds that his-her admission would cause "class size prejudice", that is to say prejudice to efficient education or efficient use of resources as a result of the measures which would need to be taken to comply with the duty to limit the size of infant classes. Appeal committees should know that a child may be refused a place in the 1999/2000 or 2000/01 school year on the basis that his/her admission to the school would cause class size prejudice in the 2001/2002 school year – when the limit starts to apply.

Appeals against refusal to admit on the grounds of class size prejudice can be upheld only where an appeal committee are satisfied that one of the following conditions applies, namely:

A. the decision was not one which a reasonable LEA/governing body ("the admission authority") would make in the circumstances of the case; or
B. that the child would have been offered a place if the admission arrangements had been properly implemented.

This letter provides more guidance to assist appeal committees in considering whether condition A applies. Condition B relates to matters of fact – essentially, whether a mistake was made – on which little general guidance can be given.

Decision was unreasonable in the circumstances of the case

Essentially, what the appeal committee have to do is to review the decision of the admission authority and the reasons for it, and to consider whether the authority have made out a reasonable case for asserting that "class size prejudice" (as defined above) would arise. In contrast to other types of appeal, the committee should not carry out a balancing process: if the admission authority make out a reasonable case for such prejudice, the committee are bound to dismiss the appeal.

The committee can allow an appeal only where they are satisfied that the authority's decision that class size prejudice would arise was one which no sensible authority, properly appraised of their responsibilities, would have made in the circumstances of the cases – i.e. circumstances such as the school's admission policy, the internal organisation of the school and its ability to accommodate pupils in compliance with the class size limit, but *not* the differential circumstances of individual children.

A committee might uphold an appeal on this ground where, for instance, the admission authority had not considered whether class size prejudice occurred but merely stated that it did, and it was clear that the child concerned could be admitted to the school without any such prejudice arising. But the committee could not uphold an appeal simply because they disagreed with the admission authority's conclusions: they could only do so where it is clear that no reasonable authority would have reached those conclusions.

Appeal procedure

As in other types of appeals, appeal committees must allow parents who are appealing against their child's non-admission to a school on class size prejudice grounds the opportunity to appear in person and make oral representations (in addition to written ones submitted to the committee before their appeal is heard). Parents may also – at the discretion of the committee – be accompanied by a friend or legal representative.

At an appeal hearing, the appeal committee should make clear to parents the circumstances in which the committee will be able to uphold a parental appeal, and that they are bound to dismiss cases which fall outside these circumstances.

Parents should be informed by letter of the appeal committee's decision and the grounds upon which it was made. Where the decision has been taken on class size prejudice grounds, decision letters should make this clear. If the appeal is not allowed, the letter should explain that neither of the two conditions cited above was met. If the appeal is allowed, the letter should say which of the two conditions applied. In either case, the letter should summarise the reasons for the committee's decision.

Where an appeal is upheld, the child has a legal right to be admitted to the school.

Examples of the operation of the new arrangements

A child may be refused a place at a school on the grounds that the admission would cause class size prejudice, namely that the class size limit could not be complied with without measures being taken, such as the need to provide an extra teacher or classroom or even a reorganisation of classes. The committee will need to consider such factors as whether an extra teacher or classroom is required and how the school is organised. To take the example of a school with a standard number of 55 organised into two classes of children in single year groups, one containing 30 children and the other 25: the admission of a 56th pupil would not on the face of it breach the limit. However, factors relevant to the admission authority's decision could be:

- whether the room for the class containing 25 children is physically large enough to accommodate an extra pupils – if not, to admit the 56th pupil could still require an extra teacher and classroom, and therefore be prejudicial;
- how the school is organised – there may be spaces in other key stage 1 classes but the admission authority may have decided against taking in the pupil on the grounds that this would introduce mixed age teaching to a school previously operating in single year group classes;
- whether the admission of the child would lead to a breach of the limit further up the system – some schools decide to have small reception classes with larger year 1/year 2 classes (standard number of 45 with 2 reception classes of 22 and 23 and 3 year 1/year 2 classes of 30). Admitting extra pupils to the reception class would not breach the limit in that year but could do so in future years.

As mentioned above, an appeal committee may not allow an appeal in a class size prejudice case simply because they disagree with the admission authority's decision. So it would not be legitimate to allow an appeal where, for example, the committee disagreed with the decision not to introduce or to expand mixed age teaching in a school – providing that decision was not a completely unreasonable one.

Where appeals are upheld, and extra children are admitted, the local education authority and the governing body must still ensure that the school complies with the limit as from the 2001/2002 school year onwards.

Bibliography

Aldrich R and Leighton P, *Education: Time for a New Act?* University of London Bedford Way Papers No. 23 1985

Brierly, D *Health and Safety in Schools* Paul Chapman Publishing Ltd 1991

Cane, P *An Introduction to Administrative Law* Oxford University Press 1986

Carr, I *Defamation on the Internet* CLT Publishing 1999

Education Law Reports Jordans

Farrington, D.J *The Law of Higher Education* Butterworths 1998

Friel, J and Hay, D *Special Educational Needs and the Law* Sweet and Maxwell 1997

Gordon, R. (Q.C) *Judicial Review and Crown Office Practice* Sweet and Maxwell 1998

Harris, N *The Law Relating to Schools* Tolley 1995

Harris, N *Special Educational Needs and Access to Justice* Jordans 1997

Head's Legal Guide Looseleaf Croner Publications

Maclure, S *Education Re-Formed* Hodder and Stoughton 1992

McManus, J.R. *Education and the Courts* Sweet and Maxwell 1998

Moore, C *Sports Law and Litigation* CLT Publishing 1997

Morrell J and Foster R, (Eds) *Local Authority Liability* Jordans 1998

Oliver, S and Austen L *Special Educational Needs and the Law* Jordans 1996

Poole, K, Coleman, J and Liell, P *Butterworths Education Law* 1997

Sunkin, M. Bridges, L and Meszaros G *Judicial Review in Perspective: An investigation of Trends in the Use and Operation of the Judicial Review Procedure in England and Wales.* Public Law Project 1993

Morris, R. *Central and Local Control of Education After the Education Reform Act 1988.* Longman 1990

Williams, S *Levelling Down* Centre for Policy Studies 1998

Official Publications

DFE *Our Children's Education The Updated Parents Charter* 1994
DfEE
Code of Practice on LEA-School Relations Draft for Consultation
   March 1998
Draft guidance on pupil health and safety on school visits, (pupil health
   and safety scheme). 1997
Final Report on the National Curriculum and its Assessment. The
   Government's Response. 1994
School Admissions, interim guidance. 1998
The Legislative Framework of Education Prof. N. Harris with Miriam
   Mokal 1997
HMSO
Elton, *Discipline in Schools* 1989
HSE
*Health and safety guidance for school governors and members of
   school boards.* 1997
Ofsted
Homework in Primary and Secondary Schools 1995
SCAA *Dearing: The Final Report* 1994

Useful Addresses

Action for Governors' Information and Training CEDC
Lyng Hall
Blackberry Lane
Coventry
CV2 3JS

Advisory Centre for Education
1b Aberdeen Studios
22 Highbury Grove
London
N5 2EA

Bar Pro Bono Unit
7 Gray's Inn Square
London
WC1R 5AZ

Centre for Policy Studies
57 Tufton Street
London
SW1P 3QL

Council on Tribunals
22 Kingsway
London
WC2B 6LE

CTC Trust
15 Young Street
London
W8 5EH

Data Protection Registrar
Wycliffe House
Water Lane
Wilmslow
Cheshire
SK9 5AF

DfEE Publications Centre
P.O. Box 5050
Sudbury
Suffolk
CO10 6ZQ

Education Law Association
39 Oakleigh Avenue
London
N20 9JE

Education Lecturing Services
Castle Quay
Castle Boulevard
Nottingham
NG7 1FW

HSE Books
P.O. Box 1999
Sudbury
Suffolk
CO10 6FS

Independent Schools Information Service
56 Buckingham Gate
London
SW1E 6AG

Independent Schools Joint Council
35–37 Grosvenor Gardens
London
SW1

National Governors' Council
Glebe House
Church Street
Crediton
Devon
EX17 2AF

National Association for Able Children in Education
Park Campus
Broughton
Northampton
NN2 7AL

National Association of Headteachers
1 Heath Square
Boltro Road
Haywards Heath
West Sussex
RH16 1BL

National Association for Special Educational Needs
NASEN House
4–5 Amber Business Village
Amber Close
Amington
Tamworth
Staffs
B77 4RP

Office for Standards in Education
Alexandra House
29–33 Kingsway
London
WC2B 6SE

Parent's Charter Unit
Department for Education and Employment
Sanctuary Buildings
Great Smith Street
London
SW1P 3BT

Professional Association of Teachers
2 St James' Court
Friar Gate
Derby
DE1 1BT

Special Educational Needs Tribunal
7th Floor
Windsor House
50 Victoria Street
London
SW1H 0NW

Index